# Indigenous and Afro-Ecuadorians
# Facing the Twenty-First Century

# Indigenous and Afro-Ecuadorians Facing the Twenty-First Century

Edited by

## Marc Becker

# CAMBRIDGE SCHOLARS

PUBLISHING

Indigenous and Afro-Ecuadorians Facing the Twenty-First Century,
Edited by Marc Becker

This book first published 2013

Cambridge Scholars Publishing

12 Back Chapman Street, Newcastle upon Tyne, NE6 2XX, UK

British Library Cataloguing in Publication Data
A catalogue record for this book is available from the British Library

ISBN (10): 1-4438-4728-3, ISBN (13): 978-1-4438-4728-5

# TABLE OF CONTENTS

Chapter One.................................................................................... 1
Introduction: Indigenous and Afro-Ecuadorians Facing the Twenty-First
Century
Marc Becker

Chapter Two..................................................................................... 7
(Neo)*Indigenismo* and the Transculturative Praxis of Ethnogenesis:
A Case Study From Urban Ecuador
Kathleen S. Fine-Dare

Chapter Three.............................................................................. 34
The Ecuadorian Indigenous Movement and the Challenges
of Plurinational State Construction
Víctor Hugo Jijón

Chapter Four................................................................................ 71
The Inheritance of Resistance: Indigenous Women's Leadership
in Ecuador
Manuela Picq

Chapter Five ............................................................................... 95
Ethnic Representation of Afro Descendant Populations in the Ecuadorian
(2008) and Bolivian (2009) Constitutions
Cristina Echeverri Pineda

Chapter Six................................................................................ 112
Afro Inclusion in Ecuador's Citizens' Revolution
Linda Jean Hall

Chapter Seven ........................................................................... 128
Reclaiming Development: Indigenous Community Organizations
and the Flower Export Industry in the Ecuadorian Highlands
Rachel Soper

Chapter Eight.......................................................................................... 150
Eucalypts in Northern Ecuador: Taking Ecological Imperialism
to New Heights
Kenneth Kincaid

Chapter Nine ........................................................................................ 173
Struggles for the Meaning of "Indigenous" within Inculturation
Theology in Ecuador
Carmen Martínez Novo

Chapter Ten .......................................................................................... 187
Power Relations and Struggles within Indigenous Churches
and Organizations
Juan Illicachi Guzñay

Chapter Eleven ..................................................................................... 201
Ángel Guaraca: 'El Indio Cantor de América'
Contesting the Ideology of the Ecuadorian Mestizo Nation
Ketty Wong

Contributors.......................................................................................... 213

# CHAPTER ONE

# INTRODUCTION:
## INDIGENOUS AND AFRO-ECUADORIANS
## FACING THE TWENTY-FIRST CENTURY

## MARC BECKER

Ecuador provides a fascinating case study for understanding the construction and emergence of race and ethnic identities. Its history, culture, and politics have become a common topic of debate for the section on Ethnicity, Race, and Indigenous Peoples (ERIP) within the Latin American Studies Association (LASA). ERIP, together with the Center for Iberian and Latin American Studies (CILAS) at the University of California, San Diego and the *Latin American and Caribbean Ethnic Studies* (LACES) journal, organized the Second Conference on Ethnicity, Race, and Indigenous People from November 3-5, 2011 at the University of California, San Diego. The event was part of a commitment to periodically organize an international conference following the establishment of ERIP and the launching of the journal LACES in 2006.

The conference covered topics related to all aspects of ethnicity, race relations, Indigenous peoples, Afro-descendants and other ethnic and racial groups in Latin America and the Caribbean. Presenters discussed issues of immigration, *indigenismo*, racism and anti-racism, along with new forms of literature, film, dance, and music of Indigenous and Afro-descendant peoples across the continent. Following the tradition of the larger LASA meetings, this conference conveyed a large diversity of perspectives, disciplines and issues reflecting the richness and complexities of the social processes that encompass the Americas.

The papers collected in this volume on Indigenous peoples and African descendants in Ecuador, as well as those from a companion volume on race and ethnicity in Latin America, draw on the strengths of the ideas presented at the conference. The volumes include contributions from junior, marginal, and lesser-known scholars in the field, including those who have not previously had the opportunity to address an English-speaking audience. While themes of ethnic identities, indigeneity, and race relations are commonly examined in our respective disciplines, it is less common to bring together essays with scholars from such a broad variety of disciplines. The first volume draws on a wide range of studies from across Latin America, including the examination of ethnohistory, the environment, and culture. This volume focuses on Ecuador, and provides an opportunity to explore indigeneity in comparative perspective with the rest of the region, as well as to highlight historically important but understudied Afro-Ecuadorian perspectives.

This volume begins with three studies that examine constructions of indigeneity in Ecuador from various perspectives and through distinctive lenses. It opens with an innovative case study from Ecuador's capital city of Quito in which anthropologist Kathleen Fine-Dare interrogates the transculturative praxis of ethnogenesis. She argues that *indigenismo*, like any "-ism," involves the theorization of a segment of reality such that action can be taken towards, on behalf of, or even in spite of it. Because a presumed state of affairs is looked into from the outside, or is organized in a conscious manner so that lived experience becomes doctrinal, "isms" are often viewed as unauthentic, transitory, or otherwise unsatisfactory approximations of reality. However derogatory the connotations of many "isms" may be, they nevertheless often serve to make visible unsatisfactory situations that would otherwise remain hidden. For example, "socialism" makes evident many underlying structural arrangements that contribute to human relational atomism and the unequal distribution of resources. "Feminism" has drawn attention to the "otherness" of femaleness and the symbolic and economic consequences of the often hidden half. Likewise, *indigenismo* has drawn attention to the historical, economic, symbolic, and lived realities of Indigenous peoples and collectives for a wide variety of purposes ranging from romantic-literary-apologetic to territorial-cultural and human rights-restorative.

From Fine-Dare's study of *indigenismo*, we turn to geologist Víctor Hugo Jijón's examination of Ecuadorian Indigenous movements and the challenges that Indigenous peoples, as well as all of Ecuadorian society, face in attempting to implement the advances codified in the new 2008 constitution. A particular challenge is to enforce the individual and collective rights that the constitution grants to Indigenous peoples, Afro-descendants and coastal peasants (*montubios*) in terms of two new paradigms: the plurinational state and the *Sumak Kawsay* or the good life. This expectation has two complementary main avenues of realization: structuring intercultural territorial circumscriptions where self-government on behalf of Indigenous peoples and nationalities is exercised, and the mainstreaming of plurinationality so that public policies for Indigenous peoples are formulated and implemented in all state bodies. Jijón argues that this process demands a truly participative corresponding legislation, a deep reconfiguration of the state-owned institutions, and an organizational strengthening of civil society.

Political scientist Manuela Picq examines the leadership that Indigenous women have provided to political resistance in Ecuador. Manuela Léon held a position of political and military leadership while coordinating an uprising in the nineteenth century. Women led important uprisings in Cayambe in the 1920s and were founders of the first Indigenous federation in 1944. These women are lasting symbols of resistance against colonization, and echo the agency of many more who also held positions of political leadership. They were feared for their military tactics and cold-bloodedness, blacklisted, and persecuted by state authorities. Icons of insubordination, these women reveal the roles of many others who consistently fought oppression. These leaders should not be understood as historical exceptions, but rather as proof of a solid legacy of political agency among Indigenous women that persists until the present. Picq also makes salient the limits of their participation in contemporary Ecuadorian politics. In analyzing the relative absence of women after the Indigenous movement was institutionalized in the mid-1990s, she examines why political mainstreaming has pushed women out of leadership positions and silenced their voices.

The contributions of Afro-Ecuadorians have been marginalized in academic studies, and two studies in the second section of this book help close that gap. Historian Cristina Echeverri Pineda examines the ethnic representation of Afro-descendant populations in the 2008 Ecuadorian and 2009 Bolivian constitutions. These constitutional processes have deepened the dynamics of public recognition of these countries' cultural and ethnic diversity, and have called the dominant model of cultural and ethnic national homogeneity into question by breaking the old unitary paradigm and declaring these countries as plurinational and intercultural states. These constitutions have acknowledged the presence of the Afro-descendant populations and contribute to their visibility. However, recognition of Afro-descendant populations has differed from the treatment received by the Indigenous populations, who have been the main and more explicit focus of the allocation of new rights. This, in turn, has generated new cultural homogenization processes on new societal groups. This chapter proposes an initial approach to the way in which the Ecuadorian and Bolivian constitutions recognized the cultural difference of Afro-descendants in contrast to that of the Indigenous groups, as well as the implications of plurinationality for Afro-Ecuadorians and Afro-Bolivians.

Anthropologist Linda Jean Hall argues that Afro-Ecuadorians will only achieve social, political, and economic equality in Ecuador's current political environment if they are cognizant of the constitutionally guaranteed entitlements of affirmative action and reparations. Affirmative action for Afro-Ecuadorians confronts discriminatory practices and disparities in education, housing, and employment. Reparations are compensatory social and economic strategies that the state can employ to make amends for racist based insults and injuries to Afro-Ecuadorians. The failure to utilize these collective rights results in a dual response that favors the continued marginalization of Blacks in Ecuador. First, leaders of the country's Afro-descendent sector begin to believe that they are now closer to the ear of political power. In response to the acceptance of these provisions as a part of the law of the land, leadership responds by relaxing their demands for tangible change. Second, feeling less threatened and more in control of civil activism, the government constructs obstacles in the form of social policies and procedures that prevent direct access to administrative power. Hall contends that awareness of this dynamic will enable civic activism and foster effective collaborative efforts to assure that Afro-Ecuadorians assume a more active role in policy-making decisions of the country.

The third section of this book examines serious environmental issues facing Ecuador. Ecuador grows more roses than any other country in the world, and sociologist Rachel Soper studies Indigenous community organizations in the flower export industry. Pedro Moncayo, a county in the northern highlands of Ecuador, has recently been awarded the title of *Capital Mundial de la Rosa*, World Capital of the Rose. Flower export production began in Ecuador in the mid-1980s during a period of neoliberal economic reform. Since then, flowers—with roses as the most popular variety—have become the nation's fourth largest export, alongside petroleum, bananas, and shrimp. As petroleum is extracted from the Amazon, and bananas and shrimp are farmed on the coast, flowers are the top export industry in the highland region. This chapter explores the tension between employment generation and environmental impacts on human health and natural resources. After introducing the dynamic of opposing industry and community norms with regard to individual productivity and global competitiveness versus collective responsibility and respect for nature, Soper addresses the question of how Indigenous community organizations have responded to the flower export industry.

Historian Kenneth Ralph Kincaid chronicles the introduction and expansion of eucalyptus trees in northern Ecuador and examines the relationship of these trees to land tenure struggles in the late nineteenth and twentieth centuries. For native Andean communities, the introduction of this exotic species changed their relationship with local ecologies as eucalyptus groves drove out native flora and violated Indigenous principles of sacred space as these trees altered revered visual alignments. Moreover, in the 1960s, hacienda owners used eucalyptus trees to sidestep land reform legislation by planting fast-growing eucalypts on their estates in order to demonstrate land use. As Kincaid illustrates, an understanding of these conflicts from an Indigenous perspective sheds light on the limits of progress as understood by the state and mainstream Ecuadorian society.

The final section of this book turns to issues of religion and culture. We begin with anthropologist Carmen Martínez's study of the meaning of "Indigenous" within Inculturation Theology in Ecuador. According to Andrew Orta's definition, the theology of "Inculturation" is part of a trend within the Catholic Church to codify and reinforce Indigenous religiosity as part of the Church's broader effort to embrace "local theologies" and "inculturate" itself within specific cultural contexts. After centuries of preaching that Indigenous peoples turn away from their traditional cultural practices to embrace Christianity, many Catholic missionaries now insist that Indigenous ways were Christian all along: Indigenous people must become more "Indian" and return to the ways of their ancestors that missionaries see as local cultural expressions of Christian values. "Inculturation" theology follows on the heels of Liberation Theology, which proposed that Christians were called upon to correct the sinful social injustices of poverty and oppression, and that tended to downplay ethnic distinctions and emphasized instead the homogenizing identity of "the poor." Martínez explores the indigenist project of Inculturation theology in Ecuador based on field and archival research in the highland and Amazonian missions of the Salesian Order. She asks whether Inculturation is an altogether different project from Liberation Theology, and whether the turn towards multiculturalism in the Catholic Church is comparable to the turn from class politics and an emphasis on redistribution to the politics of recognition. Is Inculturation, like "neoliberal multiculturalism," a form of symbolic recognition that distracts Indigenous peoples from more substantial struggles and coopts them for the church and/or the state? And, last but not least, Martínez analyzes Indigenous critiques to the indigenist project of Inculturation.

In his contribution, anthropologist Juan Illicachi examines power relations and struggles within Indigenous churches and organizations. In the late twentieth century, activists organized the Confederation of Evangelical Indigenous Peoples, Organizations, Communities, and Churches of Chimborazo (CONPOCIIECH) that followed the line of evangelical Protestants, and the Confederation of the Indigenous Movement of Chimborazo (COMICH) favored by the progressive Catholic Church in Riobamba. Illicachi contrasts Protestant and Catholic Indigenous churches, as well as their convergence in the exercise of power and authority. He examines strategies that could generate cohesion between COMICH and CONPOCIIECH, and asks why the two organizations sometimes cooperate with each other, and at other points come into conflict. Illicachi employs the concept of power as theorized by Michel Foucault to analyze the relationships and power struggles among Catholic and Protestant Indigenous churches. This implies not reducing power relations to a simple opposition between rulers and the ruled.

Indigenous music in Ecuador is often associated with Otavalo folkloric ensembles and the traditional music of Indigenous festivities such as Inti Raymi and Corpus Christi. Indigenous peoples in Ecuador, however, are not only involved in folkloric and traditional music. In fact, a large part of their musical life falls under the popular music realm. This includes a commercial and mass-mediated type of Indigenous popular music that the elites pejoratively call *chichera* music. Ethnomusicologist Ketty Wong explores the ethnic, racial, and class tensions associated with the musical production of Ángel Guaraca (b. 1975), a charismatic Indigenous singer and songwriter from the province of Chimborazo who has a large following among Indigenous peoples and lower-class mestizos. His work has been innovative in his rendition of Indigenous song-dance genres, particularly the *sanjuanito* and the *yumbo*, whose lyrics address sentiments of Indigenous pride and the experiences of Ecuadorian migrants in the diaspora.

The essays in this volume break from the common tropes and themes that scholars typically employ in their studies of race and ethnicity in Ecuador. In examining Afro-Ecuadorians and Indigenous peoples through the lens of politics, culture, religion, gender, and environmental concerns, we come to a better understanding of the problems and promises facing this country.

CHAPTER TWO

(NEO)*INDIGENISMO*
AND THE TRANSCULTURATIVE
PRAXIS OF ETHNOGENESIS:
A CASE STUDY FROM URBAN ECUADOR

KATHLEEN S. FINE-DARE

## Introduction

Indigenism (*indigenismo* in Spanish), like any "-ism," involves the theorization of a segment of reality such that action can be taken towards, on behalf of, or even in spite of it. Because a presumed state of affairs is looked into from the outside, or is organized in a conscious manner so that lived experience becomes doctrinal, "isms" are often viewed as unauthentic, transitory, or otherwise unsatisfactory approximations of reality.[1] However derogatory the connotations of many "isms" may be, they nevertheless often serve to make visible unsatisfactory situations that would otherwise remain hidden. For example, "socialism" makes evident many underlying structural arrangements that contribute to human relational atomism and the unequal distribution of resources. "Feminism" has drawn attention to the "otherness" of femaleness and the symbolic and economic consequences of the often hidden half. Likewise, "indigenism" has drawn attention to the historical, economic, symbolic, and lived realities of Indigenous persons and collectives for a wide variety of purposes ranging from romantic-literary-apologetic to territorial-cultural and human rights-restorative.

What would the world look like if we all lived more like "Indians?" some indigenists have asked, while others prefer to know when Indigenous

---

[1] MyWord.info defines an "ism" as "a word ending that indicates action, manner, condition, beliefs or prejudice" (http://myword.info/definition.php?id=ism_1-a) [accessed Jan. 25, 2013].

territories and rights to self-determination will be restored. These questions beg this one: What do "Indians" themselves think and want, and why should any voices other than their own be listened to at all? To answer this, the following must be addressed: Just who *is* an Indigenous person, in what times and places, and according to what authorities? Can there be Indigenous discourse and practice that comes equally from Indigenous, non-Indigenous, or "mixed" quarters? Can discourses about indigeneity be used to pit peoples against one another? Are the historical, anthropological, literary, sociological, artistic, and political forms of *indigenismo* just ongoing forms of colonialist discourse that fuel hidden, ongoing forms of repression and increasingly sophisticated structural racism? Can indigenist discourses and practices also be produced and performed by those seeking to create new forms of largely transculturative[2] indigeneity in collaboration, through alliance formation, and in cities as well as in the "peasant" and "subsistence" contexts long thought to be the domain of "true" indigeneity? And, finally, should we take care that our focus on "discourse" and "performance" not preclude taking a close look at just who is financially underwriting the documents, performances, museum exhibits, and other "tangible" and "intangible" expressions of indigenism in this era of NGO- and governmental support for "lite," unthreatening expressions of multiculturalism that not only serve to reduce potential conflict but also look attractive to tourists (see Dombrowski 2004)?

In this brief work I answer "yes" to most of the above questions by focusing on a case study of what can be called "indigenist" practices carried out by people who have in the past been labeled as "mestizo" or "cholo" in Quito, Ecuador's capital city. While this process is incomplete, with nearly as many drawbacks as successes, I argue that the process has

---

[2] Cuban anthropologist Fernando Ortiz has most famously employed the term "transculturation" to describe "the real history of Cuba" which has been that of "intermeshed" transcultural encounters between Caribbean Indigenous, African, Indian, Jewish, and a host of other peoples. For Ortiz (2003[1947], 17-18), transculturation is a more "fitting" term than acculturation to describe culture change as it involves not only deculturation or loss, but also "the consequent creation of new cultural phenomena" or "neoculturation." Luis Morato-Lara defines literary transculturation as "the changes, exchanges, cultural incorporations and rejections of those nationalities that share a territorial space." For Morato-Lara (1997, 65, 68), what is most valuable about Ortiz' work was his notion that rather than accept reality passively, transcultural actors "see and interpret universal reality from the starting point of their own cultural conception, which is a transculturated version of Western and Indigenous knowledge and traditions" (translation mine).

great value and that now would be a poor time to try to quell it by arguing that today's indigenist discourses are either inauthentic or just an extension of the kinds of neo-indigenism that may have de-romanticized the early twentieth century "Indianist" version of "*indigenismo*," but also have de-centered the Indian by turning indigeneity into a socio-political category useful for critiques of capitalism, Marxism, and even environmentalism. Although it is beyond the scope of this chapter to explore this thoroughly, I suggest that it may be time to center our understandings of Indigenous experience on the very place where it has been marginalized: the city.

## Indigeneity and the Hummingbird Collective

In late June of 2011 I was interviewing a couple I'll call Valentina and Miguel as we headed towards their home in Colinas del Norte, a neighborhood on the far northwest edge of Quito. As the three of us walked the several blocks from the bus stop on our way to their newly built home where they live with their three children, Miguel stopped and pointed down the street. "See that corner there? Everyone knows that if you go beyond that point you could get killed. Some places here are really dangerous." Like other neighborhoods on the north side of town, Colinas is becoming home to growing numbers of immigrants from Colombia, Haiti, and other parts of Ecuador, some of whom are known to be involved in drug trafficking.[3]

Before we entered the gate into their little garden, Miguel gave me a quick geographic sweep of the area, starting with the *Tayta* (spiritual father, Mount Casitagua) that once provided opportunities to play and explore when he was a child, down to the entire north end of Quito, which spilled out below us in shades of white and gray. Miguel pointed to sites where condominiums covered old springs, to the neighborhood where *yumbo* dancers performed near the soccer stadium, and to one of the few places where a sacred waterfall still existed, protected by a private citizen. Indoors, Valentina made lunch while we talked, covering subjects ranging from her origins in Cotopaxi province to the influence Miguel's grandmother, a *curandera* (healer), had played in his life.

Just as the interview was winding down, Miguel made an extraordinary point. We had been talking about conflict in the Kitu Kara organization, which serves as a body linking a congeries of urban and rural communities

---

[3] Their teenage son was robbed at knifepoint a few months after this interview, just a block from their home.

in the Quito Basin both to the government via CODENPE[4] and somewhat indirectly to the political party Pachakutik, particularly during election time. "Look," he said, leaning towards me, "here's something I've figured out":

> There are three lines in the thinking of Kitu Kara members. The first is that we're all connected to the Inkas and that Quito is part of Tawantinsuyu [the Inka empire]. The second is that only some people, some surnames, in this area can be legitimate members of Kitu Kara. The Simbaña, for instance, claim more legitimacy and more rights to speak for the *pueblo*. The third line is an intercultural one. It's about forming relationships, being open, working together. But there are conflicts, especially over the [speaking] Kichwa thing, so we don't have meetings very often.

As I rode home on the bus, I thought about Miguel's typology, which outlined three distinct if overlapping accounts of indigeneity. They reminded me of layers of power reflected in a photo I had taken in 1981 in Zámbiza, an Indigenous *pueblo* just west of Quito, of dancers who carried three signs of layered authority: the helmet of the Spanish soldier, the *vara* (authority staff) of the colonized ethnic polity, and the flag of the nation state of Ecuador (Figure 1).

---

[4] CODENPE is the Consejo de Desarrollo de las Nacionalidades y Pueblos del Ecuador. An Ecuadorian Executive Decree No. 386 published on December 11, 1998 and reformulated on June 13, 2005 created it. Its website, www.codenpe .gob.ec, describes the organization as a "participatory and decentralized organism." When the website was consulted in late 2011 it listed fourteen nationalities (Amazonian Kichwa, Awa´, Chachi, Épera, Tsa´chila, Andoa, Shiwiar, Huaorani, Siona, Cofán, Secoya, Shuar, Zápara and Achuar) and eighteen pueblos with a fifteenth, highland Kichwa nation (Pasto, Otavalo, Natabuela, Karanki, Kayambi, Saraguro, Palta, Kañari, Kisapincha, Tomabela, Salasaca, Chibuleo, Waranka, Panzaleo, Puruhá, Manta, Huancavilca, and the "Nación Originaria Kitu Kara"). When the site was consulted on July 30, 2012, the original fourteen nationalities were still listed, but now only sixteen "pueblos" appeared (Tomabela, Karanki, Natabuela, Otavalo, Kayambi, Chibuleo, Kisapincha, Panzaleo, Kitu Kara, Salasaka, Waranka, Puruhá, Pasto, Kañari, Saraguro, and Palta). Manta and Huancavilca had been removed. The goals of CODENPE range from monitoring cultural promotion policies to reducing extreme poverty and universalizing primary education. It also states that a major goal is to "considerably improve the life of "tugurios," or slum-dwellers. See Cervone (2009) for more information about the history, organization, and functioning of CODENPE. Also see Viatori (2009, 103-105), and Posern-Zieliński (2008).

Figure 1: *Zámbiza Capitanes*, 1981. Photo by K. Fine-Dare.

Miguel's analysis, however, was a bit different. The first, a historical/symbolic account of continuing Inka hegemony, echoed the work conducted by some middle-class Ecuadorians who were practically obsessed with the Inkas, spending their time trying to find evidence of a deeper presence of Tawantinsuyu through architecture or other signs. One investigator was searching for a Yumbada[5] that could correspond to Cuntisuyo (the roughly southwest quarter of Tawantinsuyu), thereby filling in the remaining piece of the *chakana*, or Inkaic cosmogram, whose other corners were covered by Yumbadas that took place in Cotocollao

---

[5] The Yumbada is a dance complex involving the representation of lowland Indigenous persons who wear feathers, seed ornaments, and sometimes capes made of gourds stitched together. The dance takes place at distinct times of the year primarily throughout the Quito Basin, although it appears sporadically in other zones of Ecuador, such as Cotopaxi province. Near extinction in the 1990s, the dance complex is now promoted on Ecuadorian television, in tourist marketing, and by the Ministry of Culture and the Municipality of Quito. It has recently been identified by the Kitu Kara organization as an "ancestral ritual" alongside "Coya Raymi" (late September), and "Inti Raymi" (late June). See Fine-Dare (2007) and Salomon (1981).

(northwest), San Isidro del Inka (northeast), and La Magadalena/Chibuleo (southeast) (Borja n.d.; Williams 2007). When I told this to Miguel, himself a Yumbada dancer in Cotocollao, he nodded his head. "This is what I'm talking about. There are a lot of people looking for these signs," he said, "but what do they mean to *us*?"

The second view regarding Kitu Kara membership is historical in a different sense. The emphasis on the greater legitimacy of some families over others in leading the organization may reflect pre-contact Indigenous hierarchy and the ways that the influence of local ethnic lords continued well into the colonial era and perhaps beyond. Maybe, I thought, the bitterness expressed by a family I had interviewed with one of these "legit" surnames over what they saw as the coopting of the Yumbada of Cotocollao was connected to this legacy. To Miguel, both of whose surnames are of Spanish origin, this view was exclusionary and even elitist. "A few families want to gain control of the organization," he said, "which gets in the way of our working together."

The third line, the one Miguel called "intercultural," seemed to reflect a trope that went beyond ethnic legitimacy and even Ecuadorian nationality. Identity in this line is linked to, but not defined by, language or genetics. It seems to have more to do with action and with the relationships and sociality made in the course of working towards common ends. From this perspective, to be Kitu Kara means to be something that defies the scoffing of some middle-class Ecuadorians who shake their heads whenever I talk about what is going on in the northwest barrios. "They are just putting on a show," they say. "There is no legitimacy to their claims to be Indian. They are trying to connect themselves to archaeological sites inappropriately, and they are being sucked in and duped by New Agers. They are mestizos, not Indians. They don't even speak Kichwa. And what in the world, anyway, is the "Pueblo Kitu Kara"?

This skepticism doesn't trouble Miguel, who has heard it many times before, as often from within the Kitu Kara organization as from outside of it. The internal critique claims that most of the so-called "urban Kitu Kara" people are migrants from Cotopaxi province, the birthplace of the Indigenous-surnamed Valentina. Even Miguel's own relatives and neighbors have given him grief when he has gone around collecting old stories. "Some of them called me a *hippie*," he laughs. "They didn't trust me at all, even though they knew my family."

But to him, being Kitu Kara does not mean tracing an Inka legacy or proving one is a legitimate Indian descended from one of the traditional ethnic polities. Mostly it means to dance with purpose—*"con intención"* —and to engage in a practice called *"corazonar,"* or to act from the heart.

While an Ecuadorian anthropologist who has worked with the Kitu Kara emphasizes "decolonization" in his book on the subject (Guerrero 2010, 38), Miguel gives it a less historicized connotation. "We want to be recognized for who we are by our actions, by what's in our hearts" he explained. "Being Indigenous is just *part* of who I am. It guides me, but it is not all that I am or who I will be." For Miguel, in other words, to be Kitu Kara means not to "be" at all; it means to think, do, and act. It is inclusive, it looks for partnerships, it engages with outsiders in ways that one could scarcely say involve exploitation. It also may involve rethinking the concepts of *indigenismo* and perhaps even indigeneity itself.

## *Indigenismo* in Ecuador

For the past two decades there has been an explosion in social scientific studies regarding the nature and meaning of "indigeneity." The spread and intensification of global neoliberalism in the 1990s combined with the many Columbian quincentennial observances and the development of documents associated with a transnational Indigenous peoples' movement, culminating in the 2007 United Nations Declaration on the Rights of Indigenous Peoples, have raised new questions regarding the relationships of Indigenous persons, identities, and discourses to state power, global economic exchanges, and a new internationalism (Viatori 2009, 80-81). Today, who is an Indian, where, why, and with what aims serve as central questions motivating the works of dozens of scholars. The linked question: Who *speaks* for Indians? rounds out latter day academic *indigenismo* (e.g., Lucero 2006).

Despite this growing corpus of documents, "there have been few studies made of the concrete daily dynamics of *indigenismo*, even though the discipline of anthropology prides itself on its ethnographic approach to everyday phenomena" (Saldívar 2011, 68). In this piece I address this deficit by examining the experiences of some families who sometime during the last decade formed the Hummingbird—"Kinde" in Kichwa—Collective, located in northwest Quito, Ecuador. This work is part of a larger project, the goals of which are: 1) to address the uses of concepts of indigeneity as they relate to Kinde members who descend from former *huasipungueros* or indentured hacienda servants and still retain some of the property received following the 1964 agrarian reform;[6] 2) to examine

---

[6] Before 1964 the main form of land tenure in Ecuador was the large hacienda. Labor for these haciendas came from a variety of sources, but most notable was the unsalaried residential labor force known as *huasipungueros*. Other types of labor

the relationship between class, ethnicity, sociality, and *"citadinidad"* (León 2010) in Quito; 3) to illustrate the convergence of a variety of forces, including that of state-generated *indigenismo*, global tourism, documentary filmmaking, resistance to the Catholic Church, social networking, and other factors in the lives and projects of the collective and some of the conflicts that have emerged; and 4) to compare the experiences of Andean and North American Native peoples regarding twenty-first century changes to the concept of *indigenismo* as well as the role of anthropological thought and practice in both propping up and undercutting ideas of indigeneity that may or may not be relevant or of use to peoples both Indigenous and otherwise. While I touch on some of these issues in this piece, I concentrate on the Kinde collective's experiences relating indigeneity to life in Quito's capital city (see Figure 2).

In Ecuador, pro-Indian viewpoints that fed into the Liberal Revolution of 1895 created alliances between radical liberals and Indigenous leaders against mestizo and white urban intellectuals in both the highlands and the coast. Although, as Shannon Mattiace (2007, 200) notes in an interesting article that compares the forms that *indigenismo* historically took in Ecuador to those found in Mexico,[7] the rhetoric was "steeped in paternalism," emphasizing the goal of full citizenship for all inhabitants of Ecuador (see Chávez 1993[1943] and Jaramillo 1993[1943]).[8] But as the state was actually weaker than the landholders, church, and others who held power over Indigenous persons, indigenist discourse was diffused throughout many more arenas than the state and its policies until the implementation of the 1998 Constitution, which "defined the Ecuadorian

---

were *partidarios*, *arrendatarios*, *desmonteros*, *arrimados*, and *aparceros*, none of whom owned any piece of the property on which they worked (Nieto Cabrera n.d., 1).

[7] According to Munro Edmonson (1959, 127), Alfonso Caso's approach to "the Indian problem" was acculturative, nationalistic, and dedicated to the idea that "folk art needs to be protected against undesirable commercial and tourist influences." Indigenismo should not be a romantic or egalitarian liberal project, but instead seek equality "just between equals" (Caso 1958, 102, quoted in Edmonson 1959, 127). Equality must be sought via "the transformation of [the Indians'] culture, changing the archaic, deficient—and in many cases harmful—aspects of this culture into aspects more useful for individual and community life." The ultimate goal: "An indigenist policy means, in sum, transforming three million individuals who live within the national territory and are theoretically considered Mexican into three million Mexicans who really contribute to their own progress and to the progress of Mexico" (1958, 50, quoted in Edmonson 1959, 127).

[8] For a discussion of the *costumbrismo* tradition connected to Ecuadorian *indigenismo*, see Oña (2004).

Figure 2: Indians from Quito, Ecuador, 1868 (www.loc.gov) | 1 photographic print | LOT 4831, vol. 1, no. 46 [P&P] | LC-USZ62-78963 (b&w film copy neg.). Courtesy Library of Congress.

state as 'pluricultural and multiethnic'" (Mattiace 2007, 203). A few pages earlier, Mattiace summarizes key comparative elements:

> In the 1980s and 1990s, differences between Indigenous policy in Ecuador and Mexico rested less on the relative strength of the state and its ability to penetrate the countryside and more on the strength of independent Indian organizations. Today, Indian organizations in Mexico and Ecuador frame their demands for land, autonomy, and rights as "equality in difference." This mix of demands—for equal rights and for rights to difference—is not new. What is new, in terms of Indigenous demand making, is that Indian organizations are proposing alternative models to the classic model of the nation-state, forcing states to rethink the relationship between the state and Indigenous peoples. Support for these alternative nation-building models is coming from outside as well as from within: from nongovernmental organizations (NGOs) operating on the regional and international levels, from intergovernmental organizations, such as the United Nations and the Organization of American States, and from internationally based foundations (Mattiace 2007, 197).

Despite these different histories, which resulted in different types of indigenist policy in the respective states, a type of convergence has occurred that signals the return to what might be called an "Americanist indigenism" influenced by global forces similar to the early days of the nineteenth century when the International Congress of Americanists and other organizations looked to both North and South American expressions of Indigenous culture to form general contrastive ideas to counter European dominance (Fine-Dare and Rubenstein 2009, xiii-xv). One of the biggest changes from the 1980s to the present has been the shift from ethnic identity in general and indigeneity in particular, passing from what Hernán Ibarra (2003, 1) calls a state of negativity and stigmatization to one that is more positive as identity has been collectively positioned in the middle of demands directed mainly to the State. Another key difference is that global conversations regarding indigeneity are initiated and carried out by Indigenous peoples themselves, who exchange ideas regarding differences and similarities at international meetings such as the Águila and Cóndor (Sánchez Palma and Prado 2011), or in the UN Permanent Forum (2013).

A central, if not primary, frustration of Indigenous people anywhere in the world is that they are often asked to make a choice between retaining their cultural values and characteristics and achieving access to justice and resources. This, in fact, is the dilemma facing all persons within liberal regimes, where the principle of equality is often reduced to that of sameness, while ironically claiming to prioritize the atomistic individual above the collective. Amalia Pallares (2007, 147) discusses this dilemma for Ecuadorian Indigenous peoples by characterizing it as a request that Indigenous culture be separated from its producers. *Indigenismo* as a philosophy or cultural trope in Ecuador has thus taken very different if overlapping forms over the years, which can be characterized as political, cultural, material, and what I see as a convergence of all three taking place today. In ridiculous shorthand, Ecuadorian political *indigenismo* concentrates on the liberal project of finding ways to include Indigenous peoples into the nation state while, in a fashion similar to that of Mexico, finding ways to identify the nation state with unique characteristics drawn selectively from Indigenous culture. Cultural *indigenismo* emphasizes not only the pre-Columbian past, but also the rights of Indigenous populations to express and learn their art forms, unique beliefs and practices, and especially their languages in forms appropriate to their epistemological frameworks and social organization. The right to exercise Indigenous forms of justice is included here, which dovetails with political *indigenismo* and links to material *indigenismo*, or the expression of rights to fair wages, full access to the justice system, demarcated territories, and natural resources.

## Urban Indigeneity and the Hummingbird Collective

An important but sometimes overlooked factor complicating considerations of just who can claim to be an Indian and what rights they have is where they live. In the case of Indigenous urbanites, the issue is not only that related to laws allowing the creation and retention of communal lands, but also to the widespread idea that to "be Indian" means to live in rural areas. Residing in the city connotes migration and/or a loss of Indigenous identity and cultural repertoire; in other words, it means for some to be a "cholo" who has walked away from legitimacy grounded in a rural-based collective (see Albro 2010 for an excellent study of the dilemmas of urban indigeneity in Bolivia).

As the economic and communication bases of both rural and urban areas change as a result of greater ease of transportation and a greater dissemination of information (Swanson 2010), it may be time to rethink the "rural-urban continuum." William Waters (2007, 138) states the following in his study of the aftermath of agrarian reform to communities outside of Salcedo, Cotopaxi Province, Ecuador: "The very meaning of rurality is ... open to new interpretations involving complex links between different sectors of society and the economy" (see Vicenti Carpio [2011] for a similar discussion regarding Indigenous residents of Albuquerque,

New Mexico). It is not enough, however, to rethink Tönnies; a serious material consideration must be addressed: How do Indigenous peoples who live in cities without access to communal lands claim collective rights granted to Indigenous peoples under the Ecuadorian Constitution?

One local strategy that is laying the groundwork for making claims to water and other resource and territorial rights is under construction by La Corporación Kinde—the Hummingbird Collective ("the Kindes")—centered primarily in at least five houses built on property acquired by ex-*huasipungueros* following the 1964 Agrarian Reform. The activities of this urban *ayllu*, or extended family, demonstrate, I believe, the transformed, globalized, and even coopted version of twenty-first century *indigenismo* in Ecuador. The Kindes assert both material and cultural goals in seeking recognition, access to resources, and pluriculturalism if not plurinationality and transculturalism. Their work not only calls into question understandings of indigeneity based on ethnic boundaries situated in rural areas, but also distinctions made between ruralness and urbanity, class and culture. Ironically, the experiences of residents of the capital city of Ecuador that serves as the seat of national government and CONAIE, the Indigenous federation, reflects their *distance* from both state power and national Indigenous political recognition. The Kindes seek to close this gap through a variety of interconnected means briefly outlined below.

First, the Kinde group engages with government resources—primarily via the Ministry of Culture and the Municipality of Quito—through writing grants to support educational programs, semi-private ritual activities, and widely advertised public performances of dance genres, music, sanctioned graffiti, museum exhibits, photographic displays, and the reading of brief reports. In order to provide authentic experiences to the public and to internally recuperate threatened cultural practices, this work has involved conducting interviews, oral histories, and workshops for several years as part of the cultural center they created in one of their family's houses.

Members of the collective have been actively collaborating with municipal employees (e.g., an engineer who has been working with them on their greenhouse irrigation system, and the Director of the Municipality of Quito's Cotocollao Cultural Development Center, who authorized an exposition of costumes and photos), and anthropologists. As one of the anthropologists, I am involved in complex ways as the Municipality sees me as a connection with not only the Kinde group but also the Yumbada of Cotocollao. The other anthropologist most involved teaches in an applied anthropology program at a Quito university and supervises students who conduct field research in *barrios* such as San Enrique de Velasco and make short documentary films about them. This anthropologist has also written a song about what it means to be Kitu Kara that he has taught to Kinde elementary school children and performed with them on stage when they conducted end-of-year ceremonies in the university auditorium.

This leads to a second, although now substantially transformed, key part of the Kinde Cultural Center. El Mensajero del Saber ("wisdom messenger"—a term for the hummingbird, or *kinti/kinde* in Kichwa) was an alternative or experimental elementary school centered around ideas similar to those found in the Indigenous Amawtay Wasi University (2013), but which the collective came up with on its own. They called their educational program Indigenous and "intercultural," but resisted following strict guidelines set up by the bicultural/intercultural educational office, DINEIB, saying that they should be able to define indigeneity in their own way. Two key components of this self definition are 1) appropriate and sustainable organic gardening in the city (they have two organic greenhouses on one of the family's property and sell produce at the local farmer's market set up by the municipality on Friday mornings); and 2) freedom for all people, including and especially children, from domestic violence (Taller Cultural Kinde 2007).

Although the school ran for four years, it ultimately had to change gears, as the Ministry of Education would not give them permission to operate officially because they met almost none of the basic guidelines. While many of the parents enrolled their children in other schools so that they could receive their elementary diplomas, others stayed at Mensajero del Saber, which operated during its final year as a "distance education" wing of the long-standing bilingual education school located in the south end of Quito, Tránsito Amaguaña. The school has now been transformed into an after-school program for children and an adult cultural education center for residents coming from a variety of social classes in the neighborhood. The information presented in "Casa Kinde" workshops and public "*conversatorios*" derive from oral histories and other sources of information regarding the prehistory, history, and contemporary life for residents of northwest Quito. Visiting friends, relatives, and other cultural centers in the Quito area is a particularly important activity for purposes of self-education and idea exchanges (for instance, regarding the meaning of *sumak kawsay*, instantiated in the Ecuadorian Constitution and glossed as "el buen vivir," or "the good life"), with trips to local communities such as Alaspungo, Uyachul, Catzuqui de Velasco, Santa Anita, Santa Isabel, Parcayacu, Pomasqui, Rumicucho, Kisapincha, Karapungo, Calderón, and Llano Chico, with more distant forays to communities in provinces such as Imbabura, Pastaza, and Sucumbíos growing in frequency.

Another important dimension to the collective's discourse and activities, particularly for those who also participate in the Cotocollao Yumbada, is their disagreement with and even opposition to the Catholic Church. In their view, by heightening its rhetoric against "pagan folklore" over the past decade, the Church has lessened its cooperation with and tolerance for spiritual and cultural diversity and demonstrated how out of touch it is with its potential constituents in the twenty-first century. This contributed, for example, to the Kinde members incorporating alternative spiritual practices into a Catholic mass held during the 2012 festival celebrating San Juan (St. John the Baptist) presided over by a French priest sympathetic to interculturalism and Indigenous practices who was contracted especially for the occasion.

To achieve their goals of alternative spirituality that disconnect newly inscribed indigeneity from the historical hacienda/Catholic repressive machinery, some of the activities of the Kinde group have cautiously incorporated some pan-spiritual or what might be called "New Age" rhetoric and goals into their activities. As their familiarity with the Kichwa language and practices increases, however, they have abandoned some less "Andean" rhetorical notions and practices. For instance, the Kinde members along with others who dance with the Cotocollao Yumbada have not returned to the archaeological site of Tulipe during the spring solstice, something that the Municipality once advertised prominently to tourists. Now that the site has been "opened" in an Andean spiritual way, the Yumbada dance leader says that there is no longer any need to dance at Tulipe, tourists or no tourists. In addition, the Kindes are involved in organized public activities ranging from occupying one of the two hills located in central Quito—the "female" Itchimbía—in order to effect political change through dance,[9] to hiking up the Pichincha volcano to conduct ceremonies and assert ownership of a water source they believe is at risk of being completely lost to them. They couch these activities in terms of Andean concepts such as *ayni* and *minka*, adding "*corazonar*" (linked to and partly derived from *shungu*, or heart-soul in Kichwa) to the

---

[9] The public was invited to "*corazonar*" in 2012 at Itchimbía according to an announcement posted on the social networking site, Hotlist: "Urgidos por la necesidad de aportar—sin cálculo—desde lo que somos y hacemos a la construcción del Ecuador del presente-futuro, te invitamos a Corazonar en el Yata Pajtá de Itchimbía, durante la próxima Luna Creciente (26 de julio al 2 de agosto del 2012)" (http://www.hotlist.com/e/Corazonar-en-el-Yata-Pajt%C3%A1-de-Itch imb%C3%ADa-@-Parque-Itchimbia-Quito-Quito-Ecuador/412741702104844 [no longer available online as of Jan. 25, 2013]).

mix (see Wutich 2011 regarding the "moral economy of water" in urban Bolivia).

As part of its integrated stand in support of gender equity and against domestic/intimate violence, the Kinde Corporation has a "no alcohol" (except for fermented corn beer called *chicha,* that is very female labor intensive to produce—see Figure 3*)* preference that is forwarded with great sensitivity towards elders and others who they know would find it very difficult to completely leave alcohol behind, particularly during times of festival. Their approach is one of example, stated publicly for reasons of health, but more privately for reasons of doing battle with the image of the "drunken festival Indian" still persistent throughout Latin America. Nevertheless, what must seem like a Protestant-influenced, puritanical rejection of distilled alcoholic beverages must seem like an affront to what it means to worship, to hope, and to celebrate for many residents.

Figure 3: Festival sponsor's sister making *chicha de jora (*sprouted corn flour beer) for the San Juan festival, 2012. Photo by K. Fine-Dare.

Some Kinde members are aware of the contradictions that emerge from embracing what many see as non-Indigenous, "Western" (if Asian-influenced) spiritual values while consciously doing battle with *blanqueamiento*, or "whitening," which has acculturative as well as socioeconomic connotations (see Whitten 2003). To many of the "original" residents of this neighborhood (*gente originario*), the basis of their identity lies in the devotion to Catholic saints, the predominance of masculinity throughout all domains of existence, and working hard so that their children might be educated and find meaningful if not lucrative professions. As prayer to, feeding of, and dancing for the saints is a sine qua non of worldly as well as spiritual success, advocating abandonment of such in the name of "indigeneity" or even *"sumak kawsay"* may well feel like they are moving backwards.

Finally, various members of the collective communicate their views to others by means of public graffiti and murals, and of social networking media, including email, text messaging, Facebook, and YouTube. Some of these messages are transmitted via a local organization known as the "Red Colectivo de Cotocollao" (Cotocollao Collective Network), whose active members include two women who have migrated to Ecuador from Spain.

While the Kindes maintain a connection to the Kitu Kara Consejo, or governing body, they remain skeptical and cautious regarding that organization's ability to achieve goals important for, especially, those members who reside in Quito (see Fine-Dare 2010; Gómez 2007a, 2007b). In short, the Kinde collective engages with a wide variety of outsiders to achieve goals related to recognition, cultural recuperation, community health and welfare, water rights claims, and protest against what they see as ancestral territory being usurped by state and private building projects that have torn out much of the surrounding forest supposedly protected by the city. While indigeneity is central to these goals, it is less in the sense of asserting personal or even collective "identity" as it is creating and "exercising" Indigenous forms of sociality, organization, and symbolic claim-making to territory. These activities may be more in line with the goals of the National Federation of Indigenous, Peasant, and Black Organizations (FENOCIN) than they are with those of the Confederation of Indigenous Nationalities in Ecuador (CONAIE) because of the greater inclusion, if understated, of the roles of class and what I call "transculturative acculturation," but at this point I have not heard anyone speak of such an ideological affinity. As indigeneity remains central to the discourse of the Kinde collective, a look at the relationship of non members to the collective might still be understood within the framework of class-inflected twenty-first century *indigenismo* (see Egberg 2011). In the end, the main project seems to be how to de-link *indigenismo* from racial/racist lumping ideologies as it is connected more strongly to ethnogenesis and cultural recuperation.

## Reflections upon *neoindigenismo*

For many scholars of the Americanist tradition, speaking up with authority on indigeneity has become a necessary professional task that is nonetheless fraught with the risk of opening oneself to criticisms both logico-historical and moral-ethical (see Beteille 1998 and Cruikshank 2004). Anthropologists who evince positions of advocacy for Indigenous rights are sometimes accused of paternalistically and authoritatively forcing individuals with complex histories into an identity location they might rather not assume. Some Ecuadorian archaeologists are especially skeptical and dismissive of claims to indigeneity on the part of both anthropologists and their subjects that try to establish such without lines of evidence going back to material prehistoric evidence and residence in rural communities that still speak Indigenous languages. In a kind of reverse ventriloquism, critics put other motives into the actions of their colleagues and position themselves as truer defenders of those people who have had unwanted identities foisted on them.

In the title to this chapter I place (neo) in parentheses to signal that many of the characteristics that have been identified as a new form of classic indigenism have really nothing new about them conceptually, but rather reflect the ways the category has broadened to include many others who engage in the process. One characteristic of neoindigenism as defined by researchers is that of "cultural cannibalism," whereby cultural practices and objects are eaten up by the developmental projects of late capitalism, including tourism, national branding, and justification schemes for getting large grants and reporting their success (Bretón 2007). To say that culture is cannibalized is to imply that this has been against the knowledge or will of its producers and that a new form of savagery has been unleashed. The critiques of this type of cynical indigenism connect to those of social and educational multiculturalism as well as political pluriculturalism, which are seen as asymmetrical projects that superficially acknowledge and engage with ethnic entities while selectively displaying, using, and consuming certain aspects expeditiously.

Díaz-Polanco and Swarthout (1987, 88) have articulated another interpretation of neo-indigenism as something promoted by North American institutions such as the Indian Law Resource Center "in response to a tendency on the part of Latin American ethnic movements to ally themselves with revolutionary forces."[10] This type of neoindigenism identifies Indigenous peoples as part of separate, Fourth World struggles for "self-determination," ones that should be suspicious of alliances with workers' parties, revolutionary movements, and any coalitions not specifically "Indian." While this raises a can of worms largely outside the scope of this chapter, it is in my opinion a valid issue that needs to be revisited.[11]

The whole question of forming alliances, whether those are with revolutionary movements, anthropologists, or other "friends of the Indian," must be viewed in terms of very different and complex historical and national contexts. At any rate, the issue demands consideration of the role of anthropologists in contemporary indigenist movements. Does forming alliances with non-Indians in seeking redress of environmental, labor, and other "material" concerns mean a de-centering of culture in the political arena? As Lêda Martins (2009, 249) asks, based on her work with the Indigenous Macuxi of Brazil, who are often labeled as "deculturated" *cabocos* or *caboclos*: "If Indigenous politics decenters culture, how would anthropology redefine Indians as subjects? What is the place for anthropologists in North America, in this new scenario of regional politics?" Furthermore, if "self-determination" becomes a key defining term for any claims to indigeneity, what does that mean for Indigenous peoples who live in the city and who participate in groups of association rather than "pueblos"? To speak of urban indigeneity means necessarily to talk about non-essentialized identities, multiple alliances, and other forms of border-crossing sociality that render any kind of "*indigenismo*" a process rather than a policy.

## Conclusion: Re-*Indigenismo*?

Indigenism developed as a response to the racial lumping of broad and diverse categories of people for purposes of economic gain and social control under conditions of foreign empire building that had labor and resource extraction and later colonization as central goals. In the Americas diverse peoples were categorized as "Indian" and denigrated as sub-humans who lived outside of urban and urbane places where processes of

---

[10] See also Gnerre and Bottasso (1986) for an excellent analysis of the connections between *indigenismo* and the Indigenous political movement in Ecuador.

[11] For instance, the Native American and Indigenous Studies program at the college where I work insists that one of the central educational and political goals of the program is that of promoting "self-determination" for tribal peoples throughout the world.

Catholization, civilization, and capital accumulation took place. The indigenist "movement" developed as part of this process, taking form externally as Toledan and other reforms, and internally (if often under the realm of admixed categories both biological and cultural), as various forms of armed and unarmed protest and resistance. Early nineteenth- and twentieth-century indigenism often appeared as a romantic critique of the evils of European culture, infused with imperialist nostalgia. Largely non-Indian literati and commentators held the pens. Indigenism differed in content depending on the country and history, the size of the Indigenous population, and other factors. By the mid-twentieth century, *indigenismo* had taken the form of a "neo-indigenism" that included Indigenous perspectives, even if not written by Indigenous hands (Dessau 1970; Morato-Lara 1997; Nagy-Zekmi 1997). In other words, indigenism was produced as an external, reactive ideology that served both Indians and non-Indians. It was complicated by socioeconomic class and gender, re-generated by political motivations, and has assumed many forms in diverse national, regional, and historical contexts. Today it is as much an ideology of internal ethnogenesis that negotiates meaning and power with external entities that fund projects central to the recognition sought but are often simultaneously destructive to it (see Hale 2006).

What does *indigenismo* look like in the twenty-first century as global communications connect Indigenous persons, disseminate their concerns, and generate a host of new "identities" that fall along a complex continuum made more complex by gender, generation, and income? How does a concept/doctrine born of the gross racial clustering of diverse peoples fare under new forms of diversification and the generation of new identity labels (ethnogenesis)? And how does it fare in urban areas, where Indigenous peoples for many decades were expected to be transformed into deracialized—"whitened"—national citizens whose primary life goal was upward mobility?

For members of the Kinde collective, hassling over the definitions of indigeneity just seems crazy and energy-sucking when they are living daily with increased intimate and external violence (much of it related to the drug trade), environmental degradation, removal of access to resources, growing urban sprawl, and the baroque nature of the ways the bureaucratic and cultural logic of intercultural education works to exclude more than include. Being recognized for who they are is not irrelevant by any means. It forms the backbone of their erstwhile elementary school's educational lessons and is the main theme of requests for grant assistance from the Municipality of Quito, the Ministry of Culture, and the City Museums Foundation. They refine the concept of indigeneity through very public and very private performances and ceremonies, and theorize it in documentary films, Facebook posts, and written statements. They are trying to learn Kichwa and increasingly use Kichwa terms in conversing with one another and outsiders. Indigeneity may be said to be central, but not essential. It carries great weight, but no more than that of being parents, children, co-workers, artists, and dance instructors. It permeates what they do, provides focus and definition, but does not subsume. In a process that perhaps reverses how assimilation works, they are "deconstructing" (in a culinary rather than postmodern sense) a stew into separate parts so that they might be made more instructional, more explicit, more beautiful. If there is a central metaphor to who they are it is as dancers, something they do "con intención," with purpose.

We might now ask whether *indigenismo* or even *neoindigenismo* can be appropriate characterizations of what is going on. If "indigenism" is rethought as parallel to "feminism"—i.e., as a project initiated and deployed by "natives" to close the gap between reality and dream in achieving equal access to resources and justice—then continuing to use a new version of the concept might be instructive. While once *indigenismo* was an external practice, it is now generated by those who once were only imposed upon by it. It now has class and gender elements that cannot be denied. *Indigenismo* is also produced and indigeneity internalized by some who may indeed be "inventing" or "self constructing" it. There is at least one Cotocollao *yumbo* dancer who, like other dancers—some of whom are of demonstrable Indigenous ancestry but work closely with the Catholic church, or live in middle-class suburbs, and who definitely do not speak Kichwa—incorporates this activity with many others that define him personally and as a member of a broader collective. He is the kind of person particularly made fun of by outsiders who view him as a "wannabe" with no legitimate claim to the "ancestral ritual" of the Kitu Kara. Anthropologists certainly have no right to judge this guy on a criterion of legitimacy. Who, in fact, would?

In an article that reviews current research on indigeneity, David Stoll suggests that much of what passes for "Indianness" falls more into the category of marketing brand than true culture. The exaggerated presentation of indigeneity through cultural practice and performance looks good to international donors and NGOs who "will not take up Indigenous causes unless these are tailored to their expectations." This leverage power runs the risk of "breed[ing] patron-client relationships rife with favoritism and opportunism, factionalizing the population they wish to bring together" (2011, 139). While this is a legitimate concern, those who work with Indigenous people in both North and South America may feel a bit uneasy with an analysis that seems to deny autonomy to Indigenous actors who often know precisely what they are doing in accepting "outsiders" into their midst, forming alliances with non-Indians, and trucking with everything from casinos to big NGO projects such as PRODEPINE (Bréton 2007) to get what they need for their communities.

Perhaps the most eloquent account of the importance of documenting and listening to individual voices in understanding indigenismo today comes from the work of Ecuadorian anthropologist José Yánez del Pozo, whose testimonies taken from Kichwa speakers who both live in Ecuador and have migrated out bring perspective to the urge to over-generalize or theorize what comes down to very private and personal matters. Yánez is particularly opposed to characterizing the "identity" and experience of individuals such as Jorge Lucho Maigua, a 66-year old vendor Yánez met in Washington, D.C., in terms of a "hybridism" that implies a diminished self whose sole integrity lies in some kind of romanticized traditionalism.

After a careful analysis of the transcript of the life history he gathered from Maigua's personal account, Yánez (1997, 144-147) identifies four axes that demonstrate ways that Maigua has amalgamated all of his life experiences within an existence that remains centrally "Indigenous." These axes are: 1) **vitality** (staying healthy, eating right, caring for one's body as one would the Pachamama, or earth mother); 2) **liberty** (which includes the right to move freely in the world, whether across vertical ecological zones or internationally to make a living); 3) **peace** (a state that results from maintaining good relationships with others through reciprocity and communal responsibility); and 4) **identity** (which is multiple in nature, as the states of being a human being, and Ecuadorian, a Kichwa speaker, etc. radiate from a basic core of self-esteem). Following José María Arguedas, the Quechua-speaking anthropologist, ethnomusicologist, essayist, and poet who many see as having initiated *neoindigenismo*, Yánez views "Indoamérica" as a huge tree that is grounded in some central realities that accept or reject changes that attach as leaves to its body. By viewing indigeneity this way, we can avoid the romantic essentialism and the cynical pessimism of postmodernity, both of which are characterized by reductionisms deeply colored by racism and other unenlightened forms.

Certainly there are Indigenous peoples deeply in bed with the powers-that-be to the extent that they are at the heart of "authorizing" indigeneity itself and policing its boundaries, while there are others who have no interest in what they view as pointless nonsense. As the struggle for water, territory, domestic violence safe houses, intercultural education, organic food markets, and freedom from alcohol and drug abuse heat up in Quito, it will be interesting to see and important to understand what roles indigeneity plays. Whether it is a resource, a liability, a source of conflict, or a trickster-like wild card, its survival in the minds of those whose identity was said by mid-twentieth-century to be in the throes of extinction because of urbanization and "auto-suicide" (Costales 1960, 279) is something to admire and learn from, indeed.

**Acknowledgements:** Funding for this research has been generously provided over the years by CIES Fulbright, the Fort Lewis College Foundation, the office of the Dean of Natural and Behavioral Sciences of Fort Lewis College, the Fort Lewis College Faculty Research Fund managed through the Provost's office, and the Department of Anthropology. Conversations with political scientist Byron Dare, who knows all the people and been to almost all the places discussed in this chapter has helped me enormously. Thanks also go to the always generous and visionary Marc Becker for organizing and including me in the 2011 ERIP (Ethnicity, Race, and Indigenous Peoples) session that engendered this book. Ecuadorian colleagues and students at especially the Salesiana, FLACSO, the San Francisco University and the Universidad Católica who have contributed to my understandings of political and sociocultural phenomena are too numerous to mention, but the collegiality of Alexandra Martínez, José Yánez, Ernesto Salazar, and Karina Borja has been especially important. In addition, I am grateful to members of CODENPE and Kitu Kara who allowed me to interview them and sit in on meetings, particularly Andrés Andrango and Mauricio Ushiña. The Director of the Center for Community Development (CDC-Cotocollao), Raúl Fuentes, has been generous with his time over the years when I have picked his brain about many of these issues. Members of the Cárdenas-Salazar-Barriga-López-Aguirre-Martínez extended family deserve recognition for their friendship, chauffeuring, conversational insight, and tolerance of my comings and goings. Although at this point I do not wish to mention their names publicly, I owe the largest debts of gratitude to the various residents of sectors Cotocollao and El Condado whose generosity with information, food, empathy, sympathy, and serious conversation are the sine qua non of this research. I do, however, dedicate this chapter to the memory of Segundo Pedro Morales, the *cabecilla* of the Yumbada of Cotocollao, who passed away very suddenly in March of 2013. In don Segundo's person and extraordinary life I learned many of the insights I have struggled to represent in this essay. *Que descanse en paz, mi Gobernador Grande.*

# References

Albro, R. 2010. *Roosters at midnight: Indigenous signs and stigma in local Bolivian politics.* Santa Fe, NM: School of Advanced Research Press.

Amawtay Wasi University. 2013. http://www.amawtaywasi.edu.ec/ [accessed Jan. 25, 2013].

Borja, K. n.d. Untitled paper on the Yumbada of San Isidro del Inca in possession of author.

Beteille, A. 1998. "The idea of indigenous people." *Current Anthropology* 39(2):187-91.

Bretón, V. 2007. "A vueltas con el neo-indigenismo etnófago: la experiencia Prodepine o los límites del multiculturalismo liberal." *Íconos: Revista de Ciencias Sociales* 29 (Sept.):95-104.

Caso, A. 1958. *Indigenismo.* Colección Culturas Indígenas No. 1. México, D.F.: Instituto Nacional Indigenista.

Cervone, E. 2009. "Los desafíos del multiculturalismo." In *Repensando los movimientos indígenas*, ed. C. Martínez Novo, 199-214. Quito: FLACSO y el Ministerio de Cultura.

Chávez, L.N. 1993[1943]. "Educación de espíritu indígena." *Previsión Social* 14:19-45. Reprinted in *Indianistas, indianofilos, indigenistas: Entre el enigma y la fascinación: Una antología de textos sobre el "problema" indígena*, ed. J. Trujillo, 553-82. Quito: ILDIS/Abya-Yala.

Costales Samaniego, A. 1960. *Karapungo.* México, D.F.: Instituto Panamericano de Geografía e Historia, Sección de Antropología: Plan Piloto del Ecuador.

Cruikshank, J. 2007. "Melting glaciers and emerging histories in the Saint Elias mountains." In *Indigenous experience today*, ed. M. de la Cadena and O. Starn, 355-78. New York: Berg.

De la Cadena, M. and O. Starn. 2007. "Introduction." In *Indigenous experience today*, ed. M. de la Cadena and O. Starn, 355-78. New York: Berg.

Dessau, A. 1970. "Jorque Icaza y José María Arguedas. Problemas conceptuales y artísticos del indigenismo literario." *Anuario Indigenista* (*Actas del XXIX Congreso Internacional de Americanistas, 2-9 Agosto, 1970, Lima, Perú*) XXX (Dic.):183-90.

Díaz-Polanco, H. and K. Swarthout. 1987. "Neo*indigenismo* and the ethnic question in Central America." *Latin American Perspectives* 14(1):87-100.

Dombrowski, K. 2004. "Comments." In J. Clifford, "Looking several ways: Anthropology and Native heritage in Alaska," 23-24. *Current Anthropology* 45(1):5-30.

Edmonson, M.S. 1959. "Review of *Indigenismo* by Alfonso Caso. Colección Culturas Indígenas No. 1. México, D.F.: Instituto Nacional Indigenista, 1958." *American Anthropologist* 61(1) (Feb.):127.

Egberg, M. 2011. "The Fragmentation of the Indigenous Movement in Ecuador: Perspectives on the Tension between Class and Ethnicity." Stockholm: Masters thesis in Latin American Studies, Stockholms universitet.

Fine-Dare, K.S. 2007. "Más allá del folklore: La Yumbada de Cotocollao como vitrina para los discursos de la identidad, de la intervención estatal, y del poder in los Andes urbanos ecuatorianos." In *Estudios ecuatorianos: un aporte a la discusión – tomo II*, ed. W.T. Waters y M.T. Hamerly, 55-72. Quito: FLACSO, Ecuador section of the Latin American Studies Association and Abya-Yala.

—. 2010. "Culture summary: Quito Quichua." New Haven: Human Relations Area Files. http://ehrafworldcultures.yale.edu/ehrafe/fullContext.do?method=fullC ontext&forward=searchFullContext&col=collection('/eHRAF/ethnogra phy/SouthAmer/SD15')&docId=sd15-000&page=sd15-000- 00029&offsetId=sd1500000009 [access requires password; contact author for copy: fine_k@fortlewis.edu].

Fine-Dare, K.S. and S.L. Rubenstein. 2009. "Introduction: Toward a transnational Americanist anthropology." In *Border crossings: Transnational Americanist anthropology*, ed. K.S. Fine-Dare and S.L. Rubenstein, ix-xxxi. Lincoln: University of Nebraska Press.

Gómez Murillo, A.R. 2007a. "Indígenas urbanos en Quito: el proceso de etnogénesis del Pueblo Kitukara." Paper delivered at FLACSO Social Sciences Congress, Quito, Ecuador, October 29-31.

—. 2007b. "Pueblos originarios, comunas, migrantes y procesos de etnogénesis del Distrito Metropolitano de Quito: Nuevas representaciones sobre los indígenas urbanos de América Latina." Quito: M.A. thesis, FLACSO-Ecuador.

Gnerre, M. and J. Bottasso. 1986. "Del indigenismo a las organizaciones indígenas." In *Del indigenismo a las organizaciones indígenas*, ed. J. Bottasso, 7-27. Quito: Abya Yala.

Guerrero Arias, P. 2010. *Corazonar: Una antropología comprometida con la vida*. Quito: Abya Yala y Universidad Politécnica Salesiana.

Hale, C. 2006. *Más que un Indio: Racial ambivalence and the paradox of neoliberal multiculturalism in Guatemala.* Santa Fe: School of American Research Press.

Ibarra, H. 2003. "El caso del Ecuador: Neoindigenismo e indianismo." Centro de Documentación Mapuche. www.mapuche.info/mapuint/ibarra030600.html [accessed Jan. 25, 2013].

Jaramillo Alvarado, P. 1993[1943]. "Situación política, económica y jurídica del indio en el Ecuador." *Prevision Social* 12:35-58 and 13:19-34. Reprinted in *Indianistas, indianofilos, indigenistas: Entre el enigma y la fascinación: Una antología de textos sobre el "problema" indígena*, ed. J. Trujillo, 453-493. Quito: ILDIS/Abya-Yala.

León Trujillo, J. 2010. "Las organizaciones indígenas y el gobierno de Rafael Correa." *Íconos: Revista de Ciencias Sociales* 37 (mayo):13-23.

Lucero, J.A. 2006. "Representing 'Real Indians': The challenges of indigenous authenticity and strategic constructivism in Ecuador and Bolivia." *Latin American Research Review* 41(2):31-56.

Martins, L.L. 2009. "What can Americanists and anthropology learn from the alliances between Indigenous peoples and popular movements in the Amazon?" In *Border crossings: Transnational Americanist anthropology*, ed. K.S. Fine-Dare and S.L. Rubenstein, 247-59. Lincoln: University of Nebraska Press.

Mattiace, S.L. 2007. "From *Indigenismo* to Indigenous movements in Ecuador and Mexico." *Highland Indians and the state in modern Ecuador*, ed. A. K. Clark and M. Becker, 196-208. Pittsburgh: The University of Pittsburgh Press.

Morato-Lara, L. 1997. "José María Arguedas: Fundación del movimiento literario transculturalista." In *Identidades en transformación: El discurso indigenista de los países andinos*, ed. S. Nagi-Zekmi, 63-80. Quito: Abya Yala.

Nagy-Zekmi, S. 1997. "Introducción: Algunas consideraciones sobre el neoindigenismo." In *Identidades en transformación: El discurso indigenista de los países andinos*, ed. S.Nagi-Zekmi, 7-18. Quito: Abya Yala.

Nieto Cabrera, C. n.d. "El acceso legal a la tierra y el desarrollo de las comunidades indígenas y afroecuatorianas: la experiencia del PRODEPINE en el Ecuador." FAO Corporate Document Repository. http://www.fao.org/docrep/007/y5407t/y5407t0j.htm [accessed July 31, 2012].

Oña, L. 2004. "Quito en el arte." In *La tierra, Quito . . . la ciudad, la pintura*, ed. L. Oña, 11-32. Quito: Ediciones Archipélago.

Ortiz, F. 2003[1947]. *Cuban counterpoint: Tobacco and sugar*. B. Malinowski (introduction). F. Coronil (new introduction). Durham, NC: Duke University Press.

Pallares, A. 2007. "Contesting membership: Citizenship, pluriculturalism(s), and the contemporary Indigenous movement." In *Highland Indians and the state in modern Ecuador*, ed. A. K.Clark and M. Becker, 139-54. Pittsburgh: The University of Pittsburgh Press.

Posern-Zieliński, A. 2008. "Las organizaciones indígenas como 'nuevas tribus' y sus estrategias etnopolíticas." *Estudios Latinoamericanos* 28:51-73. Varsovia-Posnań.

Saldívar, E. 2011. "Everyday practices of *Indigenismo*: An ethnography of anthropology and the state in Mexico." *The Journal of Latin American and Caribbean Anthropology* 16(1):67-89.

Sánchez Palma, F. and J.G. Prado, eds. 2011[2010]. "El encuentro del águila y el cóndor." *Somos Propuestas* (Oct.) http://www.revistasomos.cl/2011/11/el-encuentro-del-aguila-el-condor/ [accessed July 31, 2012].

Salomon, F. 1981. "Killing the Yumbo: A ritual drama of northern Quito." In *Cultural Transformations and Ethnicity in Modern Ecuador*, ed. N.E. Whitten, Jr., 162-208. Urbana: University of Illinois Press.

Stoll, D. 2011. "The obligatory Indian." *Dialectical Anthropology* 35:135-146.

Swanson, K. 2010. *Begging as a path to progress: Indigenous women and children and the struggle for Ecuador's urban spaces*. Athens: University of Georgia Press.

Taller Cultural Kinde. 2007. "Mensajero del Saber: Proyecto de educación experimental." Quito (typescript).

UN Permanent Forum. 2013. http://social.un.org/index/IndigenousPeoples /UNPFIISessions/Eleventh.aspx [accessed Jan. 25, 2013].

Viatori, M. 2009. *One state, many nations: Indigenous rights struggles in Ecuador*. Santa Fe, NM: School for Advanced Research Press.

Vicenti Carpio, M. 2011. *Indigenous Albuquerque.* P.J. Hafen (Foreword). Lubbock: Texas Tech University Press.

Waters, W.F. 2007. "Indigenous communities, landlords, and the state: Land and labor in highland Ecuador, 1950-1975." In *Highland Indians and the state in modern Ecuador*, ed. A.K. Clark and M. Becker, 120-38. Pittsburgh: The University of Pittsburgh Press.

Whitten, N.E., Jr. 2003. "Introduction." In *Millennial Ecuador: Critical Essays on Cultural Transformations and Social Dynamics*, ed. N.E. Whitten, Jr., 1-45. Iowa City: University of Iowa Press.

Williams, J.L. 2007. "Celebrando el pasado del futuro: La negociación de la identidad indígena en Lumbisí, Ecuador." In *Estudios ecuatorianos: Un aporte a la discusión—Tomo II: Ponencias escojidas del III Encuentro de la Sección de Estudios Ecuatorianos LASA, Quito 2006*, ed. W.F. Waters and M.T. Hamerly, 73-86. Quito: FLACSO and Abya-Yala.

Wutich, A. 2011. "The moral economy of water reexamined: Reciprocity, water insecurity, and urban survival in Cochabamba, Bolivia." *Journal of Anthropological Research* 67 (Spring):5-26.

Yánez del Pozo, J. 1997. "'Sinchi runami cani' (soy un hombre fuerte): Filosofía de un vendedor indígena en Estados Unidos." In *Identidades en transformación: El discurso indigenista de los países andinos*, ed. S.Nagi-Zekmi, 135-52. Quito: Abya Yala.

# CHAPTER THREE

# THE ECUADORIAN INDIGENOUS MOVEMENT AND THE CHALLENGES OF PLURINATIONAL STATE CONSTRUCTION

## VÍCTOR HUGO JIJÓN

The great challenge that not only Indigenous peoples but all of Ecuadorian society face is how to advance the implementation of the republic's new constitution that was approved by referendum in September 2008, and in particular how to enforce the individual and collective rights recognized for Indigenous peoples, Afro-descendants, and coastal peasants (*montubios*) as expressed through two new paradigms: the Plurinational State and the *Sumak Kawsay* or Good Living. This effort has two main complementary avenues of realization: the structuring of Intercultural Territorial Circumscriptions that allows the exercise of self-government on behalf of Indigenous peoples and nationalities, and the mainstreaming of plurinationality so that public policies for Indigenous peoples are formulated and implemented in all state bodies. This process demands a truly participative corresponding legislation, a deep reconfiguration of state-owned institutions, and an organizational strengthening of civil society.

The political participation of Indigenous peoples points to their willingness to influence democratically the transformation of an unjust society and exclusionary state structures. However, some laws established by initiative of President Rafael Correa's government (mining, water resources, food sovereignty, education, biodiversity, and oil) form a legislative package that threatens the acquired rights of Indigenous peoples. Furthermore, the government has done very little to fulfill another important constitutional mandate: structuring a different economy that is social and solidarity, not extractive, without losing its productive and sustainable aspects. This chapter briefly surveys the critical nodes of this experience and its possible outcomes.

## The Colonial Context and State Construction

The current situation in Ecuador emerged out of several key moments that mark its historical formation. These can be summarized into four main phases. First was the Inka invasion in the fifteenth century that led to the collapse of many native communities, their economic and political subjection to the Inka Empire, and the imposition of the Quechua language on its inhabitants (except for those living on the coast and in the Amazon region).

Second came the Spanish invasion with its dramatic consequences: the creation of the "Indian" as an image of someone who should be exploited, deprived of their lands, and have their beliefs, habits, and customs destroyed. The Indian, a term that originated from Christopher Columbus' geographical confusion who thought he had found a new route to the East Indies, was assigned attributes of inferiority, paganism, and idolatry that called into question his human character. Ideologically, this justified the conquest and presented it as a praiseworthy "civilizing" undertaking. The Spanish invasion established the discrimination and the enslavement of the population, and their religious and cultural alienation. These impacts added to the carnage of war and foreign diseases that decimated the native population, and contributed to the ethnocide and genocide of the native population.

Later, colonization had disastrous effects that derived from the violent substitution of one political, social, economic, and cultural regime by another very different one. This led to the transformation of a system of production; the elimination of a person's status; the dismantling of native peoples' organizations; their social and familial dislocation, acculturation, religious imposition; and their accompanying loss of identities. All this, however, occurred amid numerous acts of resistance, rebellions, uprisings, and multiple cultural preservation initiatives and organizational reconstruction.

Finally, the wars for independence from the Spanish Crown in which Indians played a crucial role in support of the libertarian armies launched a long and tortuous process that led to the formation of the republic and the modern state. This meant the adoption and implementation by *creole*[1] elites of a political regime imported from Europe that set up an emerging liberal and semi-feudal state that formalized and institutionalized hierarchies and guidelines foreign to the country's reality and to that of the

---

[1] Creole is the term used to refer to descendants from Spanish colonists who were born on the new continent.

continent. Schematically, two different concepts were introduced in the formation of the new republic: a *farm-state* in the sierra region (highland mountains), and an *enterprise-state* in the coastal region. Both cases were based on a *uninational* conception of the state, a selective and exclusive form of citizenship, and the formation of political parties that coincided with the predominant conservative and liberal European ideologies of the time in which Indigenous peoples simply were not included as part of the citizenship.

With the evolution of partisan and economic conflicts between landowners and merchant sectors, a series of successive constitutions sought to institutionalize the nascent republic. They were based on foreign rules that attempted to preserve the respective interests of the oligarchical sectors. This had a hard impact on the structure of official institutions that always ignored the Indigenous population. The founding fathers of independence dreamt about a *uninational state*, that is, an exclusive state of the creoles.

Colonial practices continued into the new republic, minimizing and ignoring the social and cultural diversity that would comprise the future Ecuador. In this way, each version of the constitution promulgated since the nineteenth century imposed a monocultural state. The Indigenous population was forced to work on plantations and with domestic chores in the houses of Spanish and creole families in exchange for the "huasipungo," a marginal bit of farmland that allowed for a precarious existence.

As a result, a society was formed based on an European exclusory ethnocentrism, which led to a political practice that considered only white persons or "mestizos" capable of governing. This attitude was initially expressed in constitutions where in order to be a citizen a person was required to have a certain amount of property, an amount unattainable for Indians and Blacks of the time. Literacy was also a requirement, despite that the cenacles of power knew that education was denied to them. In this way, a perverse and severe practice of discrimination was implemented that prevented Indigenous access to any public position and denied them eligibility to hold any authority. This discrimination lasted until the end of the twentieth century.

| Nationalities | Peoples | Provinces |
|---|---|---|
| **Coastal Region** | | |
| Chachi | | Esmeraldas |
| Tsachila | | Pichincha |
| Awá | | Esmeraldas, Carchi, Imbabura |
| Epera | | Esmeraldas |
| Manta-Huancavilca | | Guayas, Manabi |
| **Sierra Region** | | |
| Kichwa | Karanki | Imbabura |
| | Otavalo | Imbabura |
| | Natabuela | Imbabura |
| | Kayambi | Imbabura, Pichincha, Napo |
| | Kitu Kara | Pichincha |
| | Panzaleo | Cotopaxi |
| | Chibuleo | Tungurahua |
| | Salasaca | Tungurahua |
| | Kisapincha | Tungurahua |
| | Waranka | Bolivar |
| | Puruha | Chimborazo |
| | Kañari | Cañar, Azuay |
| | Saraguro | Loja, Zamora-Chinchipe |
| **Amazon Region** | | |
| Cofan | | Sucumbios |
| Siona | | Sucumbios |
| Secoya | | Sucumbios |
| Waorani | | Pastaza, Orellana |
| Zapara | | Pastaza |
| Shiwiar | | Pastaza |
| Achuar | | Morona-Santiago |
| | | Pastaza, |
| Shuar | | Morona-Santiago, |
| | | Zamora, Sucumbios, |
| | | Guayas, Pazt, Napo |
| Uncontacted peoples: | | |
| Tagaeri and | | |
| Taromenane | | Orellana. Pastaza |

Table 1: National Development Council of Ecuador's Nationalities and Peoples.
Source: CODENPE. Preparation: VHJ.

## Who Constitutes the Indigenous Nationalities?

In Ecuador there are 14 nationalities and 18 Indigenous peoples that belong to the Kichwa Nationality. There is no adequate census, and therefore we only have estimates that their total ranges from 7 percent to 25 percent of the country's population.

The Indigenous population is distributed throughout the country. Nevertheless, it has a stronger presence in certain regions, provinces, and cantons than others. Taking into account a combined definition of language and self-identification, the provinces with the largest Indigenous presence are: Napo (56.1 percent), Morona Santiago (41.3 percent), Chimborazo (38.7 percent), Pastaza (38.4 percent), Orellana (31.4 percent), Imbabura (25.8 percent), Cotopaxi (24.8 percent), Bolivar (24.4 percent), Cañar (17.3 percent), Tungurahua (15 percent), Zamora Chinchipe (12.8 percent), and Sucumbíos (11 percent). The distribution of Indigenous peoples across the country, however, shows that about half are concentrated in Chimborazo (17.6 percent), Pichincha (12.2 percent), Imbabura (10.0 percent), and Cotopaxi (9.8 percent). Provincial distribution of the nationalities and peoples are shown in Table 1.

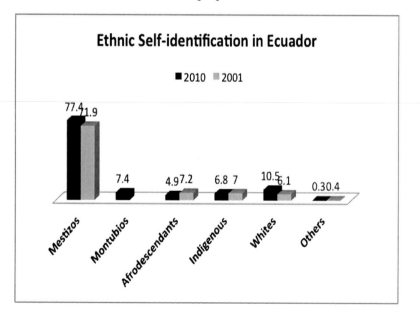

Figure 1. Source: National Institute of Statistics and Census. Preparation: VHJ.

This distribution of population is currently under discussion because the official census, based on self-identification at the time of the survey, has been questioned for not corresponding to a faithful reflection of the country's ethnic composition, and involves subjective biases of persons in respect to their ethnic status. In fact, the results of the last population census in November 2010 show that the Afro-descendant population grew from that of 2001, reaching a number greater than the Indigenous population. This is a questionable result (see Figure 1).

## Indian Movements and Their Political Participation

In Ecuador, autonomous Indigenous political participation began with the famous Indian Uprising of June 1990, led by the Confederation of Indigenous Nationalities of Ecuador (CONAIE), which represented a substantial positive break in the daily political and social life throughout the country (Jijón 1990). Indeed, the Indian Uprising shocked the Ecuadorian state and society by highlighting the strength of a social actor that had been ignored but that had been shaped over many years of resistance. The Uprising did make visible and questioned the different forms of marginalization and racism from the white-mestizo society as part of the prevailing system of domination and segregation.

The Uprising also unveiled an exclusory state and social polarization rooted in structural adjustment policies that successive governments had implemented since 1983 in obedience to the International Monetary Fund (IMF) and in the interest of the local oligarchy. Moreover, the Uprising also questioned the limits of a democracy restricted to voting that did not consider the exercise of economic and social rights, and failed to place them on par with political rights. This meant that from the beginning the Indigenous movement combined the class character of economic exploitation with the ethnic dimensions of discrimination (Macas 1999).

The emergence of the Indigenous movement also occurred in a moment of deep crisis in the labor movement that was caused by "labor flexibility" imposed by neoliberalism that reduced its historic rights. The Indigenous movement led by CONAIE, and the peasant movement led by the National Confederation of Peasant Social Security (CONFEUNASSC), emerged together with new social actors including those associated with the youth movement, the women's movement, human rights, and environmentalism.

In the first half of the 1990s, a set of developments led to the convergence of these sectors in areas of multicultural unity. These included actions in opposition to the celebration of 500 years of the alleged "Encounter of Two Worlds" led by Spain in 1992, demonstrations against a Farm Bill in 1994 that left the latifundia intact, and a referendum called by the national government in 1995 to enable the vote of persons independent of political parties.

After these developments, citizenship deepened the debate over the creation of a political organization that constituted the expression of all social forces resistant to neoliberalism, a generator of more poverty, and social exclusion. Given this, the CONAIE, which since its formation had called on its members to annul their vote in elections, deemed it necessary to reconsider its position. A call to annul votes in elections was a demonstration of its distrust of formal liberal democracy and its rejection of the demagogic utilization of Indigenous peoples by traditional political parties.

This need to intervene in elections as part of the struggle for a more just and egalitarian society and for a most inclusive participatory democracy determined the decision to pursue a political self-expression that emanated from the grassroots. It was, thus, in 1995 that an active process of dialogue and debate between the member organizations of the Coordination of Social Movements, the CONAIE, and CONFEUNASSC led to the founding of the Pachakutik Plurinational Unity Movement-New Country (MUPP-NP) (1996), which was given the mandate to fulfill several expectations, including:

a. To become a meeting point and articulation of Indigenous Peoples and Nationalities together with other sectors of the countryside, urban popular movements, public and private unions, democratic intellectuals, and church sectors who had expressed a preferential option for the poor, and above all, with a broad spectrum of society that discovered in the emergence of MUPP-NP a reflection of their longings for independence and political autonomy, and their expectation for a deep transformation of society.

b. To become a policy tool to enable an organized popular movement to get involved in the political and institutional sphere with concrete policy proposals, aimed at carrying out structural changes to benefit all society, maintaining their independence and autonomy.

c. To become stronger as a political movement, to facilitate access to institutions, and to raise the challenge to build and demonstrate alternative forms of governance and strengthen local authorities as a strategy of building a new order from the local, from the organized grassroots of civil society.

From 1996 to the present, the Indigenous population represented by the organizations belonging to the CONAIE, in alliance with other social organizations, has participated in all electoral events convoked by the Supreme Electoral Tribunal, through the Pachakutik Movement. This is in contrast to other Indigenous organizations such as FENOCIN and FEINE that have participated mainly through the Socialist Party-Broad Front without achieving any political or social change (MUPP-NP, 1999).

## Electoral participation from 1996 to 2004

As a result of the new political electoral leadership, the Pachakutik Movement came to occupy important elected offices in various periods. In 1996, it partnered with the New Country Movement led by journalist Freddy Ehlers and came in third place in the presidential vote. On that occasion Pachakutik won eight deputy seats, of which five were Indians, including a woman.

In the elections for representatives to the National Assembly in 1997, Pachakutik won seven Assembly members out of a total of 70. In 1998, Pachakutik gained eight deputies, 11 mayors, and 72 councilors and aldermen. In 2000, Pachakutik had 20 mayors in addition to seven in alliance with others parties, plus five provincial prefects, 86 counselors, 17 aldermen, and 461 parish council representatives.

In 2002, in alliance with the Patriotic Society Party, Pachakutik won the presidential election, with Colonel Lucio Gutiérrez as their presidential candidate. This alliance only lasted six months because of Gutiérrez's treason to the commitments and principles of the campaign, in particular the abandonment of the progressive social and economic policies and their replacement by submission to the IMF and World Bank. Many analysts have generally described this support of the candidacy of Colonel Gutiérrez as a political error on the part of the Pachakutik Movement's leadership. This is a superficial vision of what was really the political conjuncture.

In fact, there are several factors that led to this decision: a) the CONAIE's resolution not to participate with their own candidate to avoid internal ruptures in the organization by nominating a candidate, for which CONAIE's former leader Antonio Vargas—highly questioned at this time—competed with the Mayor of Cotacachi, Auki Tituaña; b) the short time remaining between the date of this decision and that fixed by law to register candidates, which prevented holding primary elections and implied the risk of not participating at a national level, leaving the candidates to provincial prefects and mayors without national counterparts; and c) the refusal of candidates Rodrigo Borja (social democrat) and León Roldós (socialist) to establish an electoral alliance with Pachakutik.

These circumstances left Pachakutik with no choice except to ally with Lucio Gutiérrez who, at that time, had a rebellious image and proposed radical changes to society and the state.[2] Moreover, given the Ecuadorian electoral tradition of always presenting a ticket with one candidate from the coast and the other from the sierra, it became impossible to run an Indigenous person in the vice presidential slot. Although Lucio Gutiérrez was a native of the Amazon, he was practically considered a candidate of the sierra, which therefore forced him to pair with someone from the coast. This is in fact what happened (Jijón 2004).

In the National Congress, Pachakutik won a legislative block with eleven elected members out of 100. In 2002, Pachakutik elected four provincial prefectures out of a total of 22, as well as gaining control of 32 of 215 municipalities, including those elected in partnership with other related social or political forces.

In all these elections, Pachakutik always tried to maintain ethnic and gender equity in the nomination of candidates. Indigenous peoples occupied about 50 percent of the elected positions. As for women, Pachakutik was among the political organizations that most complied with the provisions of the Elections Act in regard to a proportional allocation of candidates for different positions. Thus, in 2004, Pachakutik presented one candidate for prefect who was elected and nine candidates for mayors of whom three were elected.

It is important to note that in each of these elections the Electoral Supreme Court (now the National Electoral Council) changed the method of calculating the allocation of votes so that at the level of multi-member elections numerical comparisons cannot be done mechanically without taking into account the quantitative impact of each method. Indeed, the Court passed successively from the traditional method of ratios to the method of d'Hondt, then to the Imperial method, and finally to the

---

[2] On January 21, 2000, while still on active military duty, Lucio Gutiérrez took part in a rebellion along with the Indigenous movement and mobilized popular sectors that overthrew President Jamil Mahuad. He became a progressive political figure who various parties and social movements in Latin America courted. Once elected president in 2003, however, his vaguely nationalist and socialist messages were diluted almost immediately amid accusations of betraying the disadvantaged classes by allying with conservative parties, preserving the liberal economic model, and engaging in nepotism and corruption. This led to his overthrow in April 2005.

weighted d'Hondt method. This has a main effect of altering the real representation of the winning parties and promoting the election of minority candidates in each constituency.

| Provinces | Deputies | | Assembly | | Deputies | |
|---|---|---|---|---|---|---|
| | 1996 | % | 1997 | % | 1998 | Lists |
| Azuay | 48237 | 28.48 | 10860 | 6.72 | 125132 | 12-17-18 |
| Bolivar | 4549 | 9.85 | 10935 | 24.51 | 23923 | 18 |
| Cañar | 7622 | 14.53 | 7804 | 15.36 | 13427 | 18 |
| Carchi | 0 | 0 | 9664 | 20.81 | 8517 | 17-18-21 |
| Cotopaxi | 15159 | 15.75 | 14079 | 17.18 | 24378 | 18 |
| Chimborazo | 21947 | 18.75 | 15252 | 13.4 | 28888 | 17-18 |
| El Oro | 0 | 0 | 8606 | 6.52 | 29077 | 17-18-21 |
| Esmeraldas | 0 | 0 | 2457 | 3.5 | 0 | 0 |
| Guayas | 0 | 0 | 7792 | 0.91 | 0 | 0 |
| Imbabura | 15654 | 15.9 | 22576 | 25.43 | 43000 | 17-18-21 |
| Loja | 0 | 0 | 5478 | 5.81 | 31867 | 17-18-21 |
| Los Rios | 2821 | 1.68 | 0 | 0 | 12949 | 17-18 |
| Manabi | 0 | 0 | 10019 | 3.55 | | 17-18-21 |
| Morona S. | 4362 | 19.95 | 6408 | 27.78 | 18301 | 18 |
| Napo | 7822 | 25.69 | 5634 | 18.65 | 23449 | 18 |
| Pastaza | 1851 | 12.78 | 1414 | 10.07 | 7838 | 5-18 |
| Pichincha | 99664 | 13.46 | 47511 | 6.94 | 854966 | 17-18-21 |
| Tungurahua | 17864 | 12.1 | 15564 | 11.82 | 24413 | 18 |
| Zamora Ch. | 0 | 0 | 3463 | 20.04 | 4595 | 12-17-18 |
| Galápagos | | | | | | |
| Sucumbios | 3936 | 19.56 | 5341 | 24.4 | | |
| Orellana | | | | | | |
| Total | 251488 | 7.15 | 210857 | 6.61 | 1274720 | |

Table 2. Source: Supreme Electoral Tribunal. Preparation: VHJ.

| | Provinces | Prefects | | | Mayors | | |
|---|---|---|---|---|---|---|---|
| | | PK Voting Elected Or Not | Total Valid Votes | % | PK Voting Elected Or Not | Total Valid Votes | % |
| 1 | Azuay | 35935 | 242461 | 14.82 | 34685 | 256559 | 13.52 |
| 2 | Bolivar | 15050 | 67137 | 22.42 | 12002 | 74375 | 16.14 |
| 3 | Cañar | 16785 | 72155 | 23.26 | 18140 | 76964 | 23.57 |
| 4 | Carchi | | 72972 | 0.00 | 3605 | 77621 | 4.64 |
| 5 | Cotopaxi | 56478 | 143309 | 39.41 | 35010 | 152915 | 22.90 |
| 6 | Chimborazo | 48967 | 155630 | 31.46 | 40707 | 162387 | 25.07 |
| 7 | El Oro | 4990 | 225656 | 2.21 | 4854 | 231206 | 2.10 |
| 8 | Esmeraldas | 1101 | 126397 | 0.87 | 573 | 135172 | 0.42 |
| 9 | Guayas | 13783 | 1332157 | 1.03 | 13473 | 1441158 | 0.93 |
| 10 | Imbabura | 35883 | 138624 | 25.89 | 33074 | 142607 | 23.19 |
| 11 | Loja | | 162689 | 0.00 | 1809 | 173268 | 1.04 |
| 12 | Los Rios | | 263092 | 0.00 | 1523 | 64552 | 2.36 |
| 13 | Manabi | | 523285 | 0.00 | 12157 | 642350 | 1.89 |
| 14 | Morona S. | 20605 | 36487 | 56.47 | 10584 | 38368 | 27.59 |
| 15 | Napo | 5611 | 33517 | 16.74 | 8202 | 32676 | 25.10 |
| 16 | Pastaza | 2036 | 25731 | 7.91 | 3155 | 25329 | 12.46 |
| 17 | Pichincha | 85071 | 1047360 | 8.12 | 79939 | 1096437 | 7.29 |
| 18 | Tungurahua | 9690 | 184539 | 5.25 | 16857 | 199193 | 8.46 |
| 19 | Zamora Ch. | | 29978 | 0.00 | 3195 | 60694 | 5.26 |
| 20 | Galápagos | | 8018 | 0.00 | 97 | 7015 | 1.38 |
| 21 | Sucumbios | 9897 | 45385 | 21.81 | 8349 | 47598 | 17.54 |
| 22 | Orellana | 10732 | 29851 | 35.95 | 8825 | 30590 | 28.85 |
| Total | | 372614 | 4966430 | 7.50 | 350815 | 5169034 | 6.79 |

Table 3. Source: Supreme Electoral Tribunal. Preparation: VHJ.

At the presidential level, participation was performed with non-Indigenous candidates due to the need of reaching an under-politicized, mostly urban electorate, as well as due to a precaution of not subjecting early Indigenous leaders to the verdict of the polls, knowing that the majority of the population still carried racial prejudice and attitudes in favor of segregation. Tables 2 and 3 show the provincial distribution of the vote, which allows for identification of the areas or regions of Pachakutik's influence.

As shown in Table 3, Pachakutik's total vote in 2004 for prefects and mayors is almost the same, with a difference of 22,000 votes in favor of the former. However, there are serious provincial differences. For example, in Cotopaxi, the vote of the candidate for prefect, who was up for reelection, is far higher than that of candidates for mayor (56,478 against 35,010). Instead, in Morona Santiago, with a smaller voting base, the candidate for prefect won almost twice the votes of the candidates for mayor, 20,605 against 10,584. Pachakutik won six municipalities, thanks to the small amount of votes required to be elected. It should be noted, however, that the number of inhabitants or voters does not reflect the territorial extension of the constituencies. Some of them are very large, contributing to more responsibilities and challenges for the strategic planning of local development.

## The electoral participation in October 2006

Pachakutik participated for the first time with its own Indigenous candidate in the October 15, 2006 presidential election. It did so, however, under rather unfavorable political circumstances due to the presence of strong populist candidates that due to their demagogy could absorb part of the Indigenous electorate. An internal decision of CONAIE prevented campaigning in alliance with the Economist Rafael Correa and his Movement "Alianza PAIS." Instead, it yielded to the pressures of a indigenist current that favored the nomination of Luis Macas, a former CONAIE leader and former Pachakutik congressman, in hopes of repeating what had happened a year earlier in Bolivia with the victory of Evo Morales. This could not happen, however, since Ecuador does not have the same density of Indigenous population, or the same electoral sympathy of the non-Indigenous population as in Bolivia. Nor was there any relationship with traditional party structures and their electoral potentialities (Jijón 2006).

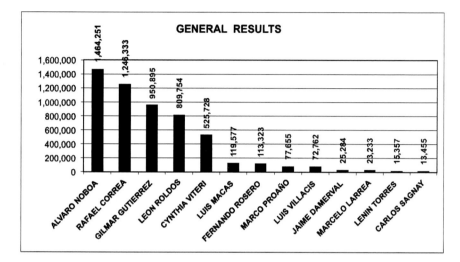

Figure 2. Source: National Electoral Council. Preparation: VHJ.

Luis Macas received nearly 120,000 votes, equivalent to 2.3 percent of the valid votes, which placed him in sixth place, but ahead of seven other candidates. These results show that in a pragmatic decision, the majority of the electorate that had been sympathetic to Pachakutik's proposals chose to vote for Correa, as evidenced by his victory and the noticeable drop off in the vote that generally had gone to Pachakutik. The coastal province of Guayas provided a paradoxical case in that it initially supported the idea of Correa running with Macas for vice president, but then assumed a disciplined position and voted for Macas for president, giving him a larger percentage of the vote than several provinces with a high Indigenous composition (see Figure 3).

This internal disaffection for the Indigenous presidential candidate becomes clear when compared to the results of the votes obtained for other dignitaries and in particular with the candidate to the Andean Parliament, Oscar Chalá, an Afro-descendant member of Pachakutik (Table 4, Figure 4).

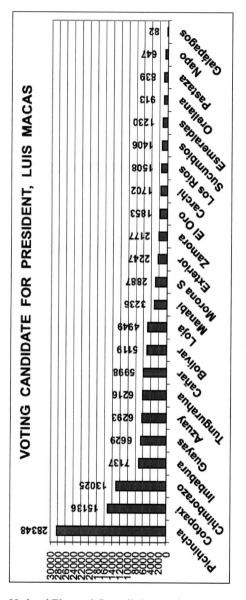

Figure 3. Source: National Electoral Council. Preparation: VHJ.

| | Deputies | President | Counselors | Andean P. |
|---|---|---|---|---|
| Azuay | 5303 | 6293 | 6359 | 5836 |
| Bolívar | 4749 | 5119 | 5461 | 5423 |
| Cañar | 6854 | 5998 | 8109 | 7079 |
| Carchi | 0 | 1702 | 0 | 1355 |
| Chimborazo | 13367 | 13025 | 13238 | 14371 |
| Cotopaxi | 18326 | 15136 | 20900 | 18531 |
| El Oro | 1756 | 1853 | 0 | 1937 |
| Esmeraldas | 1191 | 1230 | 714 | 1195 |
| Galápagos | 108 | 82 | 0 | 162 |
| Guayas | 4308 | 6629 | 0 | 5649 |
| Imbabura | 14055 | 7137 | 14098 | 8524 |
| Loja | 3521 | 4949 | 3769 | 4225 |
| Los Ríos | 1340 | 1508 | 594 | 1295 |
| Manabi | 2247 | 3236 | 2193 | 2892 |
| Morona S | 5500 | 2887 | 6136 | 5255 |
| Napo | 3182 | 647 | 2354 | 2622 |
| Orellana | 3722 | 913 | 3428 | 2707 |
| Pastaza | 1145 | 839 | 1137 | 1478 |
| Pichincha | 17450 | 28348 | 19333 | 24218 |
| Sucumbios | 2996 | 1406 | 3277 | 3433 |
| Tungurahua | 6569 | 6216 | 9910 | 7648 |
| Zamora | 3882 | 2177 | 3028 | 2769 |
| Exterior | | 2247 | | |
| Total | 121571 | 119577 | 124038 | 128604 |

Table 4. Source: National Electoral Council. Preparation: VHJ.

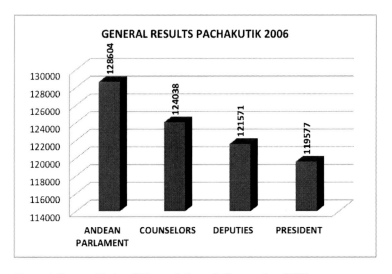

Figure 4. Source: National Electoral Council. Preparation: VHJ.

Despite these unfavorable results, the presence of Pachakutik held firm, as shown by the five posts it won in the 2007 Constituent Assembly elections. In the 2008 elections, amidst an unfavorable electoral context against the official candidates and a lack of economic resources for a campaign, five candidates were elected to the National Assembly, two men and three women, out of a total of 124 seats. It should be noted that in the same election the parties of traditional right, that before held majority power, polled very poorly with numerical results similar to those of Pachakutik.

Pachakutik also won five of 24 prefects (four men and one woman), 34 mayors out of 219 (five women), and 98 out of 420 parish presidencies, with memberships on 230 councils. This may seem very little quantitatively; what counts, however, is the territory and natural resources that exist in those areas. The total population of the five provinces with Pachakutik prefects is 990,000 inhabitants, which together with the municipalities' population of other provinces with Pachakutik mayors, reaches 10 percent of the national population. As for the geographic reach, this amounts to 25 percent of the country. This covers most of the oil reserves and mining in the Amazon, and important agricultural regions in the Central Andes.

The access of Indigenous people to local governments requires administrative techniques, transparency in public management, and strategic planning. This process has demanded intense formation, capacitation, and training to overcome shortcomings due to a lack of experience in these roles and the shortage of qualified personnel for the performance of senior management positions. To succeed in management, and to avoid repeating the same flaws and shortcomings of the traditional administration of the traditional political parties, requires employment of strategic planning and participatory budgeting as tools of decision-making, with the strong participation of Indigenous communities, peasants, the urban popular sectors, and the general citizenship.

The timely dissemination of relevant information on government policies and programs, the development of popular assemblies as mechanisms of social control over elected officials, the creation of "negotiation tables" to resolve conflicts and build consensus, and the frequent accountability of public authorities, have meant that the main beneficiary of this governance has been democracy at its most critical points: the participation of citizens and elimination of corruption. These aspects have been recognized even by international organizations such as the United Nations, the Andean Community of Nations, and others.

## Plurinational State Recognition

It was only with the constitution of 1998, and through Indigenous movement demonstrations and proposals that CONAIE and the Pachakutik Movement led, that Ecuadorian society was defined as multiethnic and pluricultural, although this was merely a simple anthropological observation without major social or political effects. The conservative and rightwing majority of the Constitutional Assembly rejected the category of plurinational at this time, arguing without factual basis that the Indigenous movement had separatist intentions that allegedly risked dividing the country.

However, the massive social mobilizations and the convincing oratory of Pachakutik deputies, although a minority, achieved formal recognition of collective rights in this constitution. Those include the right to be consulted on the plans and programs of exploration and exploitation of non-renewable resources found on their lands that could affect their environment or culture; to preserve and develop their traditional ways of living and social organization; to exercise of their own authority; to implement a bilingual intercultural education system; to practice ancestral medicine; and to administer traditional justice systems.

Convention 169 of the International Labour Organization (ILO) had already recognized some of these rights in 1989. The National Congress of Ecuador ratified this Convention in 1997, based on a proposal from

Pachakutik Movement deputies. Its content and scope was expanded and detailed later by the Declaration of the Rights of Indigenous Peoples of the United Nations Organization in September 2007.

The incorporation of the collective rights of Indigenous peoples in the 1998 constitution laid bare the limits between the discourse of parliamentary democracy and its actual practice, as the laws enacted in its implementation have often become a dead letter when it comes to even slight changes. The result is discriminatory relations that maintain economic and social inequality in the population and promote commercial overexploitation of nature.

Ecuador had to wait ten years until the Constituent Assembly of 2007 would recognize the country as a plurinational and intercultural state. This was a result of a majority of progressive deputies (82 percent of 130 seats), although the proposal required intense debate in drawing up articles for the new constitution. It was approved by referendum in September 2008. Indeed, a series of appointed Working Groups for the Thematic Committees analyzed and debated 1632 proposals that about 70,000 civil society delegations from around the country submitted to be considered for incorporation into the texts of articles that these committees should first discuss and, and then move to discussion and final adoption in plenary session (Carter Center 2008).

## What Plurinationality and Interculturality Imply

The Ecuadorian Indigenous movement that emerged in the 1990s changed the traditional denomination of the western social and political sciences in which a state corresponds to a single nation and comprises a single people with their language and culture that inhabit a territory. Instead, the Indigenous movement defined as nationality a large group of persons whose existence precedes the formation of the Ecuadorian state and its members share a set of their own cultural characteristics that are unlike the rest of society (CONAIE, 2001). They live in a determined territory; they share an identity and history through their own institutions and traditional forms of social, economic, legal, and political organization; and they have a collective communitarian authority. Within the nationalities coexist culturally diverse peoples organized in communities, associations, or centers (Maldonado 2010).

These issues contribute to a complex problematic that involves a reconceptualization of what is commonly known as the *nation-state*, and from what is derived political representation, public policies, and citizen participation. It is in this context that the current relations between *social movements, political parties*, and the *state* require special treatment. Social movements grew strongly in the 1990s in the face of the weakening of political parties because they were morally discredited and suffered a loss of representativeness. The weakened capacity of traditional parties to instrumentalize the state minimized the benefits that they could deliver to the social and economic sectors that they represented (García Linera 2002).

Thus, the traditional political mediation between society and the state that political parties previously exercised was reduced, and new social movements emerged as actors carrying policy proposals, alongside the sectorial demands that they claimed. New protagonists were formed with a mixed character, *social-political*, something unthinkable before due to a more liberal conception of parliamentary democracy that saw political parties as the only intermediaries with civil society.

Herein lies the particularity of the Ecuadorian Indigenous proposal: an institutional and political transformation of the traditional *nation-state* to another, a *plurinational state*, that incorporates the complexity of the social composition and its aspirations for substantial and egalitarian political change. It is a proposal with a vision that goes beyond the economic contradictions of class and assumed components of ancestral identity that affect production, governance, administration of justice, intercultural bilingual education, among other areas. *Plurinationality* becomes the right to exist and to live with identity versus a Eurocentric project of modernity, the expansion of capitalism, and globalization that seeks cultural uniformity, homogenization of habits and customs, and the westernization of the ways of life based on the market economy.

## Interculturality

Interculturality is not simply coexistence among different persons or different peoples, and it is not only a cultural relationship. It raises issues of respect for the personality and the culture of the "other," but this is insufficient. For the Ecuadorian Indigenous movement, an intercultural society and an intercultural citizenship create a social construction, a communicative and experiential process that is not only cultural but also political and economic, which presupposes a space of shared beliefs and values within one framework of solidarity actions with expectations of equality of all cultures to build a common project of society.

Given that social relations are power relations, it is inevitable that in intercultural relations the role played by the state and its institutions should be taken into account, since rather than promoting equity of everyone its actions may favor some cultures and harm others, which makes it untenable to interculturality (Walsh 2000).

It is equally important to note that economic globalization is based on a corporative and institutional transnationalization facilitated by multilateral credit agencies to impose "conditionalities" on economic and social policies, including the reduction of the size of the state and the privatization of public services and state enterprises. This has led to impoverishment, disarticulation of community and family structures, an institutional destructuring, the loss of values, and the destruction of local identities. The preservation of communitarian identities is thus a priority of collective existence, without the issues arising from ethnicity taken to extreme positions.

This situation requires actions of resistance to the penetration of the exploitation of oil, minerals, wood, and other natural resources, accompanied by viable alternatives to the implementation of a new model of development, avoiding adaptive attitudes or assimilation of values from external agents, usually made by companies interested in exploiting natural resources.

## The New Constitution and "Good Living"

The new 2008 constitution puts forward in its Article 1 that Ecuador is a constitutional state of rights and justice, social, democratic, sovereign, independent, unitary, intercultural, plurinational, and secular, which recognizes society's ethnic and cultural diversity. It establishes the need to make visible and concretize this definition in its economic and political strata. In turn, Articles 12 to 34 define the rights of the Sumak Kawsay or Good Living, incorporating a comprehensive vision of becoming a society whose scope and realization constitutes a substantial challenge for any new formulation of economic and social development. Thus, this approach transcends neoliberalism's simplistic views of development as growth and capital accumulation.

The Sumak Kawsay is a way of organizing a social, economic, political, and spiritual life. It consists of seeking equilibrium, knowing that a balanced life brings harmony, overall satisfaction, and happiness. The principles for achieving this equilibrium are reciprocity and complementarity, the same ones that promote and underlie redistribution and exchange, avoiding individual or sectorial accumulation.

This is why the Sumak Kawsay is sustained by the social and economic practice of reciprocity ("knowing how to give to receive"). This principle, raised as a political practice, is radically opposed to the market-driven capitalist economic system. It is for this reason that the Sumak Kawsay is presented and designed as a political, social, and economic alternative, not only in the sense of alternative development but also an alternative to development, not only for Ecuador but for all humanity.

The Sumak Kawsay proposed as paradigms of liberation by the Kichwa Indians in Ecuador and the Suma Qamaña by the Aymara Indians in Bolivia are subject to deep debate in the Andean region, even after their incorporation into the recent political constitutions of Ecuador and Bolivia. Roughly translated as "Good Living," it is not the good life or the western sense of living better that is successful at the expense of others. Rather, it refers to the construction of other types of relationships between humans, and between them and nature, by preserving it in finding other forms of complementarity rather than an unsustainable exploitation of resources, while providing for the lives of future generations. The Sumak Kawsay and the Suma Qamaña invite a rethinking of the matrix of power and, therefore, the structure of the state and the economy, namely the transformation of representative democracy to a true participatory, intercultural, and inclusive democracy, with a real social control, and a "development with identity." This means the implementation of a new productive matrix that supports a different energy matrix, less dependent on fossil fuels, respectful of biodiversity, and within a framework of a social economy that eliminates the accumulation of capital in few hands.

This Indigenous worldview poses a fundamental contradiction to economic policies aimed at the irrational extraction of natural resources, and demands a different interpretation of the notion of "resource." It considers nature as Mother Earth, the "Pachamama," that cannot be sold or treated as a commodity. The Sumak Kawsay guarantees a good living for everyone, with rights, freedoms, and opportunities that would entitle them to sufficient food and water, a healthy and ecologically balanced environment, free information and communication, and an intercultural participatory society with full respect for cultural diversity that applies modern science combined with ancient knowledge.

Likewise, in Articles 56 to 60 the constitution recognizes the collective rights of nationalities and Indigenous peoples, Afro-descendants, and montubios, opening the possibility of economic, political, and cultural expression of vast human conglomerates that historically faced discrimination, without that meaning a mere integration into a modern economy or incorporation into western thought. Similarly, in Articles 71 to 74 the constitution recognizes the rights of nature. It favors a world aimed at posing serious challenges to economic conceptions and the planning of a truly sustainable form of development. Indeed, the constitution states, "The state will apply precaution and restrictive measures for activities that can lead to the extinction of species, the destruction of ecosystems, or the permanent alteration of the natural cycles." Also it notes that "individuals, communities, peoples, and nationalities will have the right to benefit from the environment and of the natural resources that allow them the good living."

Moreover, Articles 274 to 279 establish the principles of the *Development Regime* that is defined as the organized, sustainable, and dynamic group of economic, political, sociocultural, and environmental systems which guarantee the realization of the Sumak Kawsay. And in Article 283, related to the *economic system*, the constitution states that in this new development regime,

> the economic system is socially oriented and mutually supportive; it recognizes the human being as a subject and an end; it tends towards a dynamic, balanced relationship among society, the state, and the market, in harmony with nature; and its objective is to ensure the production and reproduction of the material and immaterial conditions that can bring about the good living. The economic system shall be comprised of public, private, mixed economy, grassroots solidarity forms of economic organization.

## What is the Indigenous Peoples' Reality That is to be Transformed?

Official statistics are scarce and poorly updated in regards to the economic situation of Indigenous peoples and Afro-descendants. A general picture can be seen in the following tables.

| Poverty Based In Consumption, By Ethnic Group, 1998 - 2006 | | | | | | |
|---|---|---|---|---|---|---|
| Years | Indigenous Poverty | Non Indigenous Poverty | Total | Indigenous indigence | Non Indigenous indigence | Total |
| 1998 | 45.84% | 43.69% | 44.64% | 17.63% | 19.51% | 18.68% |
| 2006 | 69.46% | 35.57% | 38.28% | 43.07% | 10.23% | 12.86% |

Table 5. Source: INEC: Encuesta de Condiciones de Vida, 1998 and 2006.

| Income Poverty By Ethnic Group, 2001 – 2006 | | | | | |
|---|---|---|---|---|---|
| Years | Indigenous Poverty | Non Indigenous Poverty | Total | Indigenous indigence | Non Indigenous indigence | Total |
| 2001 | 80.42% | 66.99% | 67.64% | 56.95% | 39.38% | 40.24% |
| 2003 | 80.75% | 63.85% | 64.69% | 51.32% | 35.70% | 36.47% |
| 2004 | 83.96% | 68.95% | 64.69% | 51.32% | 37.70% | 36.47% |
| 2005 | 82.86% | 60.61% | 61.99% | 57.84% | 32.27% | 33.76% |
| 2006 | 83.22% | 54.94% | 56.74% | 53.55% | 26.41% | 28.13% |

Table 6: Indicators Measurement Survey of Children and Households, 2000; Survey of Employment, Unemployment and Underemployment, 2003. Source: INEC: Survey of Living Conditions, 1995 and 1999.

| Poverty By Unsatisfied Basic Needs (Ubn) By Ethnicity | | | |
|---|---|---|---|
| Ethnicity | Percentages (n/N) * 100 | Number of poor (n) | Total population (N) |
| Indigenous | 89.9% | 746,602 | 830,418 |
| Afro-Ecuadorian | 70.3% | 424,606 | 604,009 |
| Mestiza | 60.3% | 5,679,807 | 9,411,890 |
| White | 45.0% | 572,290 | 1,271,051 |
| Others | 60.9% | 23,906 | 39,240 |
| Total | 61.3% | 7,447,211 | 12,156,608 |

Table 7. Source: Census of Population and Housing, INEC 2001. Preparation: SIISE 2004.

| Extreme Poverty By Unsatisfied Basic Needs | | | |
|---|---|---|---|
| Ethnicity | Percentages (n/N) * 100 | Number of poor (n) | Total population (N) |
| Indigenous | 67.6% | 561,407 | 830,418 |
| Afro-Ecuadorian | 37.7% | 227,734 | 604,009 |
| Mestiza | 30.2% | 2,844,035 | 9,411,890 |
| White | 18.8% | 238,954 | 1,271,051 |
| Others | 30.2% | 11,863 | 39,240 |
| Total | 31.9% | 3,883,993 | 12,156,608 |

Table 8. Source: Census of Population and Housing, INEC 2001.

Among the most important factors that determine this economic situation is the high concentration of land and water in a few hands. In fact, 2 percent of farms more than 100 hectares in size account for about 43 percent of the arable land surface, while farms less than 5 hectares, representing 64 percent of total agricultural production units, have only 6 percent of the area. The average size of these is about 1.5 hectares, which is not enough to develop production processes that can generate enough jobs for a family and a good level of production and income so that farmers are able to live with dignity. Clearly there is a high correlation between a lack of access to land and poverty in Ecuador since about two-thirds of the rural population lives in poverty, and chronic malnutrition effects 26 percent of the rural population, a figure that reaches 40 percent for the Indigenous population (MAGAP 2000; COPISA 2011).

During the last twenty years, due to the concessions that the state has granted in addition to illegal use of water, 1 percent of landowners (large growers of bananas, cacao, coffee, and flowers) have captured 67 percent of irrigation water, while small producers (Indigenous, peasant associations, cooperatives, small farmers) which are 86 percent of producers have access to only 23 percent of the water (Gaybor Secaira 2008). Adding concessions for hydroelectric plants, mines, or the mere speculation of the water market in the city, 82 percent of water resources are privately owned.

In the field of agricultural production, water use is concentrated in the farming export sector, with a significant production deficit for food security. On the other side, policies designed to cover the costs of agricultural production have contributed to increasing greater dependence on the use of major inputs such as imported urea, insecticides, and pesticides, which benefit from subsidies that encourage excessive use.

In this context, it is necessary to note the precarious situation of women who neo-liberalism and a patriarchal system have marginalized in many ways. The national average of poverty for rural women is 85.5 percent, those who live in inadequate housing with services is 78.3 percent, and only 24 percent of households headed by women own land (FAO 2008).

While it is true that investment in education during the current administration has increased by 300 percent compared to the budgets of the previous decade, the situation with regard to Indigenous peoples has not realized the expected results necessary to overcome exclusion and inequity gaps. According to the 2010 census, the Indigenous population had an average of 6.4 years of schooling, while the white population reached 10.7, and mestizos 9.8. Illiteracy affects 3.7 percent of those defined as whites, and 5.1 percent of mestizos, while it affects 20.4 percent of Indigenous peoples and 26.7 percent of Indigenous women. Only 4.9 percent of the Indigenous population has some level of higher education, and only 4.1 percent of Indigenous women, while for the population self-identified as white the rate is 25.4 percent and 21.5 percent for mestizos. More alarming still, of 4.9 percent of Indigenous people who have achieved a higher education, only 2.9 percent obtained a professional qualification, and of these only 0.3 percent have a postgraduate degree (Maldonado and Jijón 2011).

With regard to housing, the census indicates that 57.6 percent of Indigenous families own their own homes, 52.3 percent have a connection to a public network of potable water, 31.7 percent are supplied with water from rivers and springs, and 9.8 percent receive their water from wells. While 82.7 percent of households have access to electricity, only 28.1 percent have access to sewage, and just 10.5 percent have telephone service, and 52.3 percent have cell phone service. The income poverty reduction achieved by the present government is shown in Figure 5.

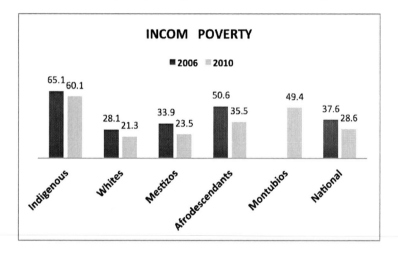

Figure 5: National Survey of Employment, Unemployment, and Underemployment. Source: National Institute of Statistics and Census. Preparation: National Secretariat of Planning and Development.

## The Plurinational State: A Mainstreaming Effort

In general, the construction of a plurinational state comprises a dynamic interplay between three main areas or dimensions: the state itself, civil society, and the market. At present, this is a complex phenomenon that varies with the political will of governments; the level of economic, industrial, and agricultural development; and levels of civil society organization, urban and rural. This dynamic can be illustrated in Figure 6, where it is possible to observe various types of relationships within the country, according to the size and type of these entities and their manner of interrelating.

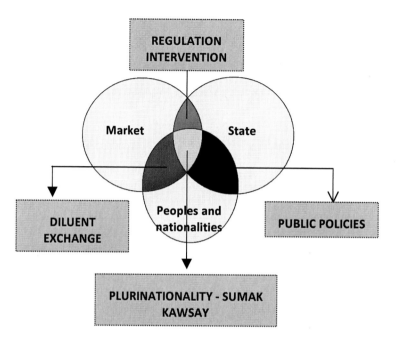

Figure 6. Preparation: VHJ.

It is important to understand that the situation of Indigenous peoples should be analyzed, understood, and resolved from a national perspective and not merely from a local or sectorial one. Understanding the problems of Indigenous peoples cannot be isolated from the historical, economic, political, social, territorial, and spiritual context of the country (Jijón 2007). For this reason, public policies and state institutions should not marginalize or dismiss the problems of Indigenous peoples. Doing so runs the risk of isolating the problems and releasing the entire state from treatment of their claims. As such, the state must respect the rights and take care of the needs of Indigenous peoples, without pigeonholing problems or demands, but seeing them as part of a whole. This allows that the formulation of Life Plans for each people or Indigenous nationality can achieve public financing by insertion into the General State Budget (GSB).

Plurinational State-building is a process that was already officially initiated when the new constitution of the republic was approved. It can be analyzed along three axes:

• A relationship Constitution – Public Institutionality - Public Policies
• A relationship Constitution - National Budget –DAG's Budget

• A relationship Government - National Assembly - Social Control

This means that the knowledge and study of the constitution becomes a very urgent need, both for public officials and for citizens, in order to have adequate knowledge of its contents. It is an unavoidable responsibility of organized civil society to realize enforcement of the guarantees and rights provided by the constitution.

Indeed, relative to the first axis, the plurinational state comes alive at the macro level in terms of an institutional restructuring, and in that sense one of the points under discussion is the creation of the National Equality Councils provided for in Articles 156 and 157 of the constitution and the fate of the National Development Council of Ecuador's Nationalities and Peoples (CODENPE). In this regard, there are two options. One is to try to maintain the same present-day institution, except with a more inflated bureaucracy and with attributions of incidence in public policies but with a budgetary allocation that is only useful to encourage small projects. The other is to think of a mainstreaming of plurinationality so that public policies for Indigenous peoples and nationalities are formulated and implemented in all state bodies, at the level of both ministerial and autonomous institutions, as well as in Descentralized Autonomous Governments (DAGs).

In the first option, peoples and nationalities are at risk of isolating themselves from ministerial or other similar instances, for example, the National Secretariat of Planning and Development (SENPLADES), and to be reduced to a kind of administrative ghetto, from Indigenous to Indigenous, with the consequent risk of pressure from the republic's presidency or other state agencies, including the Ministry of Finance.

The second option involves thinking about Indigenous participation at all levels of decision making to ensure that public policies are formulated based on goals for change and adequate funding. It must be taken into account that the GSB is structured by the Central Government, and it was sent to the National Assembly for approval without the possibility of changing the allocated amounts.

This leads in turn to consideration of the key question of a larger perspective. While there is already enough thought and elaboration about the *what, why,* and *how* of the plurinational state's construction, the most important and decisive question is *with whom*? This matter is critical from several perspectives. The essential limitation of this process is the long delay in the formation of technical and administrative professionals and, in general, the training of Indigenous, Afro-descendants, or montubios who can take significant responsibility for government, whether at a central government level or in the provinces, municipalities, and parishes.

Indeed, any substantial political or economic change involves serious confrontation with the oligarchy and with the same current administrative staff that is largely obsolete and corrupt. This constitutes a challenge of retraining and replacement that requires a strategy of training-adaptation and training-replacement, without violating the labor rights of the existing staff. This takes time and a process that requires a great deal of political will from the central government and from provincial governments. Apart from this, it is important to review the *Competencies Regime* provided in the constitution to take into account the function of the interests of Indigenous peoples and nationalities, since it sets the context of attributions of the national, provincial, and cantonal authorities to assume important responsibilities related to *local development planning* and *territorial ordering*. That issue is a realm in which too little progress has been made.

The second relational axis is rather pragmatic and demands rethinking the financing of Descentralized Autonomous Governments from the Central State. This requires participatory planning and budget preparation with the full involvement of representatives of community organizations and local governments. This is a process in which the current government has a serious political deficit, while at the provincial level there have indeed been some efforts in this direction.

In this aspect, there are two determining challenges. The first is to show a real political will from elected officials to implement a consistent and efficient participatory democracy, facilitating citizen access to decision-making and social control. This means not leaving these issues on the level of formal workshops that lack the possibility of incorporating proposals or initiatives. This simply legitimizes decisions that authorities have already taken. On the other hand, relative to social organizations, it is necessary to define the type of community participation that really enables or facilitates influence in local development planning, on its budgeting, in the tracking and monitoring of public policies, and of the application of programs or projects.

As to the third axis that refers to the central government's relationship with the National Assembly and with the so-called "Fifth Power," the *Social Control Council and Citizen Participation (SCCCP)*, the whole key lies in allowing for the development of legislation and audits. This is an issue that with the current government, and the government majority in the National Assembly has hindered and altered its democratic character. There is actually very little that the National Assembly can do on its own. Almost no draft laws that originated in their midst have been approved;

practically all of them come from the republic's presidency, without any involvement of legislators, and even less that of the citizenship.

In regard to the SCCCP, this organism has two features that the public has strongly criticized both in its formation and in its operation. In fact, the republic's presidency interfered in its formation to alter the procedures established in the constitution. Similarly, the National Electoral Council favors candidates closest to the government, in the process hindering other candidates for membership on that Council. Furthermore, this Council has not worked well when choosing authorities assigned by the constitution, in the process restricting access to these important positions to the president's friends, as in the case of the state's General Procurator and the Public Prosecutor. The same thing happened with the appointment of other high authorities of state bodies such as the state comptroller, the head of the judiciary court, the ombudsman, among others.

As a result, the mainstreaming of plurinationality has been distorted and controlled from the highest levels of government, converting public policy alternatives into a bureaucratic past time, and reducing the participation of Indigenous peoples, Afro-descendants, and montubios to a decorative or even folkloric presence. Although some members of these peoples have been appointed to high positions in major institutions, this does not follow a collective deliberative process but an agreement based on personal interests. Hence, they do not have a decisive role and can no longer question what comes as recommended policies from the presidency of the republic.

## Some Impasses of the "Citizens' Revolution"

The legal framework of the new constitution has allowed the government to act in conflictive areas confronting resistance, especially from dominant economic groups, because it breaks with some canons of neoliberal economic policies of the previous two decades. The government has revived the state's role in national development planning, and in the regulation of the economy and finance; it has increased public investment in the social arena (health, education, housing, roads, and welfare grants), and opened new credit lines for medium and small producers.

Correa's administration invested heavily in social programs, spending $1.84 billion in his first two years in office. In 2012, Correa's government estimated that it would invest $6.5 billion in social spending, representing 25 percent of the total budget. Investments include improvements in education and combating child malnutrition. The poverty rate dropped from 36.7 percent in 2007 to 29 percent in 2011 (SENPLADES 2012).

In turn, President Correa realigned the country's foreign policy by joining other South American countries that have distanced themselves from the interference of the United States. He has implemented a rapprochement with Russia, Iran, and China, and has strengthened the country's participation in regional integration through initiatives such as the Union of South American Nations (UNASUR), the Bank of the South, the South American Defense Council, and the Bolivarian Alternative for the Americas (ALBA). Most of the population has been sympathetic to some of these steps, but remains skeptical of loans from China that have replaced the IMF as a source of international credit.

Although favored by huge foreign exchange revenues from the increase in the international price of oil, the main export product that has facilitated an increase in public spending, essential contradictions remain that explain the sharp conflict between government and various important social organizations. This includes the confrontations between the government's extractive policies and the Indigenous movement's position and rejection of large-scale open pit mining because of its dangers to the environment, contamination of water, and threats to the preservation of biodiversity.

Both the Mining Law passed in January 2009 and the Amendments to the Hydrocarbon Law were adopted without debate at the National Assembly and implemented with a July 2010 law that contains articles that favor large corporations interested in the exploitation of nonrenewable natural resources. Currently, after more than a year of negotiations, on March 5, 2012 one contract was signed with the company Ecuacorriente S.A. (ECSA) in which a Chinese consortium composed of the China Railway Construction Corp. and the Tongling Nonferrous Metals Mining bought 96.9 percent of the shares.

ECSA plans to invest $1.4 billion during the first five years of the 25-year contract for the Mirador mine in the Condor range in southeastern Ecuador, an area that protesters say is one of the country's most biodiverse. The mine has an estimated reserve of 2.2 million tons (4.85 billion pounds) of copper. Ecuador stands to receive $4.5 billion over the term of the agreement. The state's share of mining income is 52 percent, higher than in countries like Chile (36 percent), Peru (32.9 percent) and Mexico (30 percent), but less than the 85 percent that applies to oil production.

Environmental activists rejected the signing of the contract because it lacks an approved environmental impact study, and Indigenous communities never had prior knowledge of it. The agreement did come just before the main aboriginal organization CONAIE started a two-week march to Quito on March 8, 2012 to protest such mining activities and other aggressive policies backed by President Rafael Correa.

In general, the government's expectations of the economic benefits of mining are large and underpin an intransigent attitude of the republic's president to any criticism of its extractive policy, having once dismissed those who mobilized to protest those policies as "childish," "fundamentalists," or "terrorists." The funds from large-scale mining are distributed as follows:

| Projects | Companies | Reserves | Prices | Revenues |
|----------|-----------|----------|--------|----------|
| **Mirador** | ECSA | 2.2 million tons copper | US$7.350/ton | US$16.17 billion |
| **Fruta Del Norte** | KIMROSS | 6.4 million ounces gold | US$1.575/oz | US$10.08 billion |
| **San Carlos Panantza** | ECSA | 3.0 million tons copper | US$7.350/ton | US$22.05 billion |
| **KIMSACOCHA** | IAMGOLD | 1.7 million ounces gold 9.5 million ounces silver | US$1.575/oz US$27/oz | US$2.67 billion US$256.5 million |
| **RIO BLANCO** | IAMGOLD | 605,000 ounces gold 4.3 million ounces silver | US$1.575/oz US$27/oz | US$952.9 million US$116.1 million |

Table 9. Source: Ministry of Non Renewable Natural Resources. Preparation: VHJ.

In regard to the oil industry, the main demand of the social sectors has been the institutional strengthening of Petroecuador and an increase in investment to step up production in the fields already in operation and for not extending the concessions to other areas of the Amazon. Instead of this, the government carried out a renegotiation of contracts with private companies and called for new bids for exploration in still virgin areas of the rainforest.

The principal objection is the renegotiation of oil contracts with foreign companies that recognize unreasonably high production costs, for which companies are compensated for their reductions in production participation and as a result obtain huge profits. The state recognizes service charges between 35 and 41 dollars per barrel in mature fields, with a small investment for exploration, without performing an audit or evaluation of environmental liabilities. All rates are higher than production costs and inflated by the companies. In comparison, production costs of the public company Petroecuador vary between 5 and 7 dollars per barrel produced (Jiménez 2011).

The government's justification is that, on average, private companies operating in Ecuador will receive two dollars less per barrel pumped, which means an increase in state revenues of more than 2.1 billion dollars, measured in net present value, for the duration of contracts and at a price of US$78 per barrel of crude (Non Renewable Natural Resources Ministry 2011).

This negotiation comes on top of a previous agreement made by President Correa with Venezuela's government in September 2009 to deliver the Sacha field, the largest in Ecuador that is already being exploited by Petroecuador, to the Venezuelan state company PDVSA. The goal was to increase oil production, which was not achieved. Indeed, the opposite occurred, and oil production decreased causing heavy economic losses to the country.

Apart from these controversial issues, there is the government's proposal to leave oil in the Ishpingo-Tiputini-Tambococha (ITT) fields underground in exchange for a contribution made by the international community to cover 50 percent of the income that would come as a result of the exploitation, that is, 3.5 billion dollars over ten years. However, the response to this initiative that responds to a long-standing request of the Indigenous movement to defend the protected area of Yasuní in the Amazon has not been what was expected. Instead of $350 million that should be the annual international contribution, so far only $116 million has been offered. This suggests that the government will launch its alternative plan to put the field into production.

Regarding the issue of water use, as was noted above, the whole problem consists in the monopolistic concentration of water resources and its illegal use, especially on the banana plantations, against which the government maintains a pragmatic indifference. Even worse, faced with this situation of injustice, the Water Act draft that the government submitted to the National Assembly is silent on the privatization of this vital resource.

In addition to these economic aspects, the government's authoritarian attitude also affects other important processes for a balanced construction of the Plurinational State. The administration of Indigenous justice remains subject to the designs of the corrupt institutions of western justice, neither recognizing the autonomy of the Intercultural Bilingual Education System nor the Ancestral Medicine System, and its functioning is subject to the will of senior bureaucratic officials of ministries that suffer from restricted budgets.

The policy of extraction of natural resources as the main source of financing for economic and social programs of the government shows several contradictions with the same objectives of its National Plan of Good Living and against the constitution, which raises the need to build an "economic, social, solidarity, and sustainable system" that will require a new structure of production as a prerequisite for a transition to a non-oil economy.

This new production matrix cannot be built without a substantial change in the country's energy matrix, a topic that has many ambiguities. Hydroelectric plants are built in territories inhabited by Indigenous people and peasants who are forced to evacuate their homes. This policy promotes the cultivation of plants for production of biofuels that displace agriculture for food. The government decided to build a new oil refinery in an area of fragile biodiversity on the Pacific coast, condemning the economy to greater dependence of the domestic oil production and oil imports to cover its refining capacity.

Concerning the institutional sphere, the "citizens' revolution" government has implemented a *Secretariat of Peoples, Social Movements, and Citizen Participation* that reports directly to the president of the republic and only follows the top-down centralizing guidelines of government. The work of this institution is limited to publicizing the regime's social policies without developing any consultation with the organizations, which only results in socialization workshops with decisions that senior bureaucrats made. It also develops a divisionist activity of organizations promoting the co-optation of Indigenous leaders for incorporation into official projects that do not correspond to the true interests of Indigenous peoples.

There is also another institution with ministerial rank, the Regional Institute for Amazon Ecodevelopment (ECORAE), that tends to a percentage of the income generated by oil that is reinvested for social organizations and some local government programs in the Amazon region to improve productivity and marketing. In general, its results have been questioned as well as its economic management, which represents several hundred million dollars.

Accompanying this contradictory situation is the permanent confrontation of President Correa with the press that he characterizes as corrupt and lying. During his administration, the president has cracked down on the media, eliciting condemnations from both the local press and international organizations such as Amnesty International and the Committee to Protect Journalists. Several lawsuits have been lodged against two local newspapers, suing journalists for millions of dollars, in an act of persecution against those who think differently or who critique public officials. Under the pretext of tax arrears, authorities have closed some private radio stations.

After an international outcry, on February 27, 2012 the president announced his decision to pardon journalists in the libel suit against the newspaper *El Universo*, its three owners, and a former newspaper columnist who was facing three years in prison. The president also dismissed a fine against the authors of a book detailing the president's alleged acts of nepotism. There are now 19 state-run media outlets in the country that were created by founding new government stations and by appropriating existing companies from banks that faced legal problems of debt to their depositors.

## Reasons for Hope

Given the rentier logic of capitalism, the development of urbanization, and the lure of irrational consumption, many philosophies and many traditions of the peoples have changed rapidly, have resisted very little, or have disappeared from the cultural and social life on every continent. Neoliberalism accentuated this phenomenon, converting participation in dominant cultural values into individual and collective aspirations. It was even said that there was no alternative.

That is why it is important to face the catastrophic results of neoliberalism that are now emerging with a giant transforming force from traditional concepts such as tools of historical memory, cultural reconstruction, and an affirmation of identity. References to the *Pacha Mama* ("*Earth Mother*") or Sumak Kawsay ("Good Living") of the Kichwa people correspond to these founding concepts of Indigenous peoples, their worldviews, and practices of respect for nature and of a shared collective life.

However, success depends on appropriate adaptations of the responsiveness of public powers to take the opportunity to combine the best of ancestral wisdom and modern knowledge, the political will to enable social participation as a right, and a renewal of the state apparatus and economic system.

A plurinational state construction is part of this challenge of the Good Living. The design and implementation of true alternative policies to a western economicist vision requires the reformulation of state institutions for citizen participation at all levels of power. It is not possible to build the Good Living without a substantial redistribution of wealth. Ecuador is ranked 83 out of 187 countries according to the *Human Development Index* (HDI). Overcoming this situation would require the efficient management of strategic sectors, democratization of land ownership, the transformation of production to reduce consumption of fossil fuels, food security, and the development of a social and solidarity economy.

Indigenous peoples, their organizations, and movements have abundantly demonstrated their patriotism in defending the sovereignty of borders; legislating for the country's development; managing with transparency; encouraging citizen participation and pluralism in regional governments; promoting interculturality in society; and overthrowing democratically submissive and corrupt governments that were responsible for bank fraud, the looting of oil resources, the docile payment of an illegal foreign debt, and the harmful policies of dollarization.

There are numerous bills that CONAIE presented to the National Assembly that are still awaiting debate and approval, which include land and water issues, food sovereignty, public transport, and enhancement of tourism.

In this period of economic and political transition, Ecuador will draw once again on the Indigenous movement's generous insistence with their actions and proposals for a more just and equitable future for all of society. It will overcome with creativity and objectivity the ambiguities of the current populist regime. It will then contribute to the strengthening of self-government in territories and provinces, a transformation of the productive matrix without harming nature, improvements in quality of life, expansion of protected area management, and development of interculturality in the educational system and in daily life. For all this, plurinationality will be a vector of peace and democracy.

# References

The Carter Center. 2008. "Informe sobre la Asamblea Constituyente de la República del Ecuador, September 5, 2008, Quito." http://www.cartercenter.org/resources/pdfs/peace/americas/.

Confederación de Nacionalidades Indígenas del Ecuador (CONAIE). 2001. *Conceptos básicos de un Estado Plurinacional.* Quito: Confederación de Nacionalidades Indígenas del Ecuador.

Consejo Plurinacional e Intercultural de Soberanía Alimentaria (COPISA). 2011. *Ley Orgánica de Tierras y Territorios. Propuesta Final*. Quito: Consejo Plurinacional e Intercultural de Soberanía Alimentaria.

Constitución de la República del Ecuador. 2008. *Registro Oficial* 449, October 20, 2008.

FAO. 2008. "Status of rural women in Ecuador." http://www.rlc.fao.org/es/desarrollo/mujer/docs/ecuador/cap01.pdf.

García Linera, Alvaro. 2002. *Autonomías indígenas y Estado Pluricultural*. Quito: FES – ILDIS.

Gaybor Secaira, Antonio. 2008. *Earth and legitimacy in Ecuador*. Quito: Water Forum.

Instituto Científico de Culturas Indígenas (ICCI). 2000. "Foro: Diez Años del Levantamiento Indígena del Inti Raymi de 1990. La Construcción de un País Plurinacional." *Boletín ICCI-Rimay* 2(20) http://icci.nativeweb.org/boletin/20/foro.html.

Jijón, Víctor Hugo, 1990. "El movimiento indígena y la cuestión étnico-nacional." In *El levantamiento indígena y la cuestión nacional*, ed. CDDH. Quito: Abya Yala.

—. 2004. "Pachakutik, la Alianza y la Democracia Disruptiva." http://www.llacta.org/notic/040131a.htm.

—. 2006. *Pachakutik 2006: los riesgos del etnicismo y del electoralismo*. Informe interno a la Dirección Nacional. Quito, mayo-2006. Archivos MUPP-NP.

—. 2007. "Propuestas y Planteamientos de una Política Pública de Participación Ciudadana Incluyente de los Pueblos Indígenas." In *Políticas Públicas para Pueblos Indígenas en el Ecuador del Siglo XXI*. Memorias del Seminario Nacional, Escuela de Gobierno y Políticas Públicas. Quito.

Jiménez, Cléver. 2011. *Demanda ante el Contralor General del Estado*. Quito: Asamblea Nacional.

Macas, Luis, 1999. *El levantamiento indígena visto por sus protagonistas*. Quito: Amauta Rupacunapac Yachai-Instituto Científico de Culturas Indígenas, ICCI.

Maldonado, Luis. 2010. *El Estado Plurinacional y la institucionalización de los pueblos indígenas*. Quito: EGOPP.

Maldonado, Luis, and Víctor Hugo Jijón. 2011. "Participación política y ejercicio de derechos en los pueblos indígenas del Ecuador." In *Participación Política Indígena y Políticas Públicas para Pueblos Indígenas en América Latina*, 171-213. La Paz, Bolivia: Fundación Konrad Adenauer.

Ministerio de Agricultura y Ganadería (MAGAP). 2000. *III Censo Nacional Agropecuario*. Quito: Ministerio de Agricultura y Ganadería.

MUPP-NP. 1996. "Documento sobre la estrategia y la táctica para el período." Archivos de la Dirección Nacional, MUPP-NP.

—. 1999. "Memoria de la Reunión del Consejo Político Nacional del Movimiento de Unidad Plurinacional Pachakutik- Nuevo País." December 22. Archivos MUPP-NP. Quito.

Non Renewable Natural Resources Ministry. 2011. "Statements of 24 January 2011." http://www.vistazo.com/webpages/pais/?id=13829

SENPLADES. 2012. *5 años de Revolución Ciudadana 2007-2011*. Quito.

Walsh, Catherine. 2000. "Interculturalidad, reformas constitucionales y pluralismo jurídico." *Boletín ICCI-Rimay* (Instituto Científico de Culturas Indígenas, Quito) 19.

# CHAPTER FOUR

# THE INHERITANCE OF RESISTANCE: INDIGENOUS WOMEN'S LEADERSHIP IN ECUADOR

## MANUELA L. PICQ

Indigenous women have long participated in acts of political resistance. In the late eighteenth century Bartolina Sisa terrified the colonial army and held Spanish officials under siege in La Paz, and Manuela Léon overpowered soldiers in the uprising of Yaruquis in the highlands of Ecuador (Ari Murillo 2003; Siles 1981). They are lasting symbols of resistance against colonization, and represent the agency of many more women who also were in positions of political and military leadership. They were feared for their military tactics and cold-bloodedness, and state authorities blacklisted and persecuted them. Women have been active participants in the long history of resisting the oppression of Indigenous peoples across the Americas. In Ecuador, many have become national icons of insubordination, some leading important uprisings in Cayambe in the late 1920s and founding the first Indigenous federation in 1944. These leaders should not be understood as historical exceptions, but rather as proof of a solid legacy of political agency that persists until the present.

Whether in positions of leadership or through daily practices of resistance, Indigenous women have consistently challenged power structures, and have built a legacy of insubordination and political engagement through centuries of active contestation. Selective histories overlooked them as passive, and throughout the New World official archives made them anonymous beings by writing them out of history in colonial processes of nation-making (O'Brien 2010; Den Ouden 2012). Even today, dressed in colorful textiles as they harvest millennia-old grains, they tend to be perceived as guardians of pre-Columbian languages and customs.[1] Indigenous women may seem to be the very antithesis of political modernity, suspended in time and isolated in marginal spaces. Yet their rebellious leadership traveled across borders and through the centuries, tangible in story-telling and popular culture if not in official histories of nation making. Women like Bartolina Sisa who once fought colonial power have been strategically revived as national heroines by electoral democracies advocating resistance against power inequalities. Far from being isolated or passive, Indigenous women are in fact dynamic actors who stand at the forefront of those forces shaping Latin American politics (Rousseau 2011; Picq 2012). They are deeply embedded in state-making, finding peripheral but creative ways to advance their agendas as municipal leaders in Oaxaca (Garcia 2011) or advocating communitarian feminism in Bolivia (Paredes 2008). In this regard, women have a long history of political mobilization and their invisibility is related more to our failure to recognize their agency than a product of their *de facto* marginalization.

This essay contends that Indigenous women have historically been key actors of political resistance. The argument focuses on the case of Ecuador, where Indigenous politics have been recognized as the most influential in Latin America and their contributions have been analyzed in depth without ever focusing on the roles of women (Van Cott 2007, 2008; Lucero 2008; Yashar 2005). This research contributes a gender perspective to the scholarship on Indigenous movements. As it emphasizes the historical significance of women's leadership, it makes salient the limits of their participation in contemporary Ecuadorian politics. In what follows, I first shed light on women's legacies of contestation, looking at colonial insubordination, the role of the leaders Dolores Cacuango and Transito Amaguaña, and women's influence through the mobilizations of the 1990s. I then turn my attention to the relative absence of women after Ecuador's Indigenous movement was institutionalized in the mid-1990s, examining why political mainstreaming has pushed women out and silenced their voices.

## Colonial Insubordination

Looking back, women's agency is tangible in varied acts of Indigenous insubordination against Spanish colonizers. Andean populations did not passively accept the colonial order. A series of small and larger uprisings

---

[1] For example, the current Venezuelan Constitution "protects" Indigenous women as "guardians of tradition."

spread through what is today Ecuador in the late eighteenth century as a reaction to Indian tribute, forced labor, and the end of caciques' political autonomy. The significant presence of women among caciques in the central highlands of the Audiencia de Quito (Coronel and Prieto 2010; Londoño 1997) evolved into active contestation as colonial pressure increased. Although records are uneven, it is clear that women played an integral part in leading and sustaining many uprisings during colonial times. Their dynamic leadership in forceful rebellions may have surprised colonial authorities, yet it was all but exceptional.

Two of the four leaders in the Guano rebellions against the 1776 census and taxes were women, Manuela and Baltazara Chiusa (Romo Leroux 1997). Their role was so crucial in the rebellion that Baltazara had her head and hands chopped off and sent to the Teniente and Corregidor to confirm her death and to serve as a public warning. In 1780, women rebelled with sticks and stones in the town of Baños to protest the imposition of taxes on alcohol. Many were sentenced to hundreds of lashes and their leader, Martina Gomes, was shaved for launching the uprising. The event became known as "the shaved women's rebellion." That same year, 1780, Rosa Señapanta fueled a rebellion in the town of Quisapincha; official archives describing her as "an Indian not embarrassed by her sex." Expressions of colonial insubordination were widespread in the late eighteen century, and women frequently played crucial roles. The extent of their leadership is little recorded because they were the Indigenous other, left out of archival history, but also because they were going against Spanish assumptions of gender roles.

One of the rebellions that marked Ecuadorian history is the large Guamote uprising against taxes on February 27, 1803. It included the leadership of Lorenza Peña, Jacinta Juaréz, and Lorenza Avemañay. Gendered leadership was no novelty, and the representative for the Audiencia de Quito reported that women were as equally present in that uprising as in prior ones. Many women mobilized, and the healer Lorenza Avemañay was a central strategist of the uprising. She believed that, in order to succeed, the rebellion needed to use similar tactics as the Spaniards, and she designed attacks according to the colonizer's military style. Taking the enemy by surprise after a Sunday mass, the Indigenous army killed multiple officials before Quito was able to react, sending two hundred men to suffocate the rebellion. Avemañay's leadership was poorly recorded in official archives, yet more than half a century after her death she was still remembered in popular songs as a heroine of Indigenous resistance (Romo-Leroux 1997, 69). Today, close to two centuries later, she has been revived as an icon in state-sponsored publications about female heroines of national history (CONAMU 2009).

Female participation was equally central to the 1871 insurgency of Yaruquis, Chimborazo, still considered one of the most significant rebellions in nineteenth-century Ecuador. Manuela Léon co-led the rebellion with Fernando Daquilema, protesting abusive church taxes and forced labor to build a national roadway. The uprising was a response to violent tactics of state-making under the presidency of García Moreno. Thousands of people mobilized across the province of Chimborazo, killing at least seven officials in charge of collecting the "diezmos," thereby igniting a strong military response from Quito. As the insurgency expanded, Manuela Léon is said to have ordered the burning of houses, battled soldiers, and killed their head Miguel Valliente, whose eyes she allegedly poked out with her own *tupo* (Costales 2002).[2] By the time soldiers were able to regain control over Cacha, hundreds of people were imprisoned in Riobamba. Manuela Léon was the first to be executed in front of a crowd of 200 people in the central square of Riobamba. Fernando Daquilema was executed later in the public square of Yaruquis. Although judicial condemnations of Daquilema and Léon have disappeared from Chimborazo's official archives and their histories consistently misplaced, social movements and the state have often revered their personas as icons of resistance.

Indigenous women were far from passive or absent, with ways of exercising leadership that were as diverse as their social backgrounds and political contexts. In a 2009 book celebrating patriotic women on the occasion of Ecuador's bicentenary of independence, the Institute for Research and Development of Women identified multiple Indigenous women as icons of national liberty. The volume opens with the Chivisa sisters Baltazara and Manuela, who coordinated the 1778 attacks against Spanish officials in Riobamba, and closes with Lorenza Avemañay, the leader in Guamote's 1803 uprising. A chapter pays homage to the many anonymous women who participated in the Guazabaras rebellion, which resisted Spanish colonization in the Amazon region through the second half of the sixteenth century. Celebrating cultural and political leadership as well, the book dedicates another chapter to the cacicazgo of María Duchicela Namguai in the seventeenth century. Born in 1620 in Yaruquis, Chimborazo, the Dhuchicela princess was an icon in Quito's social life and is remembered for promoting the legal recognition of her people.

---

[2] *Tupo* is a sort of brooch Indigenous women wear to keep their wool shawls tight around their shoulders. This accessory tends to be a long silver pin adorned with decorations.

It was not only Indigenous women, but women in general who participated in colonial politics, much to the despair of conservative politicians. Their activism did not go unnoticed, as proven by a 1835 letter from President Rocafuerte that called for the expulsion of Manuela Sáenz and warned against women's political activism. Emphasizing that women were fomenting a revolutionary spirit, he compared Sáenz to her French counterpart Madame de Stael, adding that such women were more dangerous than an army of conspirators. Women indeed led armies. They also participated in daily political matters. Kimberly Gauderman (2003) argues that seventeenth-century Spanish society was highly decentralized, giving women more opportunities to exercise political authority than is often acknowledged. Indigenous market women were strong, autonomous actors who engaged in litigation, quarreled with government officials, and manipulated competing legal jurisdictions (Gauderman 2003, 92). Rejecting the paradigm of female subordination, Gauderman insists that women in colonial Quito were entrepreneurs and legally active until the Council of the Indies shifted property rights and legal authority over to men in 1787.

The colonial order progressively disenfranchised women from political, social, and economic rights. But by rendering women invisible, the colonial order enabled—and even fueled—daily forms of resistance among women. Irene Silverblatt (1987) noted that even when they seemed most subordinated, Andean women were pursuing less obvious forms of contestation, notably through cultural practices. These forms of resistance, even when hidden, contributed significantly to building women's political culture of contestation.

Andean women, dismissed from hegemonic narratives both as women and as colonized subjects, were made into peoples without history by selective processes of memory. Pierre Clastres (in Scott 2009) posited that the history of peoples without history is that of their struggles against the state. Since they always resisted state making, first the colonial then the republican state, Indigenous women could not fit into self-aggrandizing national histories that emphasized unity. Just like peasants, one might say, their job was to stay out of archival history (Scott 2009, 34). This should not lure us to understand them as silent. After fueling insubordination during colonial times, they continued to contest oppression from the state. Some of them, in fact, were crucial for the emergence of Ecuador's modern Indigenous movement.

## Cacuango and Amaguaña: Founding the Modern Indigenous Movement

Women continued to inspire Indigenous resistance into the twentieth century. At the turn of the century, when Indigenous rebellions multiplied to protest the feudal *huasipungo* system, women organized resistance and stirred forceful agendas. In fact, two of them became the first and most lasting icons that shaped Ecuador's Indigenous movement. Dolores Cacuango (1881-1971) and Tránsito Amaguaña (1909-2009) were influential in building a national movement and are remembered for paving the way towards Indigenous emancipation. They were among the leaders of a 1931 peasant uprising in Cayambe, violently repressed by the army and retraced in Jorge Icaza's novel *El Huasipungo* (1933). In 1944, they founded the Federación Ecuatoriana de Indios (FEI), the country's first Indigenous organization. Both women fought for bilingual education, spending much of their long lives advocating for land ownership and cultural dignity across Ecuador and abroad. They were influential and indispensable, framing the alliances and setting the agendas of contemporary ethno-politics.

Dolores Cacuango is perhaps the most iconic figure in struggles for Indigenous emancipation. She was born as a *huasipunguera* in 1881 on the Pesillo hacienda, Cayambe, and never attended school. She spoke only Kichwa until age fifteen, when she was sent to Quito to work as a domestic servant for the hacienda owners. As she learned Spanish, she grasped the systematic exploitation of her people as well as the extent of the class divide. Cacuango was a young woman when she started denouncing inhumane treatment on the haciendas, including the lack of food, health, or rest. She organized labor demands and was soon persecuted by hacienda owners who tried to either send her to the Galapagos (a jail at the time) or kill her. She was forced into hiding when her *huasipungo* was burnt down, barely escaping with her youngest child (interview with Blomberg 1969). In the 1920s, the Communist party played an important role in supporting rural workers on *huasipungos*, invigorating labor demands, organizing collective action, and providing a political space for workers' rights to be claimed (Becker 2008). Cacuango actively contributed to the creation of rural unions, deepening ties with communist sectors. She became a committed communist, as well as a fierce military leader, leading, for instance, the Indigenous assault on the military base of Cayambe during the 1944 "Glorious Revolution" (Becker and Tutillo 2009).

Cacuango was a national leader who forged interethnic alliances, not a mere representative of women or Indigenous interests. Her political leadership predated the consolidation of a national Indigenous movement. She first founded and presided over the FEI, then, supported by the Communist Party, gained recognition in national politics. She became a voice for Indigenous concerns, debating with Congress and meeting the president; she traveled from Bogotá to Guayaquil to advocate for equality among workers in rural and urban areas. She spoke well, enticing large crowds, bringing together mestizos and Indigenous peoples in eloquent discourses (Carrera 2007). One anecdote recalls how she learned the Labor Code by heart, able to call upon a Minister for cheating on the content of labor laws to protect the interests of the patrons during a public audience.

As she consolidated political influence, Cacuango's political life revolved around two core issues: the redistribution of land ownership and bilingual education. In 1945, she was the one to lead the opening of four rural schools in Moyurco, San Pablo Urcu, Pucará, and La Chimba (Cayambe province). The schools enjoyed the support of the Ecuadorian Feminine Alliance (AFE), Quito's first feminist organization.[3] But since the project of bilingual education also received communist support, it was perceived as a threat in the political context of the Cold War. In 1963 the military dictatorship closed the rural schools, which were accused of fomenting communism and they fell back into being clandestine. Cacuango, who remained illiterate all her life, relentlessly stressed the importance of educating children in their native Kichwa. She died before bilingual education was formally institutionalized in 1988.[4] "Mama Dulu," as she was later remembered, fought for the respect of Indigenous peoples throughout her life. Decades after her death, her words on the force of collective action echo far beyond her native Cayambe: "we are like the grass of the highlands, always growing back even if it is torn apart."

Cacuango remains one of the pioneers of Ecuador's modern Indigenous movement. Her strength and resilience were praised across time and space. The world-renowned artist Oswaldo Guayasamin painted her portrait and at least three biographies celebrate her life (Morales 1998; Rodas and Cacuango 1998; Rodas and Cotacachi 1989). If she was at first an

---

[3] Nela Martínez and María Luisa Gómez de la Torre, communist companions of Cacuango, became central figures in the creation of the FEI schools (Becker and Tutillo 2009, 164).

[4] On November 15, 1988, Executive Decree 203 amended the General Regulation of the Education Act institutionalized intercultural education as bilingual, creating the National Indigenous Intercultural Bilingual Education (DINEIB) with its own functions and powers.

Indigenous leader, she soon became a national symbol of resistance against exploitation. Her struggles are now recognized beyond Ecuador, across Latin America, and in Europe. UNESCO paid homage to her legacy at the occasion of the 2009 International Women's Day with a photography exhibition in Paris, "The Seeds of a Dream." Mama Dulu was always aware of the universal scope of her struggles and would have said "if I die, I die, but others will continue the fight." Unequivocally influential, she paved the way for Indigenous rights to gain power and recognition on the international stage.

If Cacuango's life reveals a legacy that influences the future, it also points to the political contestation she inherited from women before her. Her leadership was not sheer serendipity. Rather, she is a testament to the engagement and agency of Indigenous women in centuries past. Cacuango was not alone. Her rebellious soul, clarity of thought, and skilled leadership were preceded by generations of women fighting against the violence and exploitation of colonization, from Bartolina Sisa to Manuela Léon. Moreover, what she learned she also transmitted, inspiring and mentoring younger women to pick up the banner. Tránsito Amaguaña was one of them, following Cacuango's footsteps in making history all the way into the twenty first century.

Tránsito Amaguaña Alba is another iconic leader in the history of Indigenous resistance in Ecuador—and probably Latin America. She was born Rosa Elena at Pesillo, Cayambe, in 1909. She was deeply influenced by the political leadership of her mother, Mercedes Alba, who organized Indigenous resistance with Dolores Cacuango in Pesillo (Mino Grijalva 2009). With a rebellious spirit against exploitation, discrimination, and violence, like Cacuango she became involved with rural unions in her teens, quickly joining the Communist Party and actively fueling the workers' strikes that preceded agrarian reform. She too was persecuted by *hacienda* patrons and by the state for mobilizing strikes, often hiding from authorities high up in the *páramos*, climbing close to the Cayambe glacier to escape reprimand, and eating vegetables left in the fields to survive clandestinely.

Amaguaña often met Cacuango during her years of hiding. Both had lost their *huasipungos* and therefore were landless and homeless. When I interviewed her late in her nineties, Amaguaña remembered walking to Quito over twenty times, barefoot to save the soles of her shoes, to support workers challenging the government, calling upon both the church and politicians to abolish *huasipungo* exploitation. She supported Cacuango's dreams of education for Indigenous children, in Kichwa by Indigenous teachers, which led to her first arrest. Twice she was made a political prisoner. Amaguaña was in the same struggle as Cacuango, and many other women accompanied them. Women were so numerous in the uprising at the Olmedo hacienda that they took over the leadership of the movement (Rodas 2009, 39). Although they had no rights in the *huasipungo* system, which were held by men, women considered themselves descendants of *cacicas,* and therefore entitled with political authority. They fought struggles initiated by their ancestors, taking over the uprisings in Olmedo with a determination anchored in historical legitimacy. Dolores Cacuango, Tránsito Amaguaña, Rosa Cachipela, Mercedes Catucumba, and Angelita Andrango commanded the actions and headed the committees that went to negotiate with Quito officials. With their enflaming speeches, Mama Dulu and Transito were central in designing alliances with the unions and organizing the logistics of food and lodging.

With Amaguaña, Ecuador's Indigenous movement gained international visibility. Bold, honest, and fierce, she voiced collective demands and Indigenous indignation from the National Congress in Quito to political forums in Europe. During her years in the FEI, she traveled first through Ecuador to organize Indigenous demands for agrarian reform, then across the Andes fueling broader workers' struggles. Like Cacuango, she attended caucuses from Riobamba to Quito to Cuenca. She often reiterated that she fought for justice everywhere and for everybody in the country, and she denied that she only acted in representation of her own province, people, or gender. She was part of the Indigenous leadership that shared their experiences with the Federation of Littoral Workers (FETAL) in the coastal region (Rodas 2009, 52). Her militancy gave her international prominence in the Communist Party, taking her first to Cuba—where she met with a young Fidel Castro in 1961—then on a trans-Atlantic journey to Moscow, Russia, as an Ecuadorian delegate to the International Communist Assembly.

Cacuango and Amaguaña were central to the consolidation of today's Indigenous movement. From the strike in Pesillo to the consolidation of rural unions and the FEI, their struggle went well beyond Indigenous exploitation on the hacienda. They were important figures in the Communist Party, linking communist ideals of worker equality with the needs of peasants living under the *huasipungo* system in the Andean highlands of Latin America. Most importantly, they expanded communist agendas with ethnic priorities. They embodied Indigenous demands that blended land and language, economics, and education. When they pressured state officials in Quito and engaged international alliances to render their struggle more salient and legitimate, they presaged contemporary struggles for self-determination and cultural recognition.

These leaders are remembered as symbols of struggles for social justice, at times revived in governmental discourses as heroic imagery of nation making. Amaguaña finished her life in poverty and mostly forgotten, taken care by her daughter-in-law Guillermina and neighbors. Yet when she died in 2009, just short of her hundredth birthday, the village of La Chimba was taken over by a national(istic) celebration. Accompanied by Bolivian President Evo Morales, Nobel Peace Laureate Rigoberta Menchú from Guatemala, and a flock of Ecuadorian state officials and press, President Rafael Correa commemorated her legacy somewhat emphatically. A dense crowd marched carrying her coffin and a shamanistic ceremony followed the presidential discourse performed out in the highlands, and reproduced on screens. Unequivocally, she was a powerful symbol of resistance to be appropriated by a government who claimed to side with the oppressed against global exploitation.

## Women's Mobilization in the 1990 Uprising

The inheritance of resistance lives on. If women were extremely visible in colonial rebellions in Chimborazo and took over the leadership of the Pesillo uprising in 1931, they were equally present in the 1990s Indigenous uprising that blocked the country and forced the government to recognize the political voice of Indigenous peoples. A large body of scholarly work addressed the significance of Ecuador's 1990 Indigenous uprising (Van Cott 2007; Lucero 2008; Postero and Zamosc 2004; Yashar 2005). The Indigenous movement revealed an enormous capacity to mobilize, drawing millions of people into their protests, blocking roads and marching towards the capital, paralyzing the country for over a week and forcing the government into negotiations. This national uprising, which was followed by smaller mobilizations throughout the early 1990s, was a critical juncture in the consolidation of ethno-politics. As its voice became tangible through a massive presence in the streets, the movement acquired undisputable visibility in public life. Suddenly able to influence national politics, the Indigenous movement became a legitimate contender in power struggles. Léon Zamosc (2005) suggested that the uprisings created the momentum to turn Indigenous politics of influence into politics of power. Donna Lee Van Cott (2007) identified the mobilizations of the early 1990s as a transition from movements to parties, later labeling emerging models of ethno-politics in the Andes as radical democracy (Van Cott 2008). Scholars explored Indigenous mobilization, variation in electoral success, and the impact of local governments in reshaping democracy at large (Lucero 2010; Cameron 2010; Madrid 2012). Despite a growing body of literature providing detailed case studies and in-depth analysis, little consideration has been given to the gendered aspects of ethno-politics, thus hiding the lasting, massive role of women.

Women were not only present throughout the 1990 uprising, but also key to its success. "The march was overwhelming...men and women of all ages walked exhausted...converting the march into a symbolic taking of the city" (Almeida 1993, 183). More than 60 thousand people chanted and demanded their requests in Kichwa in the center of Riobamba. Descriptions and images of the events reveal that women were present throughout the uprising, blocking roads and marching towards urban centers, with or without their husbands but often with their children. Women were at the front of the march that surrounded a military offense in Gatazo, Chimborazo, which ended in confrontation after one of the two hundred soldiers shot into the crowd killing a protester. Women were also among the protesters shot in Colta. In the province of Imbabura, numerous women participated in the communal assemblies that transformed the Inti Raymi into cultural armies (Almeida 1993, 177). Men and women were working together to strategically block roads, organize committees, and assure logistics behind the scenes. Women were behind the lines, assuming responsibility for intensive food logistics to support the protests across the country. They were also very active on the frontlines, participating in roadblocks, bringing children along to marches, camping in Quito, and facing the military at the frontlines. Interviews with women who participated in the *levantamiento* indicate that the mobilization brought a new sense of dignity to the traditionally excluded peasantry and strengthened women's political awareness and self-confidence.

Some women played crucial leadership roles. Blanca Chancoso, a leader from Imbabura's Indigenous and Peasant Federation (FICI), participated in the occupation of the Santo Domingo Church in Quito, where the protest started. She saw the use of extra-legal actions as necessary to pressure the government to negotiate land rights, a theme repeatedly overlooked, and maintained the occupation of the Church through the hunger strike until agreements were reached. Nina Pacari,[5] a lawyer who had long defended Chimborazo's access to land titles, was a key negotiator with the state through the uprisings of the early 1990s. In many ways, the 1990s uprisings contributed to strengthening a generation of new female leaders.

---

[5] Born María Estela Vega Cornejo in the northern province of Imbabura, Nina Pacari studied law in Quito prior to advising Kichwa communities in Chimborazo to secure land rights after the last wave of agrarian reforms in the 1970s.

The struggle belonged to women too, and they were active, central organizers. For Pacari, non-Indigenous sectors, which were often opposed to women's roles in the protests, did not understand this gender complementarity (Almeida 1993, 180). As Chancoso points out, there were always many women active beyond the individual leaders. Often fighting as a collective, women represented their communities, with nameless leaders, as the women of Cajas fought in the name of the Agricultural Association of Cajas. When a woman died, Chancoso notes, it was a full member of the community who died, not an individual woman (Almeida 1993, 135). Chancoso emphasizes that historically women were always present, but that their participation was rarely recognized and even less publicized. What changed after the *levantamiento*, she suggests, is the attention given to women. It is not that women's participation in Indigenous politics had changed; it is that those looking at Indigenous politics started recognizing the role of women.

Women's mobilizations in the 1990s evolved into a more formal political leadership. Chancoso became a political leader within ECUARUNARI, then CONAIE. Nina Pacari became arguably the most notable Indigenous woman, if not leader, of her generation. Her skills and determination gave her visibility within the movement, and her career as a lawyer switched to national politics once she joined the leadership of the movement. In 1989, she acted as CONAIE's legal advisor, supported Chimborazo in the 1990 national uprising, and became a key negotiator with the state on land rights in the following years. In 1997 she was named Director of CODENPE, the National Council of Planning for Black and Indigenous Peoples. The same year she was elected as a representative from Chimborazo for the coming Constitutional Assembly, which recognized the pluricultural and multiethnic dimension of the Ecuadorian state. In 1998, as a member of the political party Pachakutik, she was the first Indigenous woman to be elected to Ecuador's legislature and became the first Indigenous person to be appointed second vice-president of Congress, thus increasing the voice and visibility of all Indigenous peoples in Ecuadorian politics. President Lucio Gutíerrez made her Minister of Foreign Affairs in 2003, a position from which she soon resigned to protest the president's neoliberal policies. She then became a member of the United Nations Permanent Forum on Indigenous Issues, working on the portfolios of Administration of Justice, Traditional Knowledge, and Gender. In 2007, she was elected as a judge of Ecuador's Supreme Court.

Pacari represents the significant role of women in the 1990 uprising, which was large and powerful enough to provoke a collective recognition of women's roles in Indigenous struggles. In the mid-1990s, inspired by the legacy of Cacuango and Amaguaña, ECUARUNARI founded the Dolores Cacuango Leadership School for Women.[6] Created in 1996 for poor Indigenous women affiliated with ECUARUNARI, the school's objective is to form leaders who recognize their history, origins, and identity to engage in the making and re-making of Indigenous politics. It seeks to increase women's self-esteem to speak in public and propose agendas in community meetings. It is also geared towards promoting economic opportunities and cultural knowledge. Since 2003, ECUARUNARI organized a Women's Assembly to discuss the status of the leadership school and women's presence in politics. The school's mission statement says it seeks to consolidate the natural leadership that women traditionally maintained within Indigenous peoples. But if the Dolores Cacuango School celebrates Indigenous women's historical leadership, it also points to their limited opportunities to participate in current politics. In the 2005 Women's Assembly, ECUARUNARI's women leaders Blanca Chancoso and Concepción Lagua pointed out the school's achievements and weaknesses, notably discrimination by provincial leaders, weak communication, and the role of house chores in limiting women participation in workshops.

The inheritance of leadership among Indigenous women is not unique to Ecuador and can be traced across the region. In Bolivia, the organization Las Hijas de Bartolina Sisa continues to advocate gender parity (Mejía 1985). In Chile, although Indigenous women have lower educational levels and less access to computers and cell phones than their non-Indigenous counterparts, they are nevertheless more active in community organizing. In Mexico, women participate in national and ethnic movements (Chong 2007). The women of Chiapas, who combine colorful traditional Maya dress with *pasa-montañas* to hide their faces, remind us how active contestation is among Indigenous women throughout the continent. Zapatista Commander Ramona, in particular, personifies the determined leadership of women in ethnic movements for social justice (Zwarenstein 2006). Once a street seller who could not speak Spanish, Ramona became one of the seven female leaders on the Clandestine Revolutionary Indigenous Committee. She was the Zapatista army representative in the 1996 National Indigenous Congress in Mexico City, and the first Zapatista to publicly appear outside of Chiapas. She helped create the 1996 Women's Revolutionary Law, which includes women's rights to choose their partners and decide on the number of children they

---

[6] Development funds from Norway enabled the school to operate on a more regular basis since 1998.

have, participate in politics, military operations, and receive equal wages for jobs of their choice, have access to education, healthcare and nutrition, and be free from sexual violence. Chiapas' Revolutionary Law echoes women's political mobilization, yet it also reveals the extent to which violence against women is a permanent concern and priority to secure better lives.

Cacuango and Amaguaña, as well as many other Indigenous women before and after them, were fierce, admired leaders. They are emblematic of political agencies, neither marginal nor accidental, but consistent with a lasting culture of political contestation. The participation of women in contemporary Indigenous mobilizations across Latin America, therefore, is neither secondary, but the expected result of lasting political agencies. The challenge, then, is to account for the limited presence of women since Indigenous politics entered the political mainstream. Instead of strengthening women's historical influence, the institutionalization of the Indigenous movement in a formal political party seems to have dissipated women's voices and leadership.

## The Invisibility of Women in the Modern Indigenous Movement

The legacy of women's leadership in politics of contestation and liberation should contribute to a solid participation of women in Ecuador's modern Indigenous movement. Yet its recent institutionalization seems to have left most women behind. Despite women's historical leadership, Indigenous institutions count few women in their ranks, and fewer still at the top. In fact, the presidents of CONAIE and all its organizations have always been men, and females remain rare among elected party members. Women were key to the founding of the FEI, with Cacuango and Amaguaña assuming key roles. More recently, women leaders like Pacari and Chancoso contributed to the transition from movements to parties (Van Cott 2007) while Lourdes Tibán held positions of decision-making power. Yet proportionally speaking, there are few Indigenous women politicians, and rare are those involved in national-agenda setting. Overall, female leadership has grown scarce as the Indigenous movement was mainstreamed (Pacari 1993).

Zamosc (2007) pointed out undemocratic practices in the first political steps of the Indigenous movement, and this section calls attention to its gender fault lines. Discrimination based on gender is not peculiar to Indigenous groups: gender-disaggregated indicators reveal that unequal opportunities between men and women exist in every country. Women worldwide are the primary victims of poverty and suffer from social, political, and economic marginalization. This gender gap, however, tends to be more acute for Indigenous women around the world, and Ecuador's ethno-politics is no exception.

The context of economic violence and political invisibility is detrimental to Indigenous women's political participation. Women endure harsh working conditions in rural communities and are often prone to sexist customary laws that accentuate structural violence and exclusion (Cumes 2009; Sieder and Sierra 2010). They are discriminated against at the polls, and face gender and ethnic harassment.[7] They are also discriminated against publicly and privately within their communities when running for office.[8] Community politics are today considered the realm of men and are therefore a rather sexist sphere. Perhaps one of the major contradictions in the situation of Indigenous women is that they are required to vote at the national level, having the exact same political rights as any other male or *mestizo* citizen, but are most often excluded, through formal and informal mechanisms, from decision-making processes within their own communities. The communal voting system is often organized on the basis of one vote per home, but consensus rarely takes place in the private sphere.[9] As a result, women often complain that men silence them.[10] Men's opinions tend to prevail to the detriment of those of women, who are trivialized as less capable of reason and inapt at politics. Men "give orders to women," they "know better," and "explain things to the women who don't understand anything" (CESA 1993). The intangible violence that oppresses, censors, and discriminates against women's political voices adds up to physical and economic forms of violence which

---

[7] The Qellkaj Foundation, an Indigenous organization that monitors ethnic-based discrimination in elections across the country, has identified these trends. In this context, it is worth noting that men were the first to vote as a legal requirement during the agrarian reform. Thus, voting first came as a means to secure legal ownership of the land, and women took part in the process much later. Interviews with the Naula family, Guaranda, Chimborazo (November 2005).

[8] Multiple interviews with national and regional female leaders (January 2006; December 2007) and elected officials in the sector of Flores, Chimborazo (November 2005).

[9] The high levels of migration are promoting changes in this male-dominated voting system, as women become the heads of families and replace them in the voting sessions.

[10] Despite their traditional absence from decision-making arenas in the communities, women are increasingly active as they replace their husbands who migrate to the cities (CESA 1993; interviews with Naula Family; and Tránsito Chela, President of CONMIE).

leave irremediable scars on the construction of Indigenous women's identities (Poeschel-Renz 2003; Picq 2012). Efforts to even out political opportunities have so far been too slow and too occasional to really tackle women's exclusion from the political arena.

Many women who do take office endure discrimination, such as dismissal of their capacities, work, and responsibilities. They receive little encouragement to pursue work outside of their homes, are required to combine family chores with professional obligations, and are forced to ask permission from skeptical and jealous husbands. Public leadership implies more overt forms of violence. Women have reported being raped by their male counterparts—notably during the 1990 *levantamiento*, while sexual harassment was frequent—"si eres compañera, tienes que compartir todo."[11] Leaders suffer intense public discrimination for their political activities and are perceived as "public" women. At a more subtle level, politically active women tend to be ostracized within the daily life of the community.[12]

The political isolation of Indigenous women leaders is tangible in the discrimination they face both from the Indigenous movement as well as women's movements. The pervasive nature of the culture of machismo that permeates to the highest institutional levels became apparent when the Indigenous movement aborted the formation of an Indigenous women's organization. In 1996, five women, namely Nina Pacari, Teresa Simbaña, Blanca Chancoso, Vicenta Chuma, and Rosa Bacancela, founded the National Council of Indigenous Women of Ecuador (CONMIE) to advance the rights of Indigenous women. The organization was immediately perceived as a threat to the unity of the national Indigenous movement, sparking accusations among the leadership of CONAIE, FEINE, and Ecuarunari. After sustained harassment, intimidation, and threats to CONMIE's leadership, CONAIE came up with an offer: the women who abandoned CONMIE once and for all would be granted political power within CONAIE.[13] Most, including Pacari and Chancoso,

---

[11] Various women involved in political careers reported being told "if you are a *compañera*, you must share everything."

[12] Virtually all female national leaders are single. Some have children and others not, but most have never married. There is a clear trade-off between having a conjugal life or becoming engaged in politics. Although these leaders are engaged in their political careers, the personal costs are extremely high and difficult to live with. Interview with Claudia Vega.

[13] Originally, CONMIE had around 1500 members across eight provinces. The harassment and aggression that the founders of the organization suffered was also reported at the local level in the province of Cañar against women who participated

accepted, and started a new political career-path focused on ethno-politics. Since then, they have identified themselves as Indigenous rather than female representatives, advocating ethnic rights rather than a gender-oriented agenda in their political struggle.

The history of CONMIE, with its weakness and disarticulation, is the result of a conscious effort by Indigenous political elites to undermine a women's initiative perceived as a threat to the success of the larger, ethnic movement. To this day, CONMIE suffers institutional pressure and discrimination, working as it can without a budget or an office. The organization was debilitated since its start, never able to gain political relevance or to build a forceful political agenda. This case reveals only part of the tension between ethnicity and gender. As a gender-based organization, CONMIE was framed as a threat to the cohesion and power of mobilization of the Indigenous movement, and it was purposefully suffocated at its start.

Since then, Ecuarunari created a commission of Women and the Family, and CONAIE launched a program on gender. Indigenous organizations have recently shown some effort to integrate women into their agenda. In 2010, CONAIE's office still needed to draft a national agenda for Indigenous women in Ecuador. Overall, the Indigenous movement remains reticent to embrace discourses on gender, often preaching gender complementarity but doing little to redress *de facto* inequalities in terms of leadership. At times, violence is excused among Indigenous leaders themselves. This is best illustrated by Lourdes Tibán, head of CODENPE, who threatened to close the *Comisária de la Mujer* in Riobamba for trying to dismiss accusations of domestic violence against Pachakutik Congressman Estuardo Remache in 2006 (Picq 2012).

The gender gap reveals the permanence of discriminatory and violent practices, and the toleration of insidious impunity in the name of ethnic cohesion. The Indigenous movement has acquired hierarchical and *machista* practices that did not necessarily exist before. The recent silencing of women's voices in institutionalized politics may call for gender-focused reforms within Ecuador's Indigenous movement. But in order to make them efficient, we must first try to understand what pushed ethno-politics to undermine women participation, and discard political forces that contributed to the very foundation and consolidation of Indigenous legitimacy in the region.

---

in meetings. Their number has now decreased substantially. Interviews with past and present leaders from CONMIE (January 2006).

## Mainstream Politics Silencing Women

Exclusion and poverty have always affected Indigenous women, but since the 1920s rebellions in Cayambe to the massive 1990s uprisings these factors have never impeded them from resisting at the frontlines of political protest. Yet the recent institutionalization of the Indigenous movement in the mid-1990s made women's interests less tangible and their voices less present. As the Indigenous movement gained political prominence and international legitimacy, women's leadership seems to have gone dormant. Women's rebellious activism is not extinct. But some of the very achievements of the Indigenous struggle might have hampered women's participation by accentuating gender inequalities within the movement. Three factors, in particular, can be identified to explain growing gender disparities within Indigenous groups following the consolidation of the Indigenous movement.

The first factor that can explain today's gender gap is that the making of Indigenous citizens was a highly gendered process. Agrarian reform marked the end of the *huasipungo*, and with it the end of political subjugation and economic exploitation. As Indian peasants became citizens, they gained political, economic, and social rights like the rest of Ecuadorian society. But the redistribution of rights to Indigenous peoples reproduced gender fault lines that prevailed in *mestizo* society. Whereas all Indigenous peoples gained the right to vote, agrarian reform gave land titles to men. Electoral registration was necessary to exist as a citizen and thus acquire land titles, encouraging men to vote in order to get land registered in their name. Men voted for economic motives (just like they now migrate to the cities for economic motives). Since women had no opportunity to acquire land titles, they had little legal or administrative incentive to vote. This is why Señora Naula, in Chimborazo, never voted.[14] As men were pursuing legal titles to land, they were forced to engage *mestizo* society, and to learn the Spanish language, social codes, and institutions. Because the redistribution of citizenship rights was gendered, the gender gap started to grow wider as women were less involved in the process of becoming Ecuadorian citizens and increasingly were left behind. As Indigenous peasants became citizens they entered the education system. As women's literacy lagged behind that of men, their leverage to negotiate with the state also took a toll. This education gap implied not only political but economic marginalization, as women kept working non-paid jobs in the highlands while men were progressively

---

[14] Interview with the author, Chimborazo (2006).

integrated into the capitalist market economy of urban centers. The gender gap grew on political, economic, social, and cultural fronts. Men's opportunities to participate in politics grew faster than those of women. The emancipation from the *huasipungo*, for which Cacuango and Amaguaña had fought so hard, meant that Indigenous men and women were integrated in *mestizo* society and more susceptible to institutionalized gender inequalities of the nation-state.

A second influential factor in excluding women from Ecuador's modern movement is the central role of the Catholic Church in the process of agrarian reform. Liberation Theology was key to the success of the struggle for ending the exploitation of Indigenous peoples under the *huasipungo* and redistributing land. Some sectors of the Catholic Church were crucial political allies in legitimizing Indigenous demands and shifting the balance of power towards land redistribution. In Chimborazo, Monseñor Leonidas Proaño became a strong advocate of Indigenous rights, giving away church land, and contributing politically and philosophically to the emergence of today's Indigenous movement. Accused of being a Red Bishop, he fought for the poor Indians of Chimborazo, notably creating the Popular Radio Schools of Ecuador (ERPE) in 1962 for the literacy, education, and evangelization of Ecuador's Indigenous peoples. A ceremonial stone high up in the *páramo*, close to the eternal snows of the Chimborazo volcano, celebrates "the Bishop of the Indians," and Assemblywoman Lourdes Tibán stressed his influence on Indigenous peoples as a "regional and national symbol" during a 2010 commemoration in his honor. Although the Catholic Church played a positive role in supporting the making of Ecuador's modern Indigenous movement, it also emphasized a certain division of labor between men and women, further pushing hierarchical gender roles that were practiced in the hacienda system and encouraging women to stay in the private spheres (O'Connor 2007). The Church's support for Indigenous emancipation during the decades of agrarian reform came at the cost of an increasingly gendered participation in politics.

A third factor to take into account when analyzing women's receding visibility in the Indigenous movement is the gender bias prevailing in Ecuadorian mainstream politics. Mestizo politics are gendered, with few women elected to office or appointed to positions of leadership. Despite gender quotas, Ecuador's political system remains a bastion of masculine power. As the Indigenous movement consolidated its politics of influence into politics of power, it adapted to the rules of the game. Playing by the rules meant playing a patriarchal game. In the process of political mainstreaming, there is a process of normalization that takes place, which implies certain masculinization of politics. Men had more chances to succeed in the Ecuadorian patriarchal political system. Discriminated against on the basis of their gender, women stayed more frequently behind the scenes, organizing the bases, as men were favored for positions of public leadership. As Indigenous peoples entered Ecuadorian politics, gender inequalities were accentuated to conform to mainstream political standards.

All these factors combined seem to have contributed to undermining women's leadership within Ecuador's modern Indigenous movement. Indigenous women have struggled against ethnic discrimination and violence for centuries. As they gained Indigenous rights, however, they have encountered other obstacles, most notably gendered inequalities that permeated the Indigenous movement as it evolved from a social movement on the political periphery towards formal politics with national visibility. As the Indigenous movement gained ground to become a legitimate, institutionalized political voice, women benefited from newly institutionalized Indigenous rights in international norms and the Ecuadorian Constitution. Yet they also experienced intricate layers of gender-based inequalities, lingering in Ecuadorian society as a whole. Indigenous men gained more emancipation faster, whereas Indigenous women faced unequal access to property rights, education, and income.

## Conclusion

This chapter makes a case for the long-standing agency of Indigenous women in Ecuador. Examining the mobilization of women from colonial rebellions to the construction of the modern Indigenous movement, I retrace the extent, persistence, and decisiveness of their participation in politics of resistance and contestation. My historical analysis positioned at the intersections of gender and ethnicity seeks to locate the power of Indigenous women while at the same time expanding conceptual premises of political agency. In positioning Indigenous women strategically, it invites several concluding observations.

First, my core contention is that Indigenous women have always partaken in politics. The chapter accumulates historical evidence from leadership in popular rebellions, enduring social mobilization, and participation in modern politics to probe the scope and scale of Indigenous women politics. Indigenous women are by no means political bystanders. They are not novices to political struggles either, but inheritors of legitimate authority. Despite lingering gender and racial discrimination, this analysis posits Indigenous women as pivotal, enduring actors in the making of the

Ecuadorian politics. Not only have Indigenous women repeatedly mobilized in struggles against exploitation, but they have often done so in positions of leadership. Bridging historical and political perspectives, I suggest Indigenous women are political insiders who have the ability to determine power struggles. In that sense, social scientists must take their struggles seriously in order to better understand the quality of political struggles in Latin America.

Second, recognizing the enduring legacy of political leadership among Indigenous women is particularly relevant to understand their contemporary invisibility. Women were key to the founding of the FEI, Cacuango and Amaguaña are widely recognized symbols of Indigenous contestation, and Pacari strengthened the legitimacy of Ecuador's Indigenous movement. Yet female leadership is increasingly hard to find. Indigenous institutions include few women in their ranks, and even fewer at the top, and the presidents of CONAIE and all its organizations have always been men, mostly excluding women from formal corridors of power. Despite what I call the inheritance of resistance, Indigenous women appear to be increasingly lagging behind in contemporary politics in Ecuador. The double-sword of the process of institutionalization of ethno-politics in a formal political party is that it has inherited gender inequalities from the mainstream political system.

Finally, the marginalization of women sheds light on contradictions between the discourse of equality and practice of discrimination in ethno-politics. While political mainstreaming might have accentuated gender discrepancies within Ecuador's modern Indigenous movement, the movement is nevertheless responsible for practicing—and at times encouraging—gender discrimination. Retracing Indigenous women's leadership through time reveals that their invisibility is neither necessary nor anchored in the past, but rather embedded in recent political processes. As the Indigenous movement gains political authority in mainstream politics, it must be held accountable to practice the social justice it preaches. The presence of gender inequality in the Indigenous movement is not a fault of the past nor can it be written off as a mere inheritance of colonial violence. Instead, the absence of women is attached to recent developments and must be addressed with the same sense of urgency and force it inspires in non-Indigenous political contexts.

Looking forward, the story told here opens many new questions regarding the political role of Indigenous women. Recognizing Indigenous women as political actors who impact and transform political processes is essential to rethinking democratic practice in Latin America. This essay is an invitation for further research that locates what is blocking Indigenous women's leadership from attaining center-stage in the Indigenous movement, and an investigation into what forms their rebellious leadership takes today. As I contribute research seeking a less hierarchical understanding of politics, it is my hope that Indigenous women can inspire more robust forms of leadership across Latin America.

# References

Almeida V., Jose. 1993. *Sismo étnico en el Ecuador: Varias perspectivas*. Quito: Abya Yala.

Ari Murillo, Marina. 2003. *Bartolina Sisa: la generala aymara y la equidad de género*. La Paz: Editorial Amuyañataki.

Becker, Marc. 2008. *Indians and Leftists in the Making of Ecuador's Modern Indigenous Movements*. Durham: Duke University Press.

Becker, Marc and Silvia Tutillo. 2009. *Historia Agraria y Social de Cayambe*. Quito: Abya Yala/FLACSO.

Blomberg, Rolf. 1969. *Are Indians People*. Sweden.

Cameron, John. 2010. *Struggles for Local Democracy in the Andes*. New York: First Forum Press.

Chong, Natividad Gutierrez. 2007. *Women, Ethnicity, and Nationalisms in Latin America*. Burlington: Asgate.

Coronel, Valeria and Mercedes Prieto. 2010. *Celebraciones centenarias y negociaciones por la nacin ecuatoriana*. Quito: FLACSO.

Costales, Marcela. 2002. *Mensajeras Cósmicas: Grandes Figuras Femininas de Chimborazo*. Riobamba: Coordinadora Política de Mujeres de Chimborazo.

Cumes, Aura. 2009. "'Sufrimos verguenza': mujeres k'iche' frente a la justicia comunitaria en Guatemala." *Desacatos* 31(Sept-Dec):99-114.

Den Ouden, Amy E. 2012. "Colonial Violence and the Gendering of Post-War Terrain in Southern New England: Native Women and Rights to Reservation Land in Eighteenth-Century Connecticut." *Landscapes of Violence* 2(1):3.

García, Verónica Vásquez. 2011. *Usos y Costumbres y Ciudadania feminina: Hablan las presidentas municipales de Oaxaca 1996-2010*. Mexico: Porrúa.

Gauderman, Kimberly. 2003. *Women's Lives in Colonial Quito: Gender, Law, and Economy in Spanish America*. Austin: University of Texas Press.

Londoño, Jenny. 1997. *Entre la sumisión y la resistencia: las mujeres en la Audiencia de Quito*. Quito: Abya Yala.

Lucero, José Antonio. 2008. *Struggles of Voice: The Politics of Indigenous Representation in the Andes*. Pittsburgh: University of Pittsburgh Press.

Madrid, Raúl L. 2012. *The Rise of Ethnic Politics in Latin America*. Cambridge: Cambridge University Press.

Mejía, Lucila. 1985. *Las Hijas de Bartolina Sisa*. La Paz: HISBOL.

Mino Grijalva, Cecilia. 2009. *Tránsito Amaguaña: Ama Wañuna*. Quito: Abya Yala.

O'Brien, Jean M. 2010. *Firsting and Lasting: Writing Indians out of Existence in New England*. Minneapolis: University of Minnesota Press.

O'Connor, Erin. 2007. *Gender, Indian, nation: the contradictions of making Ecuador, 1830-1925*. Tucson: University of Arizona Press.

Pacari, Nina. 2002. "The Political Participation of Indigenous Women in the Ecuadorian Congress: Unfinished Business." *International IDEA*. http://www.idea.int.

Paredes, Julieta. 2008. *Hilando fino desde el feminismo comunitario*. La Paz: CEDEC/Mujeres Creando Comunidad.

Picq, Manuela Lavinas. 2012. "Between the Dock and a Hard Place: Hazards and Opportunities of Legal Pluralism for Indigenous Women in Ecuador." *Latin American Politics and Society* 54(2):1–33.

Rodas, Raquel. 2009. *Historia del voto femenino en el Ecuador*. Quito: Consejo Nacional de las Mujeres.

—. 1985. *Tránsito Amaguaña: su testimonio*. Quito: CEDIME.

Romo-Leroux, Ketty. 1997. *Movimiento de mujeres en el Ecuador*. Guayaquil: Editorial de la Universidad de Guayaquil.

Rousseau, Stephanie. 2011. "Indigenous and Feminist Movements at the Contituent Assembly in Bolivia: Locating the representation of Indigenous women." *Latin American Research Review* 46(2):5-28.

Scott, James C. 2009. *The Art of Not Being Governed: An Anarchist History of Upland Southeast Asia*. New Heaven: Yale University Press.

Siles, María Eugenia del Valle de. 1981. *Bartolina Sisa y Gregoria Apaza: dos heroínas indígenas*. Biblioteca Popular Boliviana de "Ultima Hora."

Silverblatt, Irene Marsha. 1987. *Moon, Sun, and Witches: Gender ideologies and class in Inca and colonial Peru*. Princeton: Princeton University Press.

Van Cott, Donna Lee. 2007. *From Movements to Parties in Latin America: The Evolution of Ethnic Politics*. Cambridge: Cambridge University Press.

Yashar, Deborah J. 2005. *Contesting Citizenship in Latin America: the Rise of Indigenous Movements and the Postliberal Challenge.* Cambridge: Cambridge University Press.

Zamosc, León. 2007. "The Indian Movement and Political Democracy in Ecuador." *Latin American Politics & Society* 49(3):1–34.

Zwarenstein, Carolyn. 2006. "Legacy of a Zapatista rebel." *Toronto Globe and Mail.* January 11.

# CHAPTER FIVE

# ETHNIC REPRESENTATION OF AFRO DESCENDANT POPULATIONS IN THE ECUADORIAN (2008) AND BOLIVIAN (2009) CONSTITUTIONS

# CRISTINA ECHEVERRI PINEDA[1]

The 2008 Ecuadorian and 2009 Bolivian constitutions are the most recent constitutional processes in Latin America. These processes have not only questioned the cultural and ethnic homogeneity paradigms of the previous constitutions, but have also broken the old unitary model, as both constitutions proclaim these countries to be plurinational and intercultural. This chapter proposes an initial approach to the way in which Ecuador and Bolivia constitutionally recognized ethnic differences for Afro descendant groups and their relation to the constitutional principle of a *plurinationality*. In both Ecuador and Bolivia, the state and constitutional vindication of Afros has been guided, to a great extent, by Indigenous conceptual and ancestral frameworks. The current risk is to recede into new homogenizations based on the processes of Indigenous populations, or a segment of these, since both countries have very diverse Indigenous groups. Therefore, one of the current challenges is to include other social groups, recognizing the amplified cultural diversity of these states, while avoiding new "invisibilities" of other social groups, as may be the case of Afro descendants in plurinational states. The Indigenous normative framework may not only render Afro communities invisible, but may be itself a limitation for these communities' own existence. In this sense, thinking about the presence of Afro descendant populations in the Andean region evidences the need to recognize the tensions entailed by

---

[1] I would like to thank Camilo Vargas Aguirre for assistance with the translation of this chapter.

*plurinationality* and the Indigenous model, on the one hand, with the identity and organizational dynamics of the Afro descendants in these countries, on the other. This requires considering the hybrid nature of Afro identity, delving into the heterogeneity which characterizes the way these populations inhabit the Andean region, and considering their identity from a national and global context, in the form of changing, decentralized, and relation-based constructions (Wade 2000, 129).

With this in mind, the questions that will guide this chapter are the following: Does the new plurinational conception that inspires the Bolivian and Ecuadorian constitutions include Afro Andeans? What are the implications of plurinationality for Afro Andeans? These questions will allow us to analyze how these constitutional frameworks construct the points of reference to the recognition of Afro descendant populations, and to define what type of relationships can be established with the normative elements of Indigenous recognition. In other words, we must ask ourselves if the normative framework for Afro descendants is a copy of the Indigenous framework, or if, on the contrary, it recognizes the specific characteristics of these populations and therefore avoids homogenizing their diversity. Copying the Indigenous normative framework implies not recognizing the ethnic, cultural, social, political, and even regional diversity that these countries possess, allowing for new invisibilities that hide specific traits of each of these groups that claim differential treatment. This chapter will not address the discourses that define plurinationality in the constitutional assemblies, nor the characteristics of Afro descendant social mobilization in the two countries in question. Rather, it analyzes the substance regarding Afro Ecuadorians and Afro Bolivians in each of the constitutions. In order to address these questions, this essay will initially discuss what is understood as new Latin American constitutionalism, whose main characteristic has been the recognition of ethnic and cultural diversity, which has in turn characterized the Bolivian and Ecuadorian processes. This chapter will then approach the way in which each country understands *plurinationality* and its implications for Afro Ecuadorians and Afro Bolivians, and how it can be called into question by these social groups' own conditions.

## New Latin American Constitutionalism

Since the early 1980s, Latin America has undergone an intense period of constitutional change, as a majority of its countries adopted new constitutions or introduced important reforms to existing ones (Gargarella and Courtis 2009; Uprimny 2011). The recognition of ethnic and cultural diversity of the different countries in the region was one of the main characteristics of what has been called new Latin American constitutionalism, which emerged in the mid 1980s and was especially strong throughout the 1990s. This multicultural constitutionalism (Van Cott 2000) spans throughout Latin America from the promulgation of the Honduran (1982), Nicaraguan (1987), Brazilian (1988), and Colombian (1991) constitutions, through the Bolivian constitution in 2009 (Wade 2006, 66; Rodríguez Pinto and Domínguez Avila 2011, 60). It has been since the Colombian constitution in 1991, however, that particular emphasis has been put on the elaboration of multicultural policies that stem from the recognition of the country's cultural diversity, establishing political and judicial institutions to safeguard such diversity. This is why many regard the Colombian case as the starting point for a new form of constitutionalism in Latin America (Noguera Fernández and Criado de Diego 2011, 18) that may even be regarded as a "constitutionalism of diversity" (Uprimny 2011, 4).

Under the new Latin American constitutionalism, these countries are defined as pluriethnic and pluricultural, which brings new meaning to what was previously known as the nation-state. As a result, a new heterogeneous social structure is recognized in Latin America on social, religious, cultural, and ethnic levels. This modifies the conception of a homogenous society and nation, in which diverse actors such as Indigenous peoples and the peoples of African descent had been excluded and marginalized. The tendency towards the recognition of diversity has focused on the inclusion of the rights of Indigenous peoples (Uprimny 2011 12). In fact, the granting of special rights to Indigenous communities has been most radical in the recent Ecuadorian and Bolivian constitutions, which define the countries to be plurinational states, a category that seeks to conceptualize notions derived from Indigenous traditions that question the model of cultural and political homogeneity of the nation-state, as it conceives the state as diverse in its definition, design and functions.

Both the multicultural institutional designs and the theoretical discussions of multiculturalism in Latin America have focused mainly on the recognition of rights for Indigenous peoples (Sieder 2002; Kymlicka 2003; Assies 2006 and 2000) and on the political and electoral mobilization of these groups (Van Cott; Laurent; among others). In general, in the countries that have adopted these constitutional changes, Indigenous peoples have been the main object of "otherness," as the recognition and allocation of rights has centered explicitly on these groups. However, another actor that has emerged as a differentiated political subject in these constitutional processes has been the Afro descendant groups, even if legal reforms aimed at them have been less numerous. The first precedents can be found in the constitutions of Honduras (1982) and Nicaragua (1987), where a series of ethnic rights for Indigenous and Afro descendant groups were recognized. On the other hand, Brazil (1988) and Colombia (1991) adopted legal changes that referred directly to Black communities, or *remanescentes das comunidades dos quilombos* in the Brazilian case (Wade 2006, 66). In this sense, since the 1990s there has been in Latin America a regional and international context that has been favorable to the institutional recognition of cultural diversity, as treaties and agreements that embraced the social inclusion of Indigenous and Afro descendant populations were signed (Wade 2006, 69; Assies 2006), and constitutional changes that seek to favor the recognition of a differentiated citizenship were adopted.

In this context, Ecuador established a ministry of ethnic affairs for Black and Indigenous communities in 1996 (Whitten and Quiroga 1998, quoted by Wade 2006, 66), and in its 1998 constitution Ecuador proclaimed itself as a pluriethnic and multicultural state (Art. 1), and fifteen collective rights were granted to Indigenous and Afro Ecuadorian peoples. This constitution recognized Afro descendant peoples as subjects of collective rights over their ancestral lands (Walsh 2005, 234). The 2008 Ecuadorian constitution displaced the one from 1998, defining Ecuador as an intercultural and plurinational state, which recognizes Afro Ecuadorian communities as distinct peoples and promises to protect their commonly-held lands and ancestral territories.

Bolivia, on the other hand, had proclaimed itself as a multiethnic and pluricultural country since the 1994 constitutional reform. The 2009 Bolivian constitution states in Article 3 that Bolivia shall be a "Unitary Social State of Plurinational, Community-Based Law, constituted by the Indigenous, peasant nations and peoples, and the intercultural and Afro Bolivian communities that constitute the Bolivian people." No previous constitution had recognized the presence of Afro descendants in Bolivian territory, and on this matter, one of the main demands of the Afro Bolivian people was the proper enforcement of several agreements that the Bolivian government signed or ratified at different summits and human rights conventions (Martínez Mita 2008, 12).

As noted, both Ecuador and Bolivia had previous multicultural legislative arrangements, yet the novelty of their recent constitutions is the proclamation of *plurinationality*, which therefore requires further definition. However, there is no consensual definition of the exact meaning of a plurinational state, which makes it a political and analytical category subject to ongoing debate and construction. It is therefore necessary to reflect and theorize on what plurinationality implies for the state and how it is understood in both Ecuador and Bolivia. This requires an in-depth analysis of the concept's principles and foundations, the differences in each case, and implications for state building in each country. Also, it is necessary to review the implications of plurinationality on the Afro descendant populations in Bolivia and Ecuador, and how this constitutional principle can be interrogated through this social group's own condition.

## Plurinationality and the Afro Descendant Populations

As previously mentioned, one of the novelties of these constitutional processes was the proclamation of these countries as plurinational states. This conception changes previous imageries and designs of the nation-state, since in traditional political theory the state and its reform have been in relation to a single identity that implied political unification and cultural homogenization. For this reason, there have been theoretical approaches to the constitutional principle of plurinationality in both Ecuador and Bolivia.

Coming from an intellectual stream that analyzes the critiques made from a plurinational perspective to the conceptions of nation-state that have dominated the nineteenth and twentieth centuries, political scientist Luis Tapia underscores how the nation-state has been considered the main configurational form of the organization of government and political life. This has implied a process of political unification, that is, the construction of a set of institutions that constitute a single system of administration of political power and the management of a country, as well as a process of cultural homogenization or unification (Tapia 2010, 11). The nation has been identified as a synonym of one culture and one state; that is, the nation implies that a specific community shares some social and cultural referents that have developed certain structures of political direction. To Catherine Walsh, plurinationality gives rise to identity and territorial memberships that in turn generate new forms of conceiving, organizing, and managing power, democracy, justice, and government without breaking its unitary character (Walsh 2007).

According to Tapia, plurinationality implies three elements: recognition of cultural diversity, forms of self-government, and territoriality. These elements emerge when the homogenization of the nation-state is not consolidated and cultural diversity has remained and become politicized (Tapia 2010, 12). Therefore, the plurinational character of the state is summarized in one basic principle: unity amidst the diversity of the state, in which society and its democratic political institutions recognize the existence of peoples and nationalities as political subjects within the State of Social Rule of Law (Antón Sánchez 2009, 396). Conceptualized in this way, plurinationality seeks to rethink what unifies a country (Walsh 2008), where the collective rights of communities are recognized within the unity of the state. This constitutional principle implies judicial pluralism and a common government that recognizes cultural differences and incorporates them into a set of institutions that are "always aiming at their unity, complementation and reciprocity, equity and solidarity" (Tapia 2010, 7).

In the Bolivian case, the process of the Constitutional Assembly and the constitution that ensued were born in the Indigenous and peasant marches held since the 1990s, where these communities demanded the recognition of their autonomy in terms of plurinationality. In Ecuador, the debate on plurinationality was spearheaded by the Confederation of Indigenous Nationalities of Ecuador (CONAIE), and it centered on the debate on the role of the state vis-à-vis Indigenous, Afro Ecuadorian, and Montubian peoples, as well as the degree of autonomy that plurinationality would imply (Larrea Maldonado 2008). The CONAIE has been demanding the plurinational character of the Ecuadorian state since 1994, clarifying that they did not demand its fragmentation or a shift towards some form of federalism, nor autonomies outside the national unity of the republic, but rather a change in the structure of the state in its model of development and democracy (cf. CONAIE 2007, 9). Cruz Rodríguez (2012, 1) analyzes how the Indigenous movement managed to resignify the Ecuadorian nation between 1990 and 2008 from the articulation of the Indigenous movement with other social sectors that opposed neoliberal reforms. This allowed the transition from particular demands that focused on Indigenous issues to a national struggle, defining a national project summarized in the plurinational state recognized by the political constitution of 2008. Cruz argues that the transformation that the Indigenous movement achieved in the country's social imagery is explained by its capacity to articulate the demands of diverse actors and unify them around common struggles that transcend exclusively Indigenous demands. This shows how plurinationality does not imply a process of isolation and fragmentation of certain communities from other social groups.

In Ecuador, the Afro Ecuadorian population is approximately 604,009 people that represent 5 percent of the overall population (Ponce 2006). Afro Ecuadorians achieved recognition as a "People" in the 1998 constitution, with which they gained fifteen collective rights. In 2006, the Congress of the Republic approved the Law of Collective Rights for the Afro Ecuadorian People, and in 2007 the National Government issued a national public policy for Afro Ecuadorians in the Afro National Development Plan (Antón Sánchez 2008).

In the Bolivian case, not until the 2008 constitution were Afro descendants acknowledged for their particular ethnic difference, a recognition that was a product of their social struggle. According to data from the National Afro Bolivian Council (CONAFRO), the country has a population of 35,000 Afro Bolivians, which represent less than 1 percent of a country with a general population of 9.5 million people, of which 62 percent are Indigenous. In this sense, Busdiecker (2009) argues that Bolivia has been considered as the "most Indigenous country in the Americas." Even though Afro Bolivians have inhabited Bolivia since colonial times (Crespo 1977; Criales Alcázar 1995; Gutiérrez Brockington 2009), the Indigenous majority and the white-*mestizo* population have made them invisible. Even though in both cases Afro descendants do not constitute a majority in demographic terms, they are claiming differential treatment in countries that have recognized themselves as Indigenous and *mestizo*.

In the final draft of the constitution, the recognition of Afro Bolivians appears in three of the 408 articles. Among them is Article 3 that recognizes Afro Bolivians as "communities" (not as peoples or nations) while Article 32 speaks of the "Afro Bolivian people" entitled to "the economic, social, political, and cultural rights recognized in the constitution for native Indigenous peasant nations and peoples." Finally, Article 103 protects knowledge and traditional customs through the registration of intellectual property, safeguarding the intangible rights of Indigenous, peasant, and Afro Bolivian peoples (Walsh 2008, 26). The recognition of Afro descendant populations is given in relationship to those rights recognized for Indigenous peoples. This implies that the recognition of territorial administration and self-government only applies to the Indigenous communities, and the recognition of the Afro Bolivians is guaranteed in the cultural sphere, but with no legal differentiation for these populations. It is important to point out that according to the PNUD (2010), with the exception of Brazil, Bolivia is the only country in South America that has developed advanced legislation regarding the recognition of ethnic-cultural diversity and the affirmation of rights for Afro descendants.

In Ecuador, plurinationality for Afro Ecuadorians is linked to their recognition as a "people," and in that sense beholden to collective rights over their territories. This situation is absent in the Bolivian case, where treatment of Afro descendants is equated to that of the Indigenous. As Walsh has pointed out in the case of the Ecuadorian Indigenous movement, the acknowledgement of Indigenous "nationalities" is rooted in elements such as a territory, language, history, customs, and identity that preceded the Spanish invasion and the formation of the republic. The nationality of the Indigenous communities predates the formation of the "Ecuadorian nation." In contrast,

> the identification as an Afro Ecuadorian people stems from the situation and historical and racial living conditions within the Ecuadorian nation itself…. Afros are not united by their nationality but by bonds that are a product of the slave trade and the Diaspora nature it generated, by their struggles for existence, their ancestral memory (of slavery, *cimarronaje*[2] and the territory as an element of freedom)" (Walsh 2008, 30).

This difference is key, according to this author, because it allows us to understand why Afro demands focus on the recognition and visibility of their citizenship, that is, in terms of their existence itself; these demands diverge from those forwarded by the Indigenous groups who struggled for the recognition of their territory, autonomy, nationality, and the transformation of state and social structures and institutions. According to this author, the constitutional designs for the Afro descendant population have responded to the first and second conditions, but neither of the two cases accomplishes all of the conditions.

Walsh argues that this has been a constant in history: "the recognition of the existence of the Indigenous peoples has taken place in detriment to the recognition of Afro descendants, and the establishment of African slavery had as its main purpose to save Indigenous peoples from extermination, which evidences a history that has always positioned Indigenous peoples above Blacks in a scale of social classification" (Walsh 2007, 5). It is important then to situate Afro Andean mobilizations within the broader context of the mobilization of Afro descendant communities in Latin America, pointing out the particularities implied in being an Afro Andean in the new constitutional scenarios. This situation leads us to further analyze the conceptions of the social groups that inhabit the Andes, and to think of the different ways in which the Afro descendants inhabit cities like Quito or La Paz, because the presence of Afro descendants has been associated with coastal and Caribbean regions.

One of the demands the Afro Ecuadorian movement made in the process of writing the 2008 constitution was that their recognition as a people be retained, and with it, the recognition of their collective rights.

---

[2] The practice of fleeing or escaping a condition of slavery. The term applies to the struggles of Afro descendant slaves in Central and South America, as well as the Caribbean.

Also, the new constitution included the principle of nondiscrimination, the penalization of any form of racism, the state's obligation to guarantee affirmative action to victims of racism, and the encouragement of public policies through the National Equality Councils for historically excluded ethnic communities. Antón Sánchez (2009) emphasizes that the mobilization of Afro Ecuadorian communities is not an effect of the constitutional reformation period, but can be traced back to the 1970s. This implies that Afro Ecuadorians have not been mere "indirect benefactors" of Indigenous mobilization and demands, but rather that the Afro descendant populations have had their own organizational processes, with their own set of demands and claims to economic, social, political, territorial, and cultural rights.

In general, there has been a theoretical concern to analyze how plurinationality and the new constitutions interact with other social sectors. Soruco Sologuren (2009, 19) addresses the construction of the plurinational project from the intersection of national-popular horizons. In her analysis, the author revives the category of people that the new constitution proposed as a possible way to articulate the *mestizo* sectors and the Indigenous communities and nations. Soruco Sologuren (2009, 25) argues that the project of plurinationaltiy "is an attempt to construct a political system capable of articulating these world organization schemes, these Indigenous and non Indigenous cultures, beyond the scope of capitalist coloniality." It is from the category of People that the Bolivian society will be articulated, because for Soruco Sologuren (2009, 26) the nation is a category that homogenizes, where the category of people will allow coexistence within diversity.

Likewise for Ecuador, Ramón Valarezo (2009) differs from Mayorga in establishing plurinationality as an ambiguous and insufficient concept with a lesser breadth than interculturality for three reasons: "Plurinationality recognizes diversity but does not emphasize unity within diversity; it leads the state to treat Indigenous peoples as a national minority, and does not transform the racist, unequal and monocultural and excluding structure; and plurinationality is particularly applicable to zones with territories that a single people inhabited, but it is not applicable to territories that are fluid, which are the majority in Ecuador, where several peoples and citizens cohabit" (Ramón Valarezo 2009, 125). This is why the author prefers interculturality over plurinationality which emphasizes the need to build unity from the recognition of difference, since the second constitutional principle in itself might turn out to be exclusionary since it would only apply to the cultural differences related to a specific territory, and would not include "hybrid territories" where different social groups such as Afro Ecuadorians and *mestizos* cohabit (Ramón Valarezo 2009, 127). Going deeper into the implications of interculturality, Valarerzo argues that this concept represents an advancement over other concepts such as multiculturalism and pluriculturality, as these two only describe the existence of multiple cultures in a given place, and propose their recognition, respect and tolerance in a framework of equality, but are insufficient to analyze the relations of conflict and cohabitation between different cultures (Ramón Valarezo 2009, 135). Mayorga (2010) further criticizes Bolivian plurinationality. He argues that the constitutional design that centers on "national pluralism" supposes the broadening of the state's representative capacity, which implies that the mere reproduction of plurinationality in the nomination of certain institutions will not suffice: Plurinational Legislative Assembly, Plurinational Electoral Organ, Plurinational Constitutional Tribunal. In that sense, the institutional effects of "national pluralism" are aloof and are in a way subordinate to liberal democracy and are limited to the imprecise establishment of ethnic quotas (Mayorga 2010, 30).

The approaches that Ramón Valarezo, Soruco Soroguen, and Cruz Rodríguez set forth allow us to reflect on the implications that the new constitutional designs and plurinationality have on the participation and recognition of other social sectors. Also, these approaches evidence the needs and concerns that exist both in Bolivia and Ecuador to establish an articulation of proposals for plurinationality with groups other than those of the Indigenous populations. Mayorga (2010) questions the fact that plurinationality has been limited to a nominal designation of certain institutions, which does not imply a plural design for the state. In that sense, this constitutional principle would not have any real application in the state's current institutional functioning.

Further research will have to evaluate the application of plurinationality in these countries and the articulation that it has permitted with other social sectors as a way to recognize ethnic and cultural diversity in order to avoid new forms of invisibility in relation to other social groups. In the case of Afro descendant populations, even though there are territories within these states that these communities traditionally inhabited like the Yungas region in Bolivia or Esmeraldas in Ecuador, the identity and existence of the Afro descendants is more diverse. They inhabit different cities and urban contexts in a variety of ways in which they cannot be understood as a different nation. This means that the Indigenous legal framework may not only risk rendering the Afro descendant communities invisible, but also that the model poses limitations to these communities' own living conditions. Handelsman (2001, 11) proposes thinking of the plurinational project not just in terms of the demands Indigenous peoples articulated, but as a means to the acceptance of heterogeneity. This requires the recognition of the presence of the Afro component in the plurinational discourses, since the African presence has been historically marginalized from the national and Andean cultural imagery as its presence has been considered exotic.

## Concluding Remarks

Plurinationality in Ecuador and Bolivia has taken the form of a normative, theoretical, political, and practical challenge, and is not yet a reality. It will be necessary to further examine the way it is being promoted, designed, and applied in public policies, so that plurinationality does not become a mere ornament in political discourse and constitutional design, but rather a fundamental part in understanding state building in these Latin American countries. Furthermore, it will be necessary to understand the conflicts that these different traditional and plurinational legal frameworks are generating within each country, which means reflecting on plurinationality's most concrete applications and conflicts, and not just on its discourse. Additionally, it will be necessary to articulate its meaning and its application with other constitutional arrangements such as the concepts of interculturality, community, and people; this will allow us to understand the relations that are created among different social groups in these countries.

In regard to the second challenge, this initial approach to plurinationality has evidenced the need to examine the concept's implications from the perspective of political theory, in order to contrast these constitutional arrangements with other attempts in other parts of the world where political theory has sought to understand the diverse ways to understand diversity and fragmentation of the nation-state. State construction and democracy in the Andean region might be better understood if the differences and similarities between these processes and those in other parts of the world were analyzed, giving plurinationality its place in the wider context of globalization.

The political scenarios in these two countries have been immersed in constant waves of change and political institutional reforms. Tanaka (2010) argues that democratic crises in the Andean countries are associated with bad institutional designs, which is why they have turned to reforming the political system as a means to solve periods of crisis. In this sense, when analyzing the recent constitutional changes in Ecuador and Bolivia, it is important to signal that underlying conflicts are not expressed solely in constitutional terms, but that they precede them in time. Therefore, plurinationality may be another episode in the political and institutional reforms that these countries have gone through in the past decades. This should be taken into account when analyzing the scope and the limits of plurinationality since political reform—a constant form of political action in these countries—may limit these constitutional principles. They could be subject to new institutional reforms or, on the contrary, these constitutions might have elements that may help consolidate democracy in these countries, and establish themselves in the long term.

Finally, thinking about the presence of Afro descendant populations in the Andean region evidences the need to identify the tensions that emerge between plurinationality and the Indigenous model with the identity and organizational dynamics of other social groups, and, in particular, the Afro descendant populations in these countries. This means considering the hybrid nature of their identity, further considering the heterogeneity with which these populations inhabit the Andean Region, and considering their identity in a national and global context, in the form of changing, decentralized and relation-based constructions (Wade 2000, 129).

# References

Acosta, Alberto and Esperanza Martínez, eds. 2009. *Plurinacionalidad. Democracia en la diversidad*. Quito, Ediciones Abya-Yala.

Agudelo, Carlos. 2010. "Movilizaciones afrodescendientes en América Latina. Una visión panorámica de algunas experiencias contra la exclusión y por el derecho a la identidad." *Colombia Internacional* 71 (enero a junio):109-126.

—. s/f. "Movilización política transnacional del movimiento negro en América Latina. Las redes como forma de acción." Centro de Estudios Mexicanos y Centroamericanos, CEMCA. www.cemca-ac.org/docs/Redes-CarlosAgudelo.pdf.

—. 2007. "De la democracia racial brasilera al multiculturalismo colombiano. Inclusión y exclusión de las poblaciones negras en Colombia." Ponencia presentada al simposio "Democracia racial. Experiencia brasileira, atualidade para a América latina e Europa ?" V Congreso europeo CEISAL de latinoamericanistas. Bruselas, Abril 11-14, 2007. http://www.reseau-amerique-latine.fr/ceisal-bruxelles/ESyP /ESyP-2-AGUDELO.pdf.

Afroamérica XXI. 2009. *Compendio Normativo Regional Afrodescendiente de América Latina. Acciones afirmativas a favor del pueblo*

*afrodescendiente de América Latina y legislación antidiscriminatoria.* Afroamérica XXI con el apoyo de Proyecto SociCan-Acción con la Sociedad Civil para la Integración Andina/Comisión Europea/ Comunidad Andina.
www.civilsociety.oas.org/documents/Compendio%20NORMATIVO% 20AFROLATINOAMERICANO.pdf.

Afrodescendientes de Bolivia. Rumbo a la Constituyente. 2005-2006. http://www.constituyentesoberana.org/3/propuestas/osio/6_Comunidad _Afrodescendientes.pdf.

Amariles, David Restrepo. 2009. "Entre originalidad institucional y recepción filosófica. Apuntes críticos sobre el nuevo modelo constitucional latinoamericano." *Cuadernos sobre Relaciones Internacionales, Regionalismo y Desarrollo* 4(7).

Antón Sánchez, John. 2010. "Implementación de los pactos y los convenios internacionales relacionados con los derechos civiles, culturales, económicos, políticos y sociales de la población afrodescendiente de Colombia, Ecuador, Perú y Venezuela." *Derechos de la Población Afrodescendiente de América Latina: Desafíos para su implementación.* PNUD.

—. 2009. "Multiethnic nations and cultural citizenship: proposals from the afro-descendant movements in Ecuador." In *New social movements in the African diaspora,* ed. Manning Marable and Leith Mullings. New York: Palgrave Macmillan.

—. 2009. "El proceso organizativo afroecuatoriano: 1979-2009." Quito: FLACSO-Ecuador. Programa de doctorado en ciencias sociales con especialización en estudios políticos.

—. 2008. "El lugar de los afroecuatorianos en el Estado Plurinacional."

—. 2007. "Afrodescendientes: sociedad civil y movilización social en el Ecuador." *Journal of Latin American and Caribbean Anthropology* 12(1):233-45.

—. 2007. "Afroecuatorianos: Reparaciones y Acciones Afirmativas." In *Afro-reparaciones: Memorias de la Esclavitud y Justicia Reparativa para negros, afrocolombianos y raciales. Bogotá, Universidad Nacional de Colombia.* Facultad de Ciencias Humanas. Centro de Estudios Sociales (CES).

Assies, Willen. 2000. "El constitucionalismo multiétnico en América Latina: El caso de Bolivia." Ponencia *XII Congreso Internacional "Derecho Consuetudinario y Pluralismo Legal: Desafíos en el Tercer Milenio."* Arica, Chile.

—. 2006. "El multiculturalismo lationamericano al inicio del siglo XXI."
    *Cátedra Unesco, Jornadas Pueblos Indígenas en América Latina.*
    Barcelona.
Ávila Santamaría, Ramiro. 2011. *El neoconstitucionalismo transformador.*
    *El Estado y el derecho en la Constitución de 2008.* Quito, Ediciones
    Abya-Yala
Becerra, María José. 2010. "Implementación de los pactos y los convenios
    internacionales relacionados con los derechos civiles, culturales y
    económicos, políticos y sociales de la población afrodescendiente de
    Argentina, Bolivia, Chile, Paraguay y Uruguay." In *Derechos de la*
    *Población Afrodescendiente de América Latina: Desafíos para su*
    *implementación.* PNUD.
Busdiecker, Sara. 2009. "The emergence and evolving character of
    contemporary afrobolivian mobilization: from the performative to the
    political." In *New social movements in the African diaspora*, ed.
    Manning Marable and Leith Mullings. New York: Palgrave
    Macmillan.
Castillo, Luis Carlos. 2007. *Etnicidad y Nación: El desafío de la*
    *diversidad en Colombia.* Cali: Universidad del Valle.
CONAIE. 2007. *Propuesta de la CONAIE frente a la Asamblea*
    *Constituyente. Principios y lineamientos para la nueva constitución*
    *del Ecuador.* Quito: CONAIE.
Constitución Política del Ecuador. 2008.
    http://www.asambleanacional.gov.ec/documentos/constitucion_de_bol
    sillo.pdf.
Constitución Política del Estado Plurinacional de Bolivia. 2008.
    http://www.vicepresidencia.gob.bo/Portals/0/documentos/NUEVA_C
    ONSTITUCION_POLITICA_DEL_ESTADO.pdf.
Cruz Rodríguez, Edwin. 2012. "Redefiniendo la nación: luchas indígenas
    y Estado plurinacional en Ecuador (1990-2008)." *Nómadas. Revista*
    *Crítica de Ciencias Sociales y Jurídicas.* Núm. Especial: América
    Latina. Euro-Mediterranean University Institute-Universidad
    Complutense de Madrid.
Gargarella, Roberto. 2010. "El nuevo constitucionalismo latinoamericano.
    Algunas reflexiones preliminares." *Crítica y emancipación* 3:169-188.
Gargarella, Roberto and Christian Courtis. 2009. *El nuevo constitucionalismo*
    *latinoamericano: promesas e interrogantes.* CEPAL - Serie Políticas
    sociales No 153. Santiago de Chile.
Handelsman, Michael. 2001. *Los afro y la plurinacionalidad, el caso*
    *ecuatoriano visto desde su literatura.* Quito: Ediciones Abya-Yala.

Kymlicka, Will. 2003. *La política vernácula, nacionalismo, multiculturalismo y ciudadanía.* Barcelona: Ediciones Paidos.

Laurent, Virginie. 2005. *Comunidades indígenas, espacios políticos y movilización electoral en Colombia, 1990-1998. Motivaciones, campos de acción e impactos.* Bogotá: ICAH, IFEA.

Larrea Maldonado, Ana María. 2008. "La Plurinacionalidad: iguales y diversos en busca del Sumak Kawsay." *Nuestra Constitución: Nuestro Futuro. Entre voces, Revista del Grupo Democracia y Desarrollo Local.* (Quito) 15.

Martínez Mita, María. 2008. "Impacto del pueblo afroboliviano en el reconocimiento de sus derechos humanos en el proceso Constituyente de Bolivia, 2006 – 2008." Tesis de Maestría en Derechos Humanos y Democracia en América Latina Mención Políticas Públicas. Universidad Andina Simón Bolívar, Sede Ecuador. http://repositorio.uasb.edu.ec/bitstream/10644/383/1/T680-MDH-Mart%C3%ADnez-Impacto%20del%20pueblo%20afroboliviano %20en%20el%20reconocimiento%20de%20sus%20ddhh%20en%20el %20proceso.pdf.

Medina, Henry and Mary Castro. 2006. *Afroecuatorianos Movimiento Social emergente.* Quito: Ediciones Afroamérica-Centro Cultural Afroecuatoriano.

Mosquera Claudia, Pardo, Mauricio and Odile Hoffmann. 2002. *Afrodescendientes en las Américas, 150 años de abolición de la esclavitud en Colombia.* Universidad Nacional de Colombia, ICANH, IRD, ILSA.

Noguera Fernández, Albert and Marcos Criado de Diego. 2011. "La Constitución colombiana de 1991 como punto de inicio del nuevo constitucionalismo en América Latina." *Revista Estudios socio-jurídicos* 13:15-49.

Noguera, Alberto. 2007. "El Neoconstitucioanlismo Latinoamericano: Un Nuevo Proyecto de Democratización Política y Económica para el Continente." Ponencia presentada en el Congreso socio-jurídico: Las formas del Derecho en Latinoamérica. Democracia, desarrollo y liberación." *Oñati* (España), Instituto Internacional de Sociología Jurídica (IISJ).

Paredes, Willington. 2005. *Los montubios y nosotros.* Archivo Histórico del Guayas, Corporación Montubia del Litoral.

Ponce, Juan. 2006. *Más allá de los promedios: afrodescendientes en América Latina. Los afroecuatorianos.* The International Bank for Reconstruction and Development/The World Bank.

Ramón Valarezo, Galo. 2009. "¿Plurinacionalidad o interculturalidad en la constitucion?" In *Plurinacionalidad: Democracia en la diversidad*, eds. Alberto Acosta and Esperanza Martinez, 125-60. Quito: Abya Yala.

Rodríguez Pinto, Simone and Carlos Federico Domínguez Ávila. 2011. "Sociedades plurales, multiculturalismo y derechos indígenas en América Latina." *Política y Cultura* 35:49-66.

Serna de la Garza, José María (Coord.). 2009. *Procesos constituyentes contemporáneos en América Latina. Tendencias y perspectivas.* México: Universidad Nacional Autónoma de México, Instituto de Investigaciones Jurídicas.

Sieder, Rachel, ed. 2002. *Multiculturalism in Latin America: Indigenous Rights, Diversity and Democracy.* New York: Palgrave Macmillan.

Soruco Sologuren, Ximena. 2009. "Estado plurinacional-pueblo, una construcción inédita en Bolivia." *Observatorio Social de América Latina* 10(26) (October):19-33.

Sousa Santos, Boaventura de. 2010. *Refundación del Estado en América Latina. Perspectivas desde una epistemología del sur.* La Paz: Plural Editores.

—. 2007. *La reinvención del Estado y el Estado plurinacional.* Santa Cruz de la Sierra: CENDA/CEJID/CEBID.

Tanaka, Martin and Francine Jacome. 2010. *Desafíos de la gobernabilidad democrática. Reformas político-institucionales y movimientos sociales en la región andina.* Quito: Ediciones Abya-Yala.

Tapia, Luis. 2010. "Consideraciones sobre el estado plurinacional." *Bolivian Research Review/RevistaE* 8(2) (October-November).

—. 2007 "Una reflexión sobre la idea de Estado plurinacional." *OSAL* (Buenos Aires: CLACSO) 8(22).

Uprimny, Rodrigo. 2011. "Las transformaciones constitucionales recientes en América Latina: Tendencias y desafío." *Revista Pensamiento Penal* 122. http://www.juridicas.unam.mx/wccl/ponencias/13/242.pdf.

Van Cott, Donna Lee. 2000. *The friendly liquidation of the past: the politics of diversity in Latin America.* Pittsburgh: University of Pittsburgh Press.

Viciano Pastor, Roberto and Rubén Martínez Dalmau. "¿Se puede hablar de un nuevo constitucionalismo latinoamericano como corriente doctrinal sistematizado?" http://www.juridicas.unam.mx/wccl/ponencias/13/245.pdf.

Wade, Peter. 2000 (1997). *Raza y etnicidad en Latinoamérica.* Quito: Ediciones Abya-Yala.

—. 2008. "Población negra y la cuestión identitaria en América Latina." *Universitas humanística* 65:117-137.

—. 2006. "Etnicidad, multiculturalismo y políticas sociales en América Latina: poblaciones afrolatinas e indígenas." *Tabula Rasa* 4:59-81.

Walsh, Catherine. 2008. *Interculturalidad y plurinacionalidad: Elementos para el debate constituyente.* Quito: Universidad Andina Simón Bolivar, Sede Ecuador.

—. 2007. "Dossier Actualidades: Lo Afro en América Andina: Reflexiones en torno a luchas actuales de (in)visibilidad, (re)existencia y pensamiento." *Journal of Latin American and Caribbean Anthropology* 12(1):200-212.

Walsh, Catherine, León Edizon and Eduardo Restrepo. 2005. "Movimientos sociales afro y políticas de identidad en Colombia y Ecuador." Quito: Universidad Andina Simón Bolívar. http://www.ram-wan.net/restrepo/documentos/movimientos%20sociales%20afro%20y%20politicas%20de%20indentidad%20en%20colom.pdf.

# CHAPTER SIX

## AFRO INCLUSION IN ECUADOR'S CITIZENS' REVOLUTION

## LINDA JEAN HALL

### Introduction

Afro-Ecuadorians will prosper if they understand, appropriate, and gain benefit from the exclusive constitutional rights of affirmative action and reparations. Many factors inhibit Afro citizens from taking advantage of these legal rights. This chapter examines key elements of a resistance in Ecuador to the equal exercise of these entitlements by Afro citizens: racist perceptions, political policies, and social movement favoritism practices.

Racist perceptions about Blackness influence the construction of current ideas about the worth and capabilities of Afro citizens. These misconceptions exist today, and although they may not be immediately recognizable, they continue to provide justification for mistreatment and unfairness. Negative colonial and post-colonial concepts fostered the growth of a powerful resistance to the inclusion of Afro citizens in national and local politics. Afro-Ecuadorians function as outsiders who lack the power necessary to demand equitable treatment.

The issue of power relates directly to the political policies of the state of Ecuador and the holy triad of "isms" that comprise the theoretical foundation of the nation's constitutional law: multiculturalism, pluriculturalism, and interculturalism. Afro citizen appropriation of the benefits of the 2008 Constitution will begin a process capable of eradicating unfair norms and practices that undergird discriminatory jurisprudence. Afro-Ecuadorians will be able to undertake social change and achieve economic equality when they are able to assume active roles as partners in the state's development of political procedures and protocols.

Deeply engrained social networks determine who receives equal access to employment, housing, and education. Utilization of personal and professional contacts by individuals to achieve upward mobility and economic advantage is a common cultural practice in Ecuador. However, most Black Ecuadorians do not have access to influential citizens who can help them obtain jobs, admission to universities, or even decent housing. Also, the majority of employed Afro-Ecuadorians perform labor that is not protected by powerful and politically active professional trade organizations or unions. Political pundits in Ecuador promote a civil dichotomy by positioning themselves firmly in opposition to any form of favoritism or social advantage gained through networking to support their perception of a united society or fair public alliance. However, cultural practices remain firmly seated, and the resistance to change is strong in the sector of organized labor. Afro-Ecuadorians continue to be under-represented, excluded, and disadvantaged because they are caught in the middle of a conflict between different attempts to redefine social norms.

Racist perceptions, political policies, and favoritism practices are three areas of resistance that frame the culture and daily impact the lives of Afro citizens. Therefore, these factors that represent opposition are relevant to the Afro-Ecuadorian struggle to benefit from the collective rights of affirmative action and reparations.

## Methodology and Data

During the summer of 2011, I assumed an activist role in the Ecuadorian Black community. I participated in the creation of a committee to establish academic exchanges between Afro-Ecuadorian students and faculty with various campuses in the United States. According to Hale (2006, 97), a balanced and reflexive understanding of the struggle of a group of study is enriched by the influence of culturally relative opinions obtained during all levels of data acquisition and interpretation. Speed (2012, 66) argues that an activist approach by researchers "allows us to merge cultural critique with political action to produce knowledge that is empirically grounded, theoretically valuable, and ethically viable." My role in the community continues to revolve around the telling of the issues of Afro-Ecuadorians from the perspective of Afro-Ecuadorians.

I collected data in Quito, Ecuador during the summers of 2009 and 2011. The 2009 data first appeared in the context of a Master's thesis in Latin American and Iberian Studies at the University of California at Santa Barbara. Interviews were informal, and not heavily scripted. In all cases, I remained flexible, pursuing information according to Gusterson's (1995, 116) "polymorphos engagement" approach: from a "disparate array of sources in many ways." Gusterson recommends a multi-technique participant observation strategy to obtain opinions about political, social, and economic issues. Therefore, to accomplish a balanced mixture of approaches, I examined publications and relevant media content, and interviewed non-participant sources from outside the group of study.

Some of the participants were eager to tell their personal stories but approached their interviews with apprehension. They feared retaliation from employers, neighbors, or even members of their families who favor the political policies of current Ecuadorian President Rafael Correa for their candid testimony. The sensitive nature of the testimonies from these informants required the use of pseudonyms in accordance with standard ethical practices. The utilization of the data as part of an academic project received the permission of the participants. Other sources whose names appear are public figures, and these interviews were also obtained with their understanding of the academic purpose for gathering the information.

This case study focuses on scholarly opinions, and the observations and opinions of the Afro-Ecuadorians interviewed. The ethnography reflects Afro-Ecuadorian worldviews about the issues of resistance, favoritism, and racism within the policies of isolation of Ecuador's new presidential democracy.

## Racist Perceptions and Class Construction

Afro-Ecuadorians are unable to appropriate affirmative action and claim reparations in Ecuador because of the manipulative influence of racism. The modern racist repression of Afro-Ecuadorians is a consequence of the application in Ecuadorian society of colonial and post-colonial concepts about race. Stuart Hall (1991) recognizes that there is a historical progression involved in the construction of racist, cultural, and ethnic identities. The dynamics of this move to define groups within a nation constantly responds to power relations and cultural influences (Hall 2004). The power of racism depends upon its ability to be used to retard or halt the mobilization of marginalized groups (de la Torre 2002). Afro-Ecuadorians and Indigenous peoples are Ecuador's most ostracized and susceptible groups of human beings. For this reason, Rahier (2010, 77) refers to Indigenous peoples as *otros* (others), and to Afro-Ecuadorians as the *ultimo otro* (the MOST *Other*).

Recent censuses provide statistical evidence that disparities in employment, housing, and education exist between Afro-Ecuadorians and other citizens of the republic. Afro-Ecuadorians earn substantially less, and the majority are marginalized laborers unable to provide adequate housing and access to post-elementary school educations for their children (INEC 2001 and 2010 Censuses Nacionales). The success of inter-group collaborative efforts by Indigenous peoples in Ecuador is recognized as a positive role model for ethnic-based civil activist movements whose agendas address social disparities and issues of class. Johnson (2007) argues, "class continues to dominate as the common sense way of understanding inequality in Latin America." Indigenous coalitions uprooted presidential corruption and asserted a great deal of influence in the construction of the 1998 and 2008 constitutions. Lucero and García (2007) assert that this approach paves the way to construct an ethnic unity capable of overcoming inter-group class affiliations. However, Rafael Correa's populist approach to presidential leadership is one that prefers to address civil requests and claims independent of class alliances (Ospina 2010). The result for Afro-Ecuadorian leadership is that they operate in a diplomatic quagmire in which they must contend with internal issues of class while constructing appeals for equitable treatment before the government.

## Community Action Strategies and Combined Resistance

Perez Ordóñez (2010, 88) describes Correa's discursive and populist approach to governance as one that demands that the public prioritize and unite around the common theme of anti-neoliberalism (Ospina 2010). This approach requires that activist groups form individualistic and new strategies to bring their particular issues to the attention of the administration. Laclau (2001) argues that the proliferation of independent methodologies and divergent opinions regarding how to approach problems no longer support long-term projects, but "short-term ones and that the various tactics become more autonomous." This chaotic and confusing environment does not favor the development of social movement groups, alliances between political agents, or anti-discriminatory practices to promote social fairness (Medina and Castro 2011).

Transnational influences in post-neoliberal Ecuador push forth public policy opposing activist group participation by marginalized citizens in civil processes (Stahler-Sholk et al. 2007). Global capitalists and a small group of local elites are the beneficiaries of free trade practices that oppose social activism (Friedemann 2009). Afro-Ecuadorians will not be able to exercise their exclusive constitutional rights until the 350+ social organizations representing various disjointed opinions establish a common theme (Antón 2011). Class-based discrimination, socially unfair practices, and unyielding misconceptions about Blackness in the small and culturally diverse nation jointly challenge Afro leaders to create nascent political strategies (Rahier 2008).

State administrators operate in a cloistered environment that takes advantage of the class-based and racial prejudices of the community. Only the state is judicially capable of reducing the institutional bureaucracy that separates Afro citizens from the government. A removal of these obstacles will invigorate Afro leadership to create effective social movements that are capable of addressing unequal access to education, housing, and employment before the state (de la Torre 2010).

The focal point in Ecuador of leadership for the Afro sector is officially the organization CODAE (Corporation of Afro-Ecuadorian Development). CODAE's mission defines its purpose and what it is challenged to confront:

> CODAE is an entity of the public sector whose purpose is without financial gain, created via Executive Decree Number 244 on June 16, 2005. It has the mission to press for the integral and sustainable development of the *Pueblo* (officially recognized designation before the government as an official cultural sector according to the 1998Constitution) Afro-Ecuadorian sector, and with this identity fortify the organization of the Afro-Ecuadorian Pueblo, procuring the eradication of racism and discrimination (CODEA Website 2012).

Jose Chála, Director of CODAE, in a 2011 interview, addressed the topic of racism in the context of the three-year-old intercultural and pluricultural constitution of 2008. Interculturalism and pluriculturalism are topics that will be discussed in greater detail in later sections of this chapter. I asked Chála if racism was still an issue in Ecuador. Chála's comments and observations unquestionably confirm that intercultural socio-political policies are unable by themselves to confront all forms of colonial and post-colonial racism. Chála (2011) described interculturalism as an illusion that is not effectively dealing with racism: "interculturalism is a romantic dream and it thinks of throwing racism out of here. I believe racism here is in good health."

Contrasting the above comments in 2011 to an earlier interview with Chála proves that racism is capable of adapting to the implementation of extremely liberal public policies. In 2009, Chála expressed optimism and confidence in the ability of interculturalism to bring about tangible change. Of particular importance are his reactions at that time to being in the presence of power, and how this proximity led him to believe the demands and claims of Afro-Ecuadorians were finally a part of the policy discourse of the state.

> In terms of is there an opening, a large opening for diversities, like *pueblos* as nationalities and this permits the introduction of proposals, and there's a

state, a government that is listening to us. I was with President Correa for eight days, telling him there's not enough investment by the state in the Afro-Ecuadorian pueblo and then he said to me, "ah, that's interesting but show me." And, I was in the cabinet explaining that effectively there are massive asymmetries, in spite of the fact that this government since 2006 until now has invested in very important social programs—but the funds don't arrive to the Afro-Ecuadorian pueblo. So, the president said to me that this is one of the challenges and that we're going to make politics differently so that these funds arrive to the poorest, and in that case the most impoverished are Afro-Ecuadorians. Here, we have a great event! A historical moment in which those historical demands that I commented on are actually implemented. And that in sum it represents an advance not only in terms of the constitution and the legislature, but also over the changing political will (Chála 2009).

The "political will" or the expressed priorities of Ecuador's populist regime remained unchanged during the two years between interviews. According to Chála, the claims of the citizens of African heritage for equitable treatment are still waiting in the wings to be approved based on their political worth. The latest project of CODAE requests the state uphold over twenty constitutionally guaranteed demands by Afro-Ecuadorians, including: recognition for Afro citizens as a culturally distinct group with the unique status and authority to determine priorities of development; assurance that the state end racism, discrimination, and provide restitution based on the constitutional laws of reparation; and a commitment by the state to fund the development of the Afro community in order to assure affirmative action in housing, education, and employment (CODAE 2011).

The agency's staff is small in comparison to the size of their responsibility to represent all Afro-Ecuadorians. Current federal legislation does not provide adequate funding to be able to recruit ambitious recent Afro-Ecuadorian college graduates (Antón 2009 and Chála 2011). Community activism must be sustained in order to deliver affirmative action and reparations to Afro citizens (Hooker 2008). These concessions are due to Afro-Ecuadorians under the pluricultural and intercultural terms of Ecuador's 2008 domestic contract.

## Political Policies and Strategies: The Three "isms"

Pluricultural and intercultural ideas about cultural diversity are the founding principles for Ecuador's most recent domestic contract, the Constitution of 2008. Ecuador's national leadership incorporated western ideas about how to unite the culturally diverse citizens of the nation since the adoption of the first constitution in 1830 (Carrillo and Salgado 2002).

Afro-Ecuadorian activists did not receive overwhelming and substantive
support within the context of the country's domestic contracts prior to the
landmark Constitution of 1998 (Antón 2011). Political administrators
continuously monitored and influenced by grassroots organizations created
and ratified two constitutional documents between 1998 and 2008. At the
end of the twentieth century, the primary reasons for enacting new federal
legislation were to cope with internal diversity, and to satisfy agreements
tied to the neoliberal demands of global altruistic agencies and transnational
capitalists (Cervone 2009). Three societal paradigms framed by ideas
about cultural differences drove the process of constitutional change:
multiculturalism, pluriculturalism, and interculturalism. This section will
examine how political officials began to distance themselves from
grassroots discontent by adopting multicultural and pluricultural public
policies. The appeasement projects also created substantial divisions
between activist groups and did little to effectively end discrimination and
racist practices against Afro citizens.

The Indigenous movement in Ecuador diligently sought ethnic
recognition before the government during the 1980s (Julián 2010).
According to Clark and Becker (2007, 18), demands in the new millennium
by Indigenous peoples are extensive and comprehensively designed to
address human rights violations against all marginalized groups in
Ecuador. However, Hooker (2008) indicates that the adoption of western
ideas throughout Latin America failed to deliver equality for Afro
descendants prior to 2008. Irina, an Afro-Ecuadorian government ministry
employee, recalls the painful experiences of her spouse in the mid-to-late
1990s. Cervone (2009, 200) indicates that during this era, neoliberal
concepts and multicultural ideas heavily influenced democratic
Ecuadorian public policy. Irina provides evidence that intersecting ideas
about race and class continue to shape and restrict Afro-Ecuadorian access
to public resources:

> It's been really hard. Just like when he did his military service when he
> graduated, and the first year they treated him so badly that, that they kicked
> him out he couldn't finish the service.... And that's the way they are,
> closed about class... that exists here in Ecuador, that doesn't allow, or
> rather, they [Afro-Ecuadorians] just aren't admitted (Irina, 2009).

Multi-cultural ideas became less attractive to marginalized groups at
the beginning of the new millennium. Levels of public dissention
increased, and individuals with diverse demands began to participate in
civic organizations. Kymlicka argues that personal perceptions regarding
citizenship and belonging determine individual participation in social-

political protest (Clark and Becker 2007). Women's groups and cultural groups, including Afro-Ecuadorians and unions, formed coalitions to force the government to clearly define citizenship in a way that assured all Ecuadorians access to the benefits of the state (Rapoport Center for Human Rights and Justice 2009).

Diverse grassroots organizations became skeptical of neoliberal economic policies and the accompanying socio-political concepts of multiculturalism (Radcliffe and Westwood 1996, 47). Civil discontent with these policies increased, and social concepts about diversity derived from pluricultural theory increased in importance. These ideas met the needs of ethnically distinct organizations concerned that a joint effort threatened their recognition as an individual cultural identity. The pluricultural domestic contract of 1998 embodied many of the demands of social movement coalitions. For example, juridical authorization for *pueblos* to control and resolve local conflicts appeared in the context of this same national document (Chávez V. and García 2004). Also, recognition of Afro-Ecuadorians as a *pueblo* that first appears inside this constitution marks the beginning of the process of inclusion for Afro citizens. But, institutional apparatuses changed without addressing the need to modify the distribution in Ecuador of power along racial lines. Regarding the Constitution of 1998, Walsh (2009, 64) notes that this Constitution, like its predecessors, was not constructed to end ethnic oppression and assimilation. The socio-political contract of 1998 failed to end discrimination and racist practices against Afro citizens.

Plan Operativo de los Derechos Humanos was also put into effect by the state in 1998. This law nationally curtailed discrimination and abuse by public officials. Under this legal policy, all citizens received the right to participate in the national democratic process. The same year, the International Fund for Agricultural Development (IFAD), the World Bank, and the government of Ecuador jointly founded a central agency to preserve the country's twelve distinct national identities. Afro descendants were formerly recognized as being part of the country's ethnic and cultural identity through the creation of CODAE as a separate component organization. As a result of a combination of three influences, Ecuadorian law began to incorporate and accept difference: 1) international pressures demanding universal human rights, 2) the commitment of domestic collaborative social activists to eradicate practices associated with neo-liberalism, and 3) the dedication of civic organizations to employ pluralistic methodologies to construct non-hegemonic political systems.

During the era between 1998 and 2007, the Indigenous social movements of CONAIE and Ecuarunairi exercised considerable influence in the state's reconstruction of constitutional policy (Becker 2010). Moncayo (2010, 122) argues that since the 1979 advent of a modern democratic era in Ecuador, powerful Indigenous activist groups frequently experienced resistance from an elitist influence closely tied to the seat of government (Ospina 2010). The elitist agenda favors an increase in their personal profit and a decrease in consolidations between social activists and the administrative power core. According to Ramón (2009), elite leaders, CONAIE, and CODAE began to support the ideology of interculturalism because of its core commitment to promote inter-ethnic dialogue and specific provisions opposing discrimination and racism. Ecuador's pluricultural and intercultural Constitution of 2008 addresses these issues and satisfies international scrutiny attached to financial commitments and human rights demands.

## Constructing Influence: Social Mobilization Theory

Strong disagreements within and among social sectors followed the adoption of the 2008 social contract. One of these issues relates back to the pluricultural debate about weak or strong governance by the president, his cabinet, and the elected legislature. A holistic understanding of the meaning and function of the Correa administration's governance requires consideration of authoritative opinions and the personal testimony or lived perspective of Afro-Ecuadorians. There are very few social scientist analyses of the relationship between Afro civil activist groups in Ecuador and the Correa administration. To shed light on this complex relationship, it is necessary to consider anthropological theories and strategies utilized in the research of Afro-Ecuadorian social movements, Antón's scholarly analysis of civil organization development amongst Afro-Ecuadorians, and the relationship of the groups to the executive branch of the government. Discourse about these topics supports a broad and balanced approach to future anthropological research about Afro-Ecuadorians and their efforts to form collaborative social mobilizations.

Ratification of the Constitution of 2008 required an overhaul of the entire political structure and rearrangement of relationships within political institutions (Walsh 2009). Between 2009 and 2011, diverse community groups approached the state to take advantage of what appeared to be a new opportunity to gain an audience for their particular demands. Independent attempts by activist groups eventually created a greater distance between them and other organizations, thereby resulting in an overall restriction of the growth of inter-social movement consortiums. During 2009 field interviews, a politically connected and bureaucratically influential Afro-Ecuadorian elaborated on the national dilemma facing citizens of African heritage in the post-2008 Constitutional era. Douglas Quintero (2009), legal consultant with CODAE, created an analogy in which he envisioned two strong social forces bringing their cases forward to the state for egalitarian resolution: "We're pleading for our *ciudadanización* (an educational process that works in conjunction with social change); others, they're pleading to maintain the status quo." The ultimate objective of each collective is to gain politically favorable and effective national recognition.

In establishing a methodology for his research examining Afro-Ecuadorian social movements, Antón (2011, 20) utilizes a selective approach in which he incorporates specific ideas from three widely accepted western approaches to understand collaborative efforts within social organizations in Ecuador. Initially, the anthropologist provides a disclaimer to clarify the development of logic and strategy in his analysis; "it's key not to take part in one or the other opinion without grasping from each one of them aspects that I consider indispensible." Antón's major criticism of Resource Mobilization (RM) theory as a singular explicator of Afro-Ecuadorian organizational efforts includes a strong objection of RM's support of corporatism.

> My hypothetical perception of the Afro-Ecuadorian social movement isn't summed-up or situating itself in understanding it as a network of organizations or groups of interest, perhaps corporatist. I estimate that when Afro-Ecuadorians and their organizations express themselves as a frontal struggle against racism, better inclusion in the democratic space, construction of a multi-ethnical and pluricultural nation, we're becoming a witness of a movement that should interpret itself outside the corporatist vision (Antón 2011, 21).

Edelman (2001) is in agreement with Antón that RM theory focuses "on the construction of social movement industries made up of social movement organizations, regarded collective action mainly as interest group politics played out by socially connected groups rather than by the most disaffected." Antón's theoretical approach, however, does not provide culturally relevant evidence to collaborate what is an etic opinion about the functionality of corporatism. In fact, Antón's criticism of corporatism justifies the anti-corporatist position endorsed by Correa's administration: to eradicate corporatism, or a political paradigm of influence based on group affiliation (Becker 2010). Regarding labor syndicates and organizations who represent the Indigenous and Afro citizens, Ospina (2009, 3) cautions that the government questions the democratic legitimacy of demands made by these groups based on suspicions that these claims reflect particular interests.

De la Torre (2010, 46) points to a danger in the promotion of Correa's populist regime because it is using anti-corporatism as justification to establish a firm opposition to the exercise of unilateral participant democracy. The administrative branch constructs, scrutinizes, and controls the avenues of communication with the core government in order to shape civil access. The appearance and rhetoric of the president reinforces his position on a personal level due to its constant presence and control of the media. During weekly broadcasted addresses, Correa placates marginalized groups by projecting an image that he is close to the masses that comprise the Citizens' Revolution. According to Muñoz (2010, 161), Correa's appeal as a charismatic and paternalistic figure is convincing because he repeatedly emphasizes that the common man should participate in the functioning of the state (Ospina 2010). However, opponents of the Citizens' Revolution argue that dialogue between civil groups and the president's administration fails to materialize because Correa's determination to destroy corporatism includes an "aversion to social movements" (Ospina 2009, 12).

Antón (2011, 229) argues, "Correa and his political movement Alianza País have embraced a new leftist ideological socialism of the twenty-first century, that which suggests profound reforms so much in the economic model as the political of Ecuador. We see then that the political system that Correa drives forward generates a mark of political opportunities that can be taken advantage of by the Afro-Ecuadorian social movement." Antón recognizes the political desire of the Correa administration to control civil activism. However, he situates the future success or failure of this watershed moment squarely on the shoulders of a disorganized and decentralized Afro-Ecuadorian movement: "The question is if these (same) organizations and citizens are in conditions to confront these opportunities. Above all, when one notes in that moment the weakness of the organizations and the intent from the state to control them" (Antón 2011, 230). Medina and Torres (2011, 46) affirm that the continued influence of paternalism and corporatism are factors that debilitate and shape Afro-Ecuadorian community activism in a way that is favorable to the state, "the church and cooperative international agencies." Confirmation of the vulnerability of social activist movements and the mention by Antón of the state as a controlling political actor abandons a holistic approach that is necessary to fully analyze and explain why the constitutional provisions are not being fully utilized by Afro-Ecuadorians.

Sonia Viveros, an Afro-Ecuadorian activist and director of the country's most prominent Afro cultural center, provides insight to explain that there are other factors involved that must be considered to understand the under-utilization of benefits by Afro citizens. The 2010 and current census reflect that over 7 percent of the population self-identifies as Afro-Ecuadorian, and that the majority of this disadvantaged group survives well below the level of poverty. In an interview, Viveros (2009) describes in vivid terms the suffering that is related to an imbalance of political power and the resilience of ethnic and class discrimination. According to Viveros, the result is an environment in which there is a constant polemic between two opposing sides, "on one side the economic power, on the other, a lack of power." Viveros' emic opinion speaks to meaning at the local level and challenges the positioning of an inordinate amount of civilly uncontested control in the administrative branch of the Correa regime. The danger lies in the ability of this political actor to arbitrarily exercise powers that function as obstacles to the utilization of affirmative action and acquisition of reparations by Afro-Ecuadorians.

Holistic analyses of the functionality of state policies are complete if they include the perspective of the affected group of study. According to Davis (2012), a strong analytical approach incorporates "an emphasis on political structures, processes, political opportunities, and strategic action with the NSM (New Social Movement) emphasis on culture, meaning, and identity." Holistic information acquired by an anthropologist contributes to the struggle by providing theoretically sound explanations to prove function along side the insightful perspective of those who actually live the culture. Both elements must be included in future research to analyze why Afro citizens in Ecuador are unable to improve their positions in society based on existing constitutional provisions.

## Summary

I conclude by recognizing other areas of academic study and research that are important to consider in future analyses about Afro-Ecuadorian civil efforts to appropriate collective rights. For example, human rights anthropological theory will contribute to the discussion of agency and individual response to social and political change. Political and uncertainty theory will provide essential methodologies and concepts to aid researchers to better understand governmental repression and how this socio-political aspect relates to Afro-Ecuadorian social movement participation and abstinence.

This chapter is of value to the academy because it encourages theoretical debate about methodologies that frame the process of participant observation of social movements in Ecuador. Epistemology about Afro-Ecuadorians that extends beyond the meticulous utilization of western theory to include emic perspectives is capable of accurately describing the meaning of affirmative action and reparations to Black citizens of Ecuador (Andrade 2002). The elucidation of this culturally specific information is important to Afro leaders constructing new collaborative identities to approach the state. Criticizing analyses that rely heavily on etic explanations of phenomena does not imply that I recommend approaches that abandon or ignore relevant scholarly opinions and concepts. I propose a broader anthropological approach that holistically considers relevant theory and local opinions in the form of case studies and individual life histories. In this way, anthropologists will be better able to identify ethnocentric misconceptions about Afro-Ecuadorians and this group's utilization of collective rights.

# References

Andrade, Xavier. 2002. "'Culture' as Stereotype: Public Uses in Ecuador." In *Anthropology and Beyond*, ed. R. Fox et al., 235-58. London.

Antón Sánchez, Jhon. 2009. Interview. Quito, Ecuador.

—. 2011. *El proceso organizativo afroecuatoriano: 1979-2009*. Quito, Ecuador: FLACSO.

Becker, Marc. 2010. "Correa, Indigenous Movements, and the Writing of a New Constitution in Ecuador." *Latin American Perspectives* 38(1):47-62.

Carrillo, Ricardo N. and Samyr Salgado. 2002. *Racismo y vida cotidiana*. Quito, Ecuador: Abya-Yala.

Cervone, Emma. 2009. "Los desafios del multiculturalismo." In *Repensando los movimientos indigenas*, ed. Carmen Martinez, 199-214. Quito, Ecuador: FLACSO.

CODAE Website. 2012. http://www.codae.gob.ec/index.php?option=com_content&view=articl e&id=144:que-es-la-codae&catid=34&Itemid=54.

CODAE. 2011. Anteproyecto de Ley Orgánica de Derechos Colectivos del Pueblo Afroecuatoriano. Quito, Ecuador.

Chála, José. 2009. Interview. Quito, Ecuador.

—. 2011. Interview. Quito, Ecuador.

Chávez V., Gina and Fernando García. 2004. *El derecho a ser diversidad, identidad y cambio: etnografía jurídica indígena y afroecuatoriana.* Quito, Ecuador: FLACSO.

Clark, A. Kim and Marc Becker. 2007. "Indigenous Peoples and State Formation in Modern Ecuador." In *Highland Indians and the State in Modern Ecuador*, ed. A. Kim Clark and Marc Becker, 1-21 Pittsburgh: University of Pittsburgh Press.

Davis, Diane. 2012. "The Power of Distance : Re-theorizing Social Movements in Latin America Theory and Society." *Theory and Society* 28(4):585-638.

de la Torre, Carlos. 2002. *Afroquiteños Ciudananía y Racismo.* Quito: Centro Andino de Acción Popular.

—. 2010. "¿Más allá de la democracia representativa procedimental?: Gabinetes itinerantes, enlaces ciudadanos y consejos comunales." *Ecuador Debate* 80 (Agosto):45-62.

Edelman, Marc. 2001. "Social Movements: Changing Paradigms and Forms of Politics." *Annual Review of Anthropology* 30:285-317.

Friedemann, Nina S. de. 2008. *African saga: cultural heritage and contributions to Colombia.* Santa Fe, NM: Gaon Books.

Hale, Charles R. 2006. "Activist Research v. Cultural Critique: Indigenous Land Rights and the Contradictions of Politically Engaged Anthropology." *Cultural Critique* 21(1):96-120.

Halebsky, Sandor and Richard L. Harris, eds. 1997. *Capital, Power, and Inequality in Latin America.* Boulder, CO: Westview Press, Inc.

Hall, Stuart. 2004. In *Researching race and racism*, ed. Martin Bulmer and John Solomos. London: Routledge.

Hernández, Guillermo Julián. 2010. *Antropología y Desarrollo Encuentros y Desencuentros. Centro Nacional De Superación Para La Cultura, 2010.* Habana: Centro Nacional de Superación para la Cultura.

Hooker, Juliet. 2008. "Afro-descendant Struggles for Collective Rights in Latin America: Between Race and Culture." *Souls* 10(3):279-91.

INEC: Instituto nacional de estadistica y censos (National Institute of Statistics and Census). 2012. Accessed via Internet, 05/21/12. http://www.inec.gob.ec/inec/.

Irina (pseudonym). 2009. Interview. Quito, Ecuador.

Johnson, Ethan. 2007. "Schooling, Blackness and National Identity in Esmeraldas, Ecuador." *Race Ethnicity and Education* 10(1):47-70.

Laclau, Ernesto. 2001. "Can Social Immanence Explain Struggles?" *Diacritics* 31(4):2-10.

Lucero, José António and María Elena García. 2007. "The Shadows of Success: Indigenous Politics in Peru and Ecuador." In *Highland Indians and the State in Modern Ecuador*, ed. A. Kim Clark and Marc Becker, 234-47. Pittsburgh, PA: University of Pittsburgh Press.

Medina, Henry Vallejo and Mary Torres Castro. 2011. *Afroecuatorianos: un movimiento social emergente*. Saarbrucken, GR:LAPPLAMBERT Academic Publishing.

Moncayo, Patricio. 2010. "Una democracia de rostro populista." *Ecuador Debate* (Agosto):121-36.

Muñoz, Janeth Patricia E. 2010. "Gabinetes itinerantes, enlaces ciudadanos y consejos comunales." *Ecuador Debate* 80 (Agosto):155-78.

Ospina Peralta, Pablo. 2009. "Corporativismo, estado y revolución ciudadana el Ecuador de Rafael Correa." Unpublished MS, History Department Universidad Andino Simón Bolívar, Downloaded 12/12/2010. http://www.flacsoandes.org/web/imagesFTP/1263401619.Corporativis mp.pdf.

—. 2010. "Diálogo Sobre La Coyuntura: Vicisitudes Del Presidencialismo y De La Intervención Estatal." *Ecuador Debate* 80 (Agosto):7-22.

Pérez Ordóñez, Pilar. 2010. "El presidente Rafael Correa y su política de redención." *Ecuador Debate* 80 (Agosto):77-94.

Quintero, Douglas. 2009. Interview. Quito, Ecuador.

Radcliffe, Sarah A and Sallie Westwood. 1996. *Remaking the Nation: Identity and Politics in Latin America*. London: Routledge.

Rahier, Jean. 2008. "Races, Fútbol, and the Ecuadorian Nation: The Ideological Biology of (Non-)Citizenship." *e-Misférica* 5(2) (December):1-20.

—. 2010. "Mami, ¿que será lo que quiere el negro?: representaciones racistas en la revista Vistazo. 1957-1991." In *Ecuador racista: Imágenes e identidades*, ed. E. Cervonne and F. Rivera, 73–110. Quito: FLACSO-Sede, Ecuador.

Ramón Valarezo, Galo. 2009. "¿Plurinacionalidad o interculturalidad en la constitucion?" In *Plurinacionalidad: Democracia en la diversidad*, eds. Alberto Acosta and Esperanza Martinez, 125-60. Quito: Abya Yala.

Rapoport Center for Human Rights and Justice. 2009. *Territorios olvidados, derechos incumplidos: Afroecuatorianos en áreas rurales y su lucha por tierra, igualdad y seguridad*. (Un reporte de la delegación Rapoport en derechos de tierra afroecuatorianos).

http://www.utexas.edu/law/academics/centers/humanrights/projects_an
d_publications/Ecuador%20Report%20Spanish.pdf.
Speed, Shannon. 2006. "At the Crossroads of Human Rights and
Anthropology: Toward a Critically Engaged Activist Research."
*American Anthropologist* 108(1):66-76.
Stahler-Sholk, R., H. E. Vanden, and G. D. Kuecker. 2007. "Globalizing
Resistance: The New Politics of Social Movements in Latin America."
*Latin American Perspectives* 34(2):5-16.
Viveros, Sonia. 2009. Interview. Quito, Ecuador.
Walsh, Catherine. 2009. *Interculturalidad, Estado, Sociedad: Luchas (de)
colonials de nuestra época.* Quito: Universidad Andina Simón Bolívar.

# CHAPTER SEVEN

# RECLAIMING DEVELOPMENT: INDIGENOUS COMMUNITY ORGANIZATIONS AND THE FLOWER EXPORT INDUSTRY IN THE ECUADORIAN HIGHLANDS

# RACHEL SOPER[1]

Ecuador grows more commercial roses than any other country in the world. Pedro Moncayo, a county in the northern highlands of Ecuador, has recently been awarded the title of *Capital Mundial de la Rosa*, World Capital of the Rose. Flower export production began in Ecuador in the mid-1980s during a period of neoliberal economic reform. Since then, flowers—with roses as the most popular variety—have become the nation's fourth largest export, alongside petroleum, bananas, and shrimp. As petroleum is extracted from the Amazon, and bananas and shrimp are farmed on the coast, flowers are the top export industry in the highland region.

Most flower production in Ecuador takes place north of Quito in the adjacent highland counties of Cayambe and Pedro Moncayo. Located along the Pan-American Highway on old hacienda lands, flower plantations grow and package fresh cut flowers year-round to be shipped out of the Quito airport. Flower firms in this region employ tens of thousands of workers, many of whom live in the hundreds of rural Indigenous communities that extend out across the Andean countryside.

Whereas California and the Netherlands used to supply Europe and North America with fresh cut flowers, production has largely been relocated to South America and East Africa—principally to Colombia,

[1] This research was supported by the Tinker Pre-Dissertation Research Travel Grant, awarded by the Center for Iberian and Latin American Studies at the University of California, San Diego.

Ecuador, Kenya, and Tanzania. As a result, 90 percent of the roses sold in the United States are now imported from abroad (Ziegler 2007). Flowers are just one of many highly perishable crops whose production has been relocated from Northern countries to areas of the global South in order to take advantage of cheaper labor and natural resource costs. Lengthened commodity chains provide year-round supplies of fresh fruits, vegetables, and flowers to Northern consumers—but at what cost? Although the international development agencies behind the spread of agricultural exports praise the strategy for bringing employment to impoverished areas, there is growing scholarly attention to the negative social and environmental consequences of export production, especially in relation to the heavy use of harsh pesticides.

This chapter explores the tension between employment generation and environmental impacts on human health and natural resources. After introducing the dynamic of opposing industry and community norms with regard to individual productivity and global competitiveness versus collective responsibility and respect for nature, I answer the question of how Indigenous community organizations have responded to the flower export industry based on my field research in the Ecuadorian highlands.

## Labor-, Water-, and Pesticide-Intensive Flower Production

Export-oriented flower production is known to be labor-intensive, water-intensive, and chemical-intensive in the use of chemical fertilizers and pesticides. These three features of the cut flower production process exist in tension with one another, creating an employment-environment dialectic that the local population must face. The production of fresh cut flowers for the global market involves planting, fumigation, and harvesting inside greenhouses, followed by a chemical wash, trimming, and packaging inside post-harvest processing facilities. The *cultivación*, *cosecha*, and *post-cosecha* steps of the commodity chain all take place on flower plantations, or *florícolas*, that line the Andean countryside. The flower industry in Ecuador employs twelve people per hectare of land. This number is more than any other export crop in the country.[2] The

---

[2] According to a chart published by the Association of Flower Growers and Exporters of Ecuador, flower production employs 12 workers per hectare, while the cocoa, banana, palm oil, shrimp, and broccoli export industries only employ between 0.1 and 1.1 workers per hectare.

hundreds of flower firms in Cayambe and Pedro Moncayo alone employ over 40,000 workers.

The amount of labor required to supply the global market with an abundant supply of fresh flowers can be analyzed in two lights: (1) as a way for international investors to lower production costs by relocating production from the global North to cheaper labor markets in the global South; and (2) as an economic development initiative to bring employment and income into areas with high rates of poverty and unemployment. Regardless of motive, the export-oriented agricultural development of the Ecuadorian highlands assuredly came from international development institutions as part of the market-based economic restructuring of the Ecuadorian and larger global economy.

Larry Sawers (2005) tells us that neoliberal trade liberalization and international development aid are the primary factors behind the emergence of the flower export sector in Ecuador. Flower production began in 1985 during the administration of León Febres Cordero, the first president to adopt a free-market model, and took off during the Borja administration between 1988 and 1992. In addition to reducing barriers to international trade and investment, this political-economic model fostered export growth through governmental and non-governmental promotional programs. For example, the U.S. Agency for International Development financed a study to identify which agricultural export commodity had potential to become a competitive new industry, then offered promotional credit to business entrepreneurs to start up operations (Sawers 2005, 49).

While requiring a constant supply of permanent and seasonal wage labor, flower production is also chemical- and water-intensive. It relies on the use of chemical fertilizers and pesticides, and requires large and constant flows of irrigation water. The cut flower industries in South America and Africa are frequently described as harsh and exploitative because of the use of toxic chemical fertilizers and pesticides, flexible labor contracts which hinder labor organizing, and outright union suppression (Hughes 2001; Korovkin 2003; Korovkin 2005; Dolan 2005; Hale and Opondo 2005; Wright and Madrid 2007; Madrid and Lovell 2007; Korovkin and Sanmiguel-Valderrama 2007; Riisgaard 2009). This literature provides detailed accounts of the various forms of exploitation that flower workers endure in Ecuador, Colombia, Kenya, and Tanzania, including direct exposure to chemicals, lack of proper safety gear, denial of health services and other benefits, less-than-minimum wages, and forced overtime. For example, in Ecuador, "most flower companies use fumigation several times a week, using products that have been banned in Europe and North America" (Korovkin 2005, 55).

In addition to the unsafe working conditions of flower plantation employees, a detailed study from a research institute in Cayambe highlights the contamination of natural resources and health effects that surrounding populations of rural communities face (IEDECA 1999). These include respiratory disease, headaches, eye infections, cancer, and birth defects, as well as soil and water contamination. Although poor working conditions have improved since the industry first emerged—in terms of safety gear, minimum wage, and overtime pay—pesticide runoff and the growing demand for water to irrigate depleted plantation soil remain serious environmental problems that affect the local population.

## Highland Livelihood and the Employment-Environment Trade-off

Despite the negative environmental impacts on workers, communities, and natural ecosystems, the flower export industry has been a means for Indigenous community members to return home to their communities of origin. It has reunited families. Flower plantations provide a source of local employment so the rural population is no longer forced to migrate to cities to find work.

When the flower industry began in the 1980s, a context of limited employment opportunities marked the rural highlands. With the agrarian modernization of the countryside during the 1960s and 1970s, large haciendas replaced labor-intensive staple food crop production with mechanized cattle and dairy operations (Ramón Valarezo 1990). Despite the modest re-distribution of land in the Andean countryside, peasant agriculture did not provide a viable source of livelihood for the large rural Indigenous population (Zamosc 1994; Colloredo-Mansfeld 2009). For one, land reform provided Indigenous peasants with the highest, driest, and least fertile land (Zamosc 1994, 43). In addition, new generations brought the sub-division of family plots into smaller land units, insufficient to generate enough income to support household needs. These household livelihood trends were paired with a decreased demand for rural wage labor as large landowners moved towards mechanized dairy production. Consequently, temporary migration to urban areas in search of employment became a widespread phenomenon among Indigenous youth, leaving older generations to farm the land (Colloredo-Mansfeld 2009).

From this context, the reorientation of highland agriculture toward cut flower production involved several major changes in the local land and labor structure. For one, although flower plantations reside on old hacienda lands, they are, for the most part, not owned by the traditional landed agrarian class, but rather by urban entrepreneurs. Flower plantations average ten to twenty hectares in size; they are operated by Ecuadorian engineers, but owned by *socios*, or partnerships, made up of several, mostly foreign, investors. Some small-scale flower production does take place; however, urban entrepreneurs also run these small farms. As such, the local Indigenous population is incorporated into the flower export industry only by way of their position as wage labor employed on the plantations.

Current rural livelihoods in Indigenous communities are characterized by small-farm subsistence and commercial production, combined with wages from employment in the flower industry. There is still a generational difference in that older community members often farm household plots of land while younger family members are employed in the flower industry. However, because of the proximity of industry and community, younger generations of wage laborers still reside in their home communities rather than urban areas.

Thus it can be seen that flower plantations both offer opportunities to and threaten the local Indigenous population. While flower production provides a source of rural employment, the flower industry is also water— and pesticide—intensive, presenting a threat to human health and local ecology. This tension that exists between the opportunity of local employment and environmental threat to the surrounding area poses the question of how the local population—made up of rural Indigenous communities—has reacted to the entrance and expansion of the flower export industry.

## Political-Organizational Context of the Highlands

Agrarian reform not only brought a capitalist modernization of the countryside—setting the stage for the entrance of agricultural export production—it also established Indigenous peasant communities as the primary unit of organization in the highlands. While agrarian reform has been considered an economic defeat for Indigenous populations in terms of real re-distribution of land and wealth, the program was a "clear victory in political-organizational terms," creating an "organizational explosion" in the number of communities and community associations (Korovkin 1997, 29).

In 1964, the *Ley de Reforma Agraria* legally ended the debt peonage system of landlord-labor relations on haciendas. This reform measure allowed Indigenous tenant workers to gain ownership of their plots of land "on the condition that they group themselves into territorialized communities" (Krupa 2010, 334). Agrarian reform effectively divided the rural highlands into a dual structure of property rights: selling land under free market principles, except in Indigenous communities where land is collectively owned under communal rather than individual property rights (Ramón Valarezo 1990). The *Ley de Comunas*, which defines *comunas* as the smallest political-administrative unit in Ecuador, dates back to the 1930s, but had limited impact until the 1960s when Indigenous peasants took advantage of the corporatist policy as a space for local autonomy to practice their own customary traditions (Yashar 2005).

Indigenous community norms and institutions are based on a tradition of mandatory participation in community assemblies and communal work projects, or *mingas*. One member of each household must participate in Saturday *mingas* and vote on community affairs during assemblies; other community responsibilities include volunteering for elected leadership positions that rotate every few years (Colloredo-Mansfeld 2009). These communities are also the building blocks of larger Indigenous networks. What I refer to as Indigenous community organizations in this paper are Organizaciones de Segundo Grado (OSGs), or second-tier Indigenous organizations, which work in the realm of community development projects and local political reforms. Each OSG is made up of various *comunas* and incorporated into the larger Indigenous movement network.

Indigenous community organizations are a prominent feature of the highlands of Ecuador. Tanya Korovkin (1997, 27) refers to these community organizations as the basis of rural civil society and "institutional means" to collective action. Second-tier community organizations are affiliated with local Indigenous federations—which are themselves part of larger regional and national Indigenous confederations that represent the interests of Indigenous people in national politics. Indigenous communities are the building blocks of the nation's Indigenous movement, often taking to the streets to form roadblocks and march in nation-wide mobilizations that the Confederación de Nacionalidades y Pueblos Indígenas de Ecuador (CONAIE) led. Since 1990, the Ecuadorian Indigenous movement has held a series of successful national campaigns to defend territorial autonomy, to demand access to land, to support agrarian livelihoods, and to petition for constitutional recognition of cultural diversity and the rights of nature.

The political-organizational context of the Andean highlands is thus marked by cultural norms of participation and communal obligation, with political goals to maintain the right of Indigenous communities to communal property and local autonomy. Based on literature published on the Ecuadorian cut flower industry, it can be seen that in addition to employment-environment tension, individualistic, profit-oriented agribusiness poses an opposing cultural logic of economic development-at-any-cost that clashes with Indigenous community norms of collective responsibility and respect for nature.

## Opposing Cultural Logics of Industry and Community Norms

In her research on the flower industry in Ecuador, Tanya Korovkin (2003) points to the competing cultural values of company and community life. She describes the strict disciplinary culture of flower companies in Ecuador, including the use of individual productivity systems. Under this system, each worker is assigned a quota of flower beds to cultivate or cut flowers to pack; if a worker has not completed her assigned tasks by the end of the day, she is forced to stay late without overtime pay. Rather than working collaboratively in groups, each worker is responsible for her own share of work, with managers keeping detailed records of how productive and efficient each individual performs.

A distinguished scholar of highland livelihoods and Indigenous organizing, Korovkin (2003, 31) argues that the productivity quotas, strict supervision, and corporate industrial discipline foster an individual achievement orientation among flower workers that "clashes with the norms of solidarity and cooperation that constitute the cultural foundation of Indigenous organization life." More than a situation of competing influences on the Indigenous flower workers that straddle both company and community life, scholars have pointed to the potential for Ecuador's flower industry to undermine community norms and weaken local civil society in the flower-growing region.

Korovkin (2003, 2005) argues that the cut flower industry holds the potential to undermine Indigenous community institutions and local civil society. She finds that community members employed in the flower industry are significantly less likely to participate or hold leadership positions in community associations than are other community members. She attributes this empirical finding to the fact that flower employees work six days a week, including Saturdays when *mingas* and meetings are typically held. Christopher Krupa (2010, 340) also touches on the potential for the flower industry to hinder community cohesion. He argues that flower industry managers compete for the loyalty of Indigenous community workers by providing services, benefits, and behavioral rewards. For example, plantations use a system of scorecards, rewarding good behavior with tokens that workers can use to buy vacation days.

On top of winning loyalties, these tactics used by flower companies have the potential to undermine participation in community and Indigenous movement activities. Krupa (2010, 340) explains that "Management frequently denies workers the chance to cash in these tokens, however, when they suspect the free day will be used to attend community work projects or protests called by the national or regional Indigenous movement." Drawing the connection between community-level and wider Indigenous activism, Korovkin (2005, 61) extends the implications of her findings on participation rates to argue that the "erosion of communal organization...has signaled a weakening of civil society in flower-growing cantons." She further contends that "over the previous decades, Ecuador witnessed the rise of a powerful Indigenous and peasant community movement. In flower-growing areas, however, community organizations are falling apart." Given these assertions, the question remains whether opposing cultural norms between industry and community have led to a weakening of community organizing, local civil society, and Indigenous movement networks.

## Research Question and Methodology

Development institutions have put forth agricultural export production as a form of rural development in areas of high poverty and unemployment, yet the flower export industry in Ecuador is associated with social and environmental practices that clash with the cultural norms of highland Indigenous communities. The tension between employment and environmental justice is exacerbated with the threat to community traditions of participation in *mingas* and meetings. In this paper, I address the implications of Korovkin's (2003) findings of decreased community participation among flower workers through a series of questions. Namely, what has been the Indigenous community's response to the flower industry? (a) Have communal norms of participation and collective responsibility been eroded? Has local civil society weakened? Are Indigenous organizations from the flower-growing region less involved in national Indigenous movement campaigns? (b) Does the local Indigenous population embrace or reject the flower industry? Are they trying to rid the area of this type of production? Have Indigenous civil society organizations formed to oppose the flower industry, or do they embrace it as a means to income generation and rural development?

To answer these questions regarding the employment-environment trade-off and clashing cultural norms as a potential threat to Indigenous community organizing, I performed two months of field research during the summer of 2011 in the flower-growing counties of Cayambe and Pedro Moncayo—the same region where Korovkin and Krupa's research was based. While residing in this area, I lived with Indigenous community members through family homestays in four different communities across both counties. Through these interactions with the local population I gained information about what Indigenous organizations exist in the region and on what agendas they are working. Methodologically, I combined participant observation of meetings and workshops, document analysis of materials from various organizational archives, and interviews with host families and neighbors, Indigenous community organizations and federations, municipal government offices, and flower grower associations.

## Reclaiming Development

Although Korovkin (2003) has found evidence that Indigenous community members employed in the cut flower industry are participating less in community obligations, this threat to local civil society has not put an end to active community organizing in the flower-growing region. Neither has it dismantled engagement with the national Indigenous movement. Rather, new organizations are emerging in response to the flower industry to reform its practices and defend local autonomy and access to resources.

Through field research in Cayambe and Pedro Moncayo, I found that Indigenous community organizations have formed in response to the negative impact of flower industry practices—but these organizations are not rejecting or opposing the industry outright. There is not a widespread local sentiment that the industry should leave. Rather, community organizations are acting to limit growth, reform production practices, and propose alternatives to export-oriented development. In this sense, Indigenous community organizations are *reclaiming* development in various ways. In doing so, they maintain a cultural logic of participation, respect for nature, and collective responsibility. These community organizations are also active in CONAIE's nation-wide protests, both in terms of marching on the street and drafting policy demands.

The following sub-sections provide examples of Indigenous community organizing that has taken place in reaction to the flower export industry: regulating environmental practices and regaining control of local productive resources in order to put forward an alternative vision of sustainable rural development. Two OSGs have formed in recent years in direct response to local environmental inequalities associated with the flower industry. UCCIBT formed in response to pesticide contamination of the area surrounding plantations, and CODEMIA formed in response to the unequal distribution of irrigation water between flower firms and Indigenous communities. These two, along with other OSGs in the area, are part of the local Indigenous federation, Pueblo Kayambi. Pueblo Kayambi is part of both ECUARUNARI, the highlands regional federation, and CONAIE, the nation-wide confederation. Contrary to the hypothesis that local civil society and participation in national Indigenous movement campaigns are weakening as a result of the flower industry, Indigenous community organizations in Cayambe and Pedro Moncayo are actively involved in CONAIE's recent *Ley de Aguas* campaign for water rights and food sovereignty, thereby reclaiming development at the local and national level.

## Regulating Industry Practices: UCCIBT

The Unión de Comunidades Campesinas, Indígenas y Barrios de Tabacundo (UCCIBT, Union of Indigenous Peasant Communities and Neighborhoods of Tabacundo) formed in 2009 when a group of community members came together to foster social and environmental responsibility in the flower export sector. Concerned with the negative impacts of flower production and the lack of industry regulation, local residents in the *parroquia* of Tabacundo in *cantón* Pedro Moncayo formed a *veeduría comunitaria*, or community watch group, to monitor industry practices. The group's initial objective was to investigate whether the numerous flower plantations located in their *parroquia* had obtained legally mandated environmental licenses. UCCIBT is now working to decrease pesticide contamination by pressuring plantations to undergo environmental impact reports and to improve the social responsibility of plantations with regard to neighboring communities.

*Licensias Ambientales* became mandated by the national government in 2003. Prior to this, the flower industry was not held accountable to any government regulations. Plantations could do "whatever they pleased," reveals the director of Pedro Moncayo's Department of the Environment. Industry practices went completely unregulated—resulting in the use of highly toxic chemicals, improper disposal of waste, and contamination of the soil, water, and air. Under national environmental legislation, to be enforced at the municipal level, the environmental licensing program requires an environmental impact report, a plan for environmental management, and yearly inspections to verify compliance.[3]

UCCIBT's *veeduría comunitaria* held the objective "to monitor compliance with obtaining Environmental Licenses...and demonstrate the lack of a sentiment on the part of flower companies to prevent contamination."[4] The group reached out to the national Council of Citizen Participation to demand information from the municipal government on how many plantations were complying with the environmental legislation. Despite mandatory legislation since 2003, in December of 2009 the *veeduría* found that not one flower plantation in the county had obtained an environmental license, and only six (out of 148) were in the process of applying for one. The community organization has since succeeded in drawing attention to the issue throughout both Cayambe and Pedro Moncayo.

As of August 2011, 75 percent of flower companies in Pedro Moncayo have their licenses.[5] Similarly, in Cangahua, a flower producing *parroquia* in *cantón* Cayambe, a local government official informed me that all nine flower plantations in the *parroquia* held environmental licenses, but had only received them within the last year.[6] During my time in the area, the Department of the Environment, community members, and several flower companies came together in meetings open to the public to discuss the results of environmental impact reports and the firms' plans for social and environmental responsibility.

Part of the social responsibility requirements of the environmental impact reports has to do with strong relations with the neighboring communities. Toward the goal of improving flower firm responsibility to the people and ecology of the surrounding area, UCCIBT has put forward a program of *convenios*, or agreements, between plantations and communities in which flower plantations agree to certain activities that benefit the surrounding communities based on "the necessity that flower companies in the sector give support as compensation for the harm caused by environmental contamination."[7] These *convenios* involve helping to

---

[3] Interview with Pedro Moncayo's director of the Department of the Environment, July 27, 2011.

[4] Article posted on the wall of UCCIBT office.

[5] Interview with the president of UCCIBT, August 7, 2011.

[6] Interview with vice president of the *junta parroquial*, Cangahua, August 10, 2011.

[7] Convenio de Cooperación entre las Empresas y la Union de Comunidades Campesina, Indigenas y Barrios de Tabacundo, December 2010, UCCIBT archives.

repair secondary roads that lead to both plantations and communities, participating in reforestation efforts, and purchasing local farm products. Several flower companies have agreed to purchase vegetables, milk, and bread from surrounding communities to serve to their employees during lunch.

While these actions can be seen as a way to gain social benefits and spread the wealth of the export sector, UCCIBT is also limiting the expansion of the industry. At a meeting, representatives from the communities in Tabacundo that are part of UCCIBT voted to limit the entrance of new flower firms in their *parroquia* to plantations under three hectares that are at least 70 percent organic and socially responsible to the surrounding community. The president of the organization reported that, based on informal household surveys, 80 percent of the community members in the *parroquia* do not want any more flower plantations in the area. However, one community representative at the meeting spoke out in favor of the flower industry. He asked: how many people are employed by ten hectares of flower production? 100. What if those same ten hectares were used for dairy farming, how many people would be employed? Two or three. [8]

Other people at the meeting were concerned that the entire area would soon become covered with plantations and argued that land should be used to grow crops to feed the area, not just for flowers for export. In the end, a compromise was made to permit new industry growth, but in a regulated manner that follows the above stated guidelines. It can be seen that while the tension between employment and environmental contamination is a very real one felt by the local population, Indigenous community organizations are reclaiming development by regulating industry practices and limiting industry growth rather than supporting business-as-usual or fighting for the industry to leave the area all together.

## Gaining Control of Local Resources: CODEMIA

A second OSG in the Cayambe-Pedro Moncayo flower-growing region formed in response to another environmental inequality: unequal distribution of irrigation water. Although community members in rural *parroquias* that extend far up the mountainside from the plantations experience environmental side effects of flower plantations less in terms of runoff and more in terms of pesticide exposure to workers and their families, many different communities, far from and close to plantations,

---

[8] Observation at UCCIBT meeting, August 5, 2011.

experience environmental inequality in terms of the distribution of this
natural resource. The Consorcio de Desarrollo de Manejo Integral de Agua
y Ambiente, Cayambe-Pedro Moncayo (CODEMIA) is a community-
based organization, recognized as part of the Indigenous movement, that
assumed management of the county's irrigation canal from the municipal
government after years of unregulated water use by flower plantations.

The municipal government had previously managed the large irrigation
canal bringing water into the county of Pedro Moncayo from the *volcán*
Cayambe volcano. This system of management did not respect a system of
canal users taking turns. To meet the needs of the booming flower
industry, many community water users argue, the municipal government
mismanaged the irrigation canal, giving unregulated access to the large
flower plantations. Rather than respecting water limits determined by size
of property, they allowed companies to pay more in order to use more.
Consequently, distribution schedules were not enforced and small farmers
at the tail end of the canal were left without access to the vital resource.
An elderly peasant farmer reveals that under municipal management,
irrigation water did not arrive to her house for several months, while ten
minutes away the situation was drastically different: "the flower plantations,
which produce roses for export, have stems that grow taller than two
meters high! For those companies...access to the liquid is guaranteed" (*El
Comercio* 2007).

The unequal distribution of water during this period was not only due
to the unlimited use of canal water by the growing number of plantations,
but also the lack of infrastructure to bring irrigation water to rural
Indigenous communities farther away from the central canal. The canal
was originally built in the mid-twentieth century to supply haciendas with
irrigation; therefore, the flower plantations that now reside on the old
hacienda land are located right alongside the irrigation canal. In order to
access the central canal, community water users had to build their own
secondary canal infrastructure, with little help from the municipal
government.[9]

In 2005, a group of Indigenous community leaders from across the
region came together and formed an organization with the goal of taking
management responsibilities over from the municipal government. The
600 members of the *Pre-directorio del sistemas de agua de riego,
Cayambe-Pedro Moncayo* (Pre-directorate of Cayambe-Pedro Moncayo
irrigation systems) came from five different OSGs in five neighboring
*parroquias* located along the route of the canal: two within the border of

---

[9] La Acequia Tabacundo: Un Recorrido Historico; CODEMIA archives.

Cayambe and three inside Pedro Moncayo. Objecting to the highly unequal distribution of water between large plantations and small farmers, the pre-directorate stated "we are facing an injustice in the distribution of water...the deficient administration by the municipality of Pedro Moncayo has triggered the awaking of the rural people of the communities."[10] They collected signatures from community water users, showing preference for community over municipal management of the canal. After assuming de facto responsibility of canal management from 2005 onward, the community pre-directorate gained legal recognition as administrator of the canal in January 2008 under the title CODEMIA.

CODEMIA is a decentralized, participatory consortium of community water-user organizations. No longer able to pay more to receive more irrigation water, flower plantations must respect limits on how much water they can use.[11] In addition to regulating turn taking, CODEMIA differs from the centralized municipal control of the previous administration in several respects: participatory decision-making, collective works projects, and priority access to food production. An Indigenous leader from a rural community in Cayambe informed me that since the change in management, people have a more participatory role in deciding the how the canal will be run.[12] Before, they were not involved in decision-making at all; now, CODEMIA holds public meetings every two weeks to discuss user concerns and future infrastructure projects to bring irrigation water to more communities. In the first two years after the pre-directorate formed, the number of canal users grew from 1100 to 2600 (*El Comercio* 2007).

The objective of the pre-directorate and subsequently CODEMIA is to increase participation and collective responsibility of all water users, including flower companies. All canal users, including both flower plantations and Indigenous communities, are required to participate in collective work projects, such as canal cleaning, reforestation of the *páramo*, and construction of secondary canals to bring water to communities without access.[13] These activities are indicative of the organization's stated vision to carry out work projects "with a friendly relationship with the environment, maintaining the ancestral culture of the minga."[14]

---

[10] Informe General del Predirectorio de la Acequia Tabacundo, February 17, 2007; CODEMIA archives.

[11] Interview with the secretary of CFT, the Corporation of Flower Growers of Tabacundo, July 11, 2011.

[12] Personal interview, August 8, 2011.

[13] Interview with the vice president of CODEMIA, July 26, 2011.

[14] Retrieved from website <codemia.org>, July 14, 2011.

CODEMIA also manages the Cayambe-Pedro Moncayo canal "with the goal of improving agricultural production of the small farm sector, promoting Food Sovereignty."[15] They administer the canal to grant priority access to users who contribute to food sovereignty, limiting the amount of water available to flower plantations. During the dry summer months, preference is given to canal users who use irrigation water to grow food. This commitment to food sovereignty is spreading to other areas as well. In Cangahua, the largest flower growing *parroquia* in Cayambe, the local water board is developing a proposal that 70 percent of the canal water in the area must be allocated to users who grow food crops, while only 30 percent can go to flower plantations.[16]

Indigenous communities are reclaiming their right to water by ensuring that small farmers have access to the resource, governed by their own rules. To access canal water, flower companies must help out in canal cleaning, reforesting the *páramo*, and *mingas* to construct and repair secondary canals. What is remarkable about this is how an Indigenous community organization has brought the community norms of participation in meetings and *mingas* to a wider sphere. In the confrontation between company and community cultural logics, flower companies may be instilling an ethic of individual productivity in their flower workers, but Indigenous communities are also mandating a spirit of collective responsibility among flower plantations through their management of local resources.

## Alternative Development Initiatives: Pueblo Kayambi

CODEMIA's policy of priority water rights to users who contribute to food sovereignty, as well as their goal of expanding irrigation canal access to rural agrarian communities, are just some examples of food sovereignty initiatives as alternative growth strategies among Indigenous organizations in the area. Similarly, the sentiment put forth during UCCIBT's meeting regarding land use for local food production, not just export commodities, is widespread. This sentiment has been translated into practice through various local development projects. Pueblo Kayambi, the local Indigenous federation with which UCCIBT, CODEMIA, and numerous other OSGs in Cayambe and Pedro Moncayo are affiliated, has put forth a series of

---

[15] Retrieved from website <codemia.org>, July 14, 2011.

[16] Interview with vice president of the *junta parroquial*, Cangahua, August 10, 2011.

projects to bolster the small farm sector as an alternative source of income to decrease reliance on flower plantation employment.

Support for the small farmers in Indigenous communities has been at the forefront of the agendas of Indigenous community organizations and federations. Pueblo Kayambi is developing a series of food sovereignty projects to diversify land use in the area because "no se puede comer las flores" (you can't eat flowers). These projects are intended to generate sustainable livelihoods through local food production and to decrease dependence on flower employment. In one program to increase staple food production of corn, beans, and potatoes, the principal objective "is to depend not on the flower plantations, but on our own land." Another article in Pueblo Kayambi's periodical quotes a member of a women's group which has recently formed to collectively raise cuy (guinea pigs): "before we worked on flower plantations, and now we raise organic farm products instead."[17]

These initiatives reveal that employment generation is not seen as an end-all appropriate response to rural livelihood sustainability. Development agencies have framed export-plantations as responding to rural development needs by providing a reliable source of employment; yet many locals do not see wage income with which to buy food as the answer. They believe in the importance of the small-farm sector and culturally appropriate local food production, and act towards bolstering agrarian-based livelihoods.

## Local Participation in National Campaign: Ley de Aguas

The issue of water rights and food sovereignty is salient not only locally, but on a national scale as well. Between November 2008 and May 2010, CONAIE held a series of nation-wide protest marches and roadblocks with respect to national water legislation. Initially marching to present congress with their proposed *Ley de Aguas*, subsequent protests were held to oppose the government-sponsored draft water law that did not incorporate their full demands.

The Indigenous movement proposed legislation that would, among other things, (1) create a government fund to invest in rural water infrastructure; (2) rank the uses of water, giving priority to water users who produce food crops for domestic consumption; and (3) ensure decentralized and participatory water management through a model that is both *público y comunitario*. Although the government administration's

---

[17] Pueblo Kayambi periodical, *Nukanchik Shimi*, June 2011.

draft law met the Indigenous demand to prioritize water users who contribute to food sovereignty, CONAIE opposed the final draft legislation because it created the position of a central water authority appointed by the president to govern the nation's water, instead of a decentralized, community-based model. Fearing that community water rights would be taken from them, 25,000 people nation-wide participated in protests that succeeded in stalling the congressional vote and eventually shelving the law.

In the flower-growing region of the northern highlands, Indigenous activism around water rights was particularly strong (*El Norte* 2009). The initial march to present congress with the Indigenous movement's proposed *Ley de Aguas* took place in Pedro Moncayo. Many local residents I spoke with while living in Indigenous communities—including those who currently or formerly worked in the flower plantations—told me they participated in the mobilization. One neighbor in a rural community in Cayambe told me "casi toda la gente de aqui" marched in the *Ley de Aguas* protests.[18]

The local population of Cayambe and Pedro Moncayo not only contributed to CONAIE's *Ley de Aguas* campaign by marching in the protests, they were actively involved in drafting the proposed water law. During 2008, each OSG of Pueblo Kayambi held workshops with their member communities to brainstorm and write their own versions of a fair water law; then they all came together in a meeting to unify their drafts into one proposal and submit it to CONAIE.[19] The vice-president of CODEMIA explains that they put forth the proposal to guarantee water as a fundamental right to communities, managed through a *modelo comunitario*. This measure was then submitted to CONAIE and included in their final draft law presented to the national government.[20]

Even after congressional voting on the *Ley de Aguas* was shelved, water rights remained a central political issue throughout all the tiers of the Indigenous movement. During my trip, Pueblo Kayambi was in the process of drafting a new water law to present to the government—affirming that water should be dedicated first and foremost to the production of food and administered locally by community water boards.[21] In addition, OSGs throughout both counties listed water rights, support for small farmers, and protecting the *páramo* (the source of water) as the

---

[18] Personal interview, July 10, 2011.
[19] Interview with small farmer and president of Ñurukta, an OSG in Cayambe, July 27, 2011.
[20] Interview with the vice president of CODEMIA, July 26, 2011.
[21] Interview with vice president of Pueblo Kayambi, July 11, 2011.

primary items on their agenda. The president of Pueblo Kayambi even announced at a youth leadership workshop that he had limited time to spend on other issues since he was so busy meeting with local *juntas de agua,* or community water boards. He continued to say that people who have not previously taken interest in participating in CONAIE campaigns are passionate about, and mobilize around, the topic of water.[22]

The example of the *Ley de Aguas* reveals that Indigenous community organizations in the flower-growing region are not just locally active, they are actively participating in national level campaigns. These findings speak to the potential of flower employment to weaken the local Indigenous population's engagement with national Indigenous movement organizing. Although many flower workers did not risk their jobs by leaving work to join the protests, in the region as a whole, community organizations were very active with the national Indigenous movement in this particular campaign. The flower export industry does not appear to be weakening the local civil society in Cayambe and Pedro Moncayo, but rather deepening the environmental injustice around which Indigenous communities are motivated to act.

## Land as a Cultural, Material, and Political Resource

These findings are not surprising when analyzed in the light of the central demands of Ecuador's Indigenous movement: territory and autonomy; or, in other words, the ongoing struggle to maintain community ties to land as a cultural, material, and political resource. Deborah Yashar (2005) discusses the historically different approaches to land between the class-based peasant organizations of the highlands and the ethnic-based Indigenous organizations of the Amazon. When the two groups came together in the 1980s and formed the nation-wide confederation CONAIE, they maintained land as a central concern, in both the cultural/political and material sense.

Yashar (2005, 139) explains that for Amazonian groups, the demand for land meant the fight to delimit territorial spaces in which they could live according to their own practices. On the other hand, Andean groups demanded land as a material resource: as a plot of land to farm. Highland organizations, influenced by their Amazonian allies, have since expanded their class-based understandings of land to include local spaces of autonomy and the right of the *comuna* to govern itself. Yashar (2005, 140) elaborates to say that "those Andean leaders in ECUARUNARI who had

---

[22] Observation at a Pueblo Kayambi workshop, July 14, 2011.

initially seen land as a largely productive material resource were convinced by their peers…that land was also a cultural and political basis for Indigenous survival."

It can be seen that within the Indigenous movement land has multiple, overlapping meanings: as *political* space of local autonomy in which to practice *cultural* traditions, such as protecting nature and farming the land in the *material* sense. Indigenous leaders have described this legacy of movement organizing as such: "for us, the indigenous, the claims to land were of double significance, we used them as the basis for our subsistence, but also as Pacha Mama, the source of our culture (CONAIE 1989, 276, quoted in Yashar 2005, 101).

Based on the findings in this study, it is clear that local autonomy and small-farm agrarian livelihoods both remain central to the Indigenous agenda. This can be seen in the recent *Ley de Aguas* campaign, enforcement of environmental regulation, and other food sovereignty alternatives to flower employment. In terms of land as a material resource for livelihood sustainability and food production, community organizations are proposing alternative development projects to bolster the small farm sector as a way of supporting rural agrarian livelihoods and local food self-sufficiency

The *Ley de Aguas* campaign seeks to secure land rights in both its (a) material significance as a productive resource (priority access to small farmers) and (b) as a political space (decentralized community-based management of local water boards). The Indigenous-movement drafted water law proposed a decentralized community-based model rather than centralized management of natural resources: in this sense, it not only prioritizes water for small farmers who produce for domestic consumption, but gives community water boards rather than government officers the authority to enforce priority access.

The cultural significance of land as Pachamama is evidenced in both UCCIBT's environmental regulation efforts and CODEMIA's collective responsibility of canal cleanings and reforesting the *páramo*. This strong affinity between rural Indigenous populations and land—as a cultural, material and political resource—explains why community organizations are reclaiming rather than openly embracing or outright rejecting agro-export production.

## Conclusion

Given the tension between agro-export employment, environmental justice, and the cultural norms of Indigenous communities, the building blocks of Ecuador's Indigenous movement, exploring how the local highland population has reacted to the flower export industry presents a valuable line of inquiry. Although some scholars have found evidence that Indigenous civil society networks are falling apart in the flower-growing region, my findings demonstrate that community-based organizations are currently active and thriving. Indigenous movement participation in Cayambe and Pedro Moncayo remains strong.

In response to local environmental injustice, Indigenous community organizations are actively targeting—and shaping—industry practices. Reacting to pesticide runoff and unequal distribution of water, Indigenous communities are organizing not only to enforce existing regulations (*Licensias Ambientales*) but to implement new ones (*convenios*; reforesting the páramo; priority access to water users who contribute to food sovereignty). This not only sets parameters on industry practices, it also transfers cultural norms.

Korovkin (2003) points to the potential of demanding schedules, corporate discipline, and individualistic norms to undermine community institutions. While I am not refuting that agribusiness has an effect on the cultural orientations and practices of flower workers, I am asserting that cultural transfer is a two-way process. Indigenous community norms of participation and collective responsibility are being spread to industry practices, as flower plantations must help in public works projects to clean, repair, and build new canal infrastructure.

What I mean by reclaiming development is twofold: (1) Indigenous community organizations are *regulating* industry practices to reduce environmental injustice and to be more socially and environmentally responsible. At the same time, they are also (2) limiting industry expansion and *proposing alternatives* to flower employment. These alternatives offer an alternative logic to exploiting local productive resources for export-oriented production: they encourage small-scale production of food for local consumption as a way to bolster rural agrarian livelihoods.

The local organizational response has been to change industry practices and propose alternatives to export employment, but community organizations do not completely oppose the flower industry. Community response to the flower export sector can thus be described as a middle-ground approach: neither embracing nor rejecting, but reforming. Community organizations are not attempting to rid the area of labor-intensive flower production, nor have they allowed the chemical- and water-intensive production processes to continue unregulated.

Limiting growth, regulating environmental practices, and proposing development alternatives—while still holding on to current prospects of employment—can be seen as a way to stay rooted in communities. Reconciling the goal of staying connected to family and rural life with the objective of protecting nature, agrarian livelihoods, and food sovereignty, Indigenous community organizations have put forth a clear agenda of maintaining local autonomy over natural resources in order to steer the direction of development.

# References

Colloredo-Mansfeld, Rudi. 2009. *Fighting Like a Community: Andean Civil Society in an Era of Indian Uprisings*. Chicago, IL: University of Chicago Press.

*El Comercio*. 2007. "El agua en Tabacundo divide a campesinos y a floricultores" (June 8); CODEMIA archives.

Dolan, Catherine S. 2005. "Benevolent Intent? The Development Encounter in Kenya's Horticulture Industry." *Journal of Asian and African Studies* 40(6):411-437.

Hale, Angela and Maggie Opondo. 2005. "Humanising the Cut Flower Chain: Confronting the Realities of Flower Production for Workers in Kenya." *Antipode* 37(2):301-323.

Hughes, Alex. 2001. "Global Commodity Networks, Ethical Trade and Governmentality: Organizing Business Responsibility in the Kenyan Cut Flower Industry." *Transactions of the Institute of British Geographers* 26(4):390-406.

Instituto de Ecología y Desarrollo de las Comunidades Andinas (IEDECA). 1999. *Impacto de la floricultura en los campesinos de Cayambe*. Quito: IEDECA.

Krupa, Christopher. 2010. "State by Proxy: Privatized Government in the Andes." *Comparative Studies in Society and History* 52(2):319-350.

Korovkin, Tanya. 1997. "Indigenous Peasant Struggles and the Capitalist Modernization of Agriculture: Chimborazo, 1965-1991." *Latin American Perspectives* 24(3):25-49.

—. 2003. "Cut-Flower Exports, Female Labor, and Community Participation in Highland Ecuador." *Latin American Perspectives* 30(4):18-42.

—. 2005. "Creating a Social Wasteland? Non-traditional Agricultural Exports and Rural Poverty in Ecuador." *Revista Europea de Estudios Latinoamericanos y del Caribe* 79(1):47-68.

Korovkin, Tanya and Olga Sanmiguel-Valdaramma. 2007. "Labor Standards, Global Markets and Non-State Initiatives: Colombia's and Ecuador's Flower Industries in Comparative Perspective." *Third World Quarterly* 28(1):117-135.

Madrid, Gilma and Terry Lovell. 2007. "Working with flowers in Colombia: The 'lucky chance'?" *Women's Studies International Forum* 30(3):217-227.

*El Norte*. 2009. "Paro indígena paralizaría la provincial" (September 27).

Ramón Valarezo, Galo. 1990. "Indios, Tierra y Modernización: Cayambe 1950-1988." In *Transferencia de tierras en Ecuador: Tres estudios de caso*, 1-99. Quito: Centro Andino de Acción Popular.

Riisgaard, Lone. 2009. "Global Value Chains, Labor Organization and Private Social Standards: Lessons from East African Cut Flower Industries." *World Development* 37(2):326-340.

Sawers, Larry. 2005. "Nontraditional or New Traditional Exports: Ecuador's Flower Boom." *Latin American Research Review* 40(3):40-66.

Wright, Caroline and Gilma Madrid. 2007. "Contesting Ethical Trade in Colombia's Cut-Flower Industry: A Case of Cultural and Economic Justice." *Cultural Sociology* 1(2):255-275.

Yashar, Deborah J. 2005. *Contesting Citizenship in Latin America: The Rise of Indigenous Movements and the Postliberal Challenge*. Cambridge, England: Cambridge University Press.

Zamosc, León. 1994. "Agrarian Protest and the Indian Movement in the Ecuadorian Highlands." *Latin American Research Review* 29(3):37-68.

Ziegler, Catherine. 2007. *Favored Flowers: Culture and Economy in a Global System*. Durham, NC: Duke University Press.

# CHAPTER EIGHT

# EUCALYPTS IN NORTHERN ECUADOR: TAKING ECOLOGICAL IMPERIALISM TO NEW HEIGHTS

# KENNETH KINCAID

Since its introduction to Ecuador's highlands in the late nineteenth century until today, the eucalyptus tree has been an iconic symbol of progress for state authorities and economic elites. Native to Australia, this adaptable, fast-growing hardwood has enjoyed the patronage of government authorities, development planners, and plantation and hacienda owners alike for more than a century. The eucalyptus tree has also had its share of detractors, primarily amongst environmentalists and Indigenous communities.

Conflicts between rural communities and state projects that have sought to promote tree monoculture are neither new nor specific to any one part of the world. In northern India and Java, for example, pine and teakwood plantations, respectively, have been the source of contestation between peasants and governing officials since the late 1980s (see Guha 1989 and Peluso 1992). At the heart of these conflicts are ideological differences over what constitutes progress.

In Ecuador, discontent over eucalypts and their social and ecological impacts were first reported in the early 1990s. In June 1990 after several attempts to negotiate with President Rodrigo Borja's government over issues relating to bilingual education, land reform, and legal recognition of Ecuador's pluricultural composition, the Confederación de Nacionalidades Indígenas del Ecuador (CONAIE) launched an uprising. Coinciding with the Indigenous celebrations of Inti Raymi, hundreds then thousands of Indigenous protestors in Quito and other highland towns and cities occupied buildings, haciendas, churches, and squares in protest. These events cast native peoples in the public eye, nationally and internationally, for the first time. As Indigenous communities and organizations began mobilizing en masse in favor of advancing political rights, they also began expressing greater concern over water rights, land claims, and quality of soil. Often a key component of highland complaints was the negative environmental and cultural impact of eucalyptus trees. Many Indigenous leaders drawing from environmental studies argued that eucalyptus groves were negatively affecting ecosystems and contended that eucalypts had thrived on Ecuadorian soil at the expense of native species.

In the early twenty-first century eucalypts were again the center of controversy in Ecuador; this time, however, it was on the coast. In the Muisne canton, located in the province of Esmeraldas, peasant protests developed after it became apparent that land acquisition and expansion by the foreign-owned Eucalyptus Pacific S.A. (EUCAPACIFIC) was being achieved at the expense of peasant holdings and local ecologies. From 2000-2010, that company acquired upwards of 14,000 hectares of which 75 percent was to be used for a eucalyptus plantation (Gerber and Veuthey 2010, 464). As the company's holdings have grown, it has been able to use its economic power and political influence to coerce small landholding peasants to sell their lots.

Peasant discontent first became manifest against the company over issues such as manipulating the value of lots, which led to underpayment and misrepresenting the potential for employment with the company. The environmental complaints, however, were what have sparked widespread protest and the decision to seek out support from other agencies on local, national, and international levels. These complaints centered around three concerns: first, the eucalyptus plantation has obstructed access to communal lands and forests enjoyed by the peasants; second, the company has continued to expand the eucalyptus plantation, even illegally, thus displacing forested areas which provide essential foods, fuel, construction materials, and medicine for peasant populations; and third, the eucalypts have greatly reduced aquifers and polluted nearby streams causing detriment to those who still rely on the land for subsistence. Of particular concern is the impact that the eucalyptus trees have had on the mangrove reserves.

Contemporary concerns in Ecuador about eucalypts are important in that they address issues relating to development and modernization, and who are the beneficiaries of projects designed to foment "progress." They also allow native peoples and peasants to present alternative strategies for development based on traditional and local ecologies. Indeed, eucalypts seem to have become another but more recent chapter in the age-old narrative of elite territorial dominion at the expense of Indigenous peoples and peasants.

Nevertheless, eucalyptus trees have been part of the Andean landscape since the 1900s. Many of the issues surrounding eucalypts and the conflicts that they have precipitated have their origins in the early and middle twentieth century. Using the basin of Lake San Pablo in northern Ecuador as a case study, this chapter attempts to trace this history and introduce some of the principal themes relevant to a study of this polarizing tree. In particular, it examines the impact that development projects (state and private) had on the Lake San Pablo basin. For some, the introduction of eucalyptus trees represented progress, aesthetically and functionally; for others, the benefits of this exotic wood were subordinated to the negative impact that it had on native species and on sacred landscapes. An understanding of the introduction of eucalyptus trees in the San Pablo basin not only provides insight into the ecological consequences of imposing exotic species into traditional environments, but it also sheds light on Indigenous-elite relations in the early twentieth century.

## Modernizing Lake San Pablo

In highland Ecuador, the eucalyptus tree is ubiquitous on the Andean landscape. It has transcended its humble roots as a transplant from across the Pacific to establishing itself as the most versatile and adaptable hardwood in the Andes. In fact, "Eucalyptus trees are so common in the Sierra that people think they are native to the region: they are that highly integrated. And that is why it is hard to believe that it was less than 150 years ago that the roots of these plants first came into contact with Ecuadorian soil" (Cuvi 2005).

This perspective of highland Ecuador contrasts greatly with that of Friedrich Hassaurek (1967, 148), U.S. President Abraham Lincoln's ambassador to Ecuador, who wrote the following upon his visit to Lake San Pablo basin:

> No grove, no forest, relieves the wandering eye. The noises of railroads, sawmills, or steamboats are listened for in vain. All is silence below. Not a boat, not a sail, not even a canoe, ruffles the waters of the melancholy lake; not a coach, not a wagon enlivens the deserted highways. The cattle slowly moving along the shores or on the hills are the only evidence of life the scenery presents. But it is the gloomy life of the brute; and there are no vestiges of the active, struggling, intelligent life of enterprising man.

Hassaurek's glimpse of Lake San Pablo one hundred fifty years ago has little resemblance to the lake basin today as roads, eucalyptus trees, and houses are sketched all over the countryside. His words do, however, provide insight into the unofficial western criticism of Andean landscapes during the latter half of the nineteenth- and early twentieth-centuries. Attitudes such as these towards the "backwards" Andean world aptly reflected U.S. and elite Ecuadorian notions of progress, and the role that modernization might play in delivering Ecuador into the league of modern nations. As such, Ecuador's political authorities and economic planners at various stages in this country's turbulent turn of the century, embarked on a series of "proyectos del embellicimiento," projects designed to transform its rural landscapes from being "dreary" and "barren" to being "beautiful" and "productive" through the introduction of new species, in particular eucalyptus trees.[1]

## The Eucalyptus Project

In 1865, Ecuador's President García Moreno received an assortment of seeds as a gift from France's Acclimation Society. The president forwarded the box to Dr. Nicolás Martínez of Ambato who conducted a germination test on them. Of the batch only three eucalyptus seeds actually germinated (two gigantangion eucalyptuses and one longifolia eucalyptus). Martínez sent one of the gigantangion eucalyptuses to Juan Molinero, and the other he planted himself. Within fifteen years the eucalyptus tree on Martínez's estate had grown to a height of 14 meters and had a circumference of 3 meters, 80 centimeters.[2] The next generation grew even faster. Having fallen from the original trees in April of 1874, the seedlings achieved a height of 30 meters and circumference of 1 meter, 70 centimeters by June 1880 despite heavy frosts in November 1874 and December 1875 (Acosta Solís 1949, 8).

Martínez, citing the medicinal effects of the leaves, the multiple uses of the wood, and the rapidity with which it grew, called for authorities and landowners to begin large-scale eucalyptus cultivation (Acosta Solís 1949, 8). He also proudly proclaimed that that first tree would be preserved and venerated by the Martínez family and his descendants.

Highland Ecuadorian lore maintains that most eucalyptus trees in the sierra descended from those first two trees in Ambato. Many considered Ecuador's first eucalyptus tree as a "living monument" until 1949 when it was felled for firewood (Acosta Solís 1949, 7).

---

[1] Another exotic species that shaped Ecuadorian pisciculture and Indigenous access to bodies of water was California rainbow trout. See Kincaid (2005) for a cursory treatment of this subject.

[2] Ecuador became the first American nation with eucalyptus trees, outpacing Brazil by three years.

Martínez's concerns regarding the need to generate more forest in highland Ecuador anticipated those of Ecuador's father of conservation and Director of Ecuador's Forestry Department, Dr. Misael Acosta Solís. An economist and botanist, Acosta Solís traveled throughout Ecuador's highlands in the 1930s and 1940s studying and cataloging "useful flora." Central to his investigation was an economic analysis of native and exotic trees as potential solutions for Ecuador's deforestation problem.

Acosta Solís, like Martínez before him, recognized that population growth, urbanization and poor rural planning had put heavy strains on Ecuador's highland ecologies. Native tree populations, in particular, were subject to exhaustion, resulting from a combination of construction demands, energy needs with failure to replace fallen trees with saplings, and slow arboreal growth rates of native species.

Acosta Solís (1960, 141) was critical of the national government, municipalities, and agricultural centers, as well as of landowners, hacendados, and farmers, for their lack of concern regarding reforestation and for their failure to take steps to limit soil erosion. His philosophy was "to return to the earth the wealth that man uses is not only a natural obligation; it is also a practical economic policy."

Acosta Solís (1949, 10) celebrated the hardiness of the Australian import pointing out that in Ecuador's rocky soils with its high levels of ash, sand, and even arsenic, the eucalyptus thrived. He added that in areas where it is able to sink its roots deeper, the trees grow larger yet. Because of the variety of species of eucalyptus trees and their abilities to adapt to different climates and conditions, Acosta encouraged widespread planting of these trees, not only throughout the sierra, but also along Ecuador's western regions and even in the Galapagos Islands. Acosta's call would be heeded as landowners and estate managers planted eucalyptus groves throughout the sierra, from their ideal altitude of 2000 to 2900 meters above sea level to regions as low as 1800 meters above sea level at Baños near the Guayllabamba river and as high as 3300 meters at Alto Pilahuín in the Province of Tungurahua and San Juan in the Province of Pichincha.

According to Acosta Solís, the industrial and domestic applications of eucalyptus trees for highland societies were numerous. These included its uses as construction material for buildings and furniture. Acosta Solís also asserted that rows of the Eucalyptus globulus tree could have functional value as windbreaks, shade casters, or natural fencing, as well as aesthetic value, adorning city landscapes and highland roads. Lastly the tree could be used as fuel, particularly important in highland Ecuador where firewood was often difficult to find. For Acosta Solís (1960, 141), although the eucalyptus was alien to Ecuadorian soils, there was no other tree foreign or native better acclimated to Andean topography and climate. He concluded that "without the eucalyptus, many interandean sections would be truly uncultivable" and that the tree "has been the wood-yielding salvation of the Sierra."

Eucalyptus trees found a fertile home in Ecuadorian soil and began to thrive in the highlands, but it was not until the 1920s that they began to be grown on a commercial scale (Acosta Solís 1960, 141). Citing a 1927 investigation by Italo Paviolo, Pio Jaramillo Alvarado (1997, 2:64) lists eucalyptus as one of the principle rural or forest products in the republic. According to Jaramillo the value of the eucalyptus industry in 1927 was about 3.25 million sucres. Though its relative value to overall agricultural and forest production for that year is miniscule (less than one percent of the 410 million sucres generated), its mere presence on the list indicates quick growth of an industry (in less than half of a century), and its recognition as a national asset.

In Otavalo and the Lake San Pablo basin, by 1909 eucalyptus groves had already taken root on municipal and hacienda lands (Herrera 2002, 111). Public lands were rented to individuals who grew the trees and sold them from 5 to 10 sucres each.[3] Thus, in the period of about forty years from when they were first introduced to Ambato soil, eucalypts had expanded their domain at least one hundred sixty kilometers through the Andean highlands and went from being a novelty to a commercial item.

Landowners, public and private, and *minifundistas* (small landholders) as well as *latifundistas* (large landholders) also sought to take advantage of the "savior of the Andes" by planting eucalyptus trees on their lands. Images taken from the cameras of Aníbal Buitrón and John Collier in 1946 for their publication *El valle del amanecer* (*The Awakening Valley*, 1949) make it clear that in the regions around Lake San Pablo the tree had proliferated extensively. Studies of property titles around the lake from the late nineteenth century to the mid-twentieth century also demonstrate clearly that estates had taken the advice of Martínez and Acosta.

## Otavalos and Lake San Pablo

Contrary to western and elite notions of what constitutes suitable uses of lands, native peoples valued space and subsoil ecologies in different ways. The introduction of eucalyptus trees in the Lake San Pablo basin

---

[3] Archivo Histórico del Institutio Otavaleño de Antropología (AHIOA)/Libro Copiador de Actas de la Municipalidad de Otavalo (LCAMO), June 11, 1941, p. 84.

had profound implications for the ways of life of Indigenous communities. In order to comprehend the extent to which eucalypts in the basin affected native peoples it is necessary to outline the relationship of Indigenous communities with their environment and with sacred landscapes.

San Pablo Lake, known by many native peoples as Imbacocha and Chicapán, is one of the two most important bodies of water in the province (the other being Yaguarcocha). The lake served as the cradle of civilization to scores of Indigenous groups that settled in the region. The lake's inhabitants ascribed certain powers to it and made it the recipient of ritual sacrifices. The most notable example of this is rooted in its name Chicapán. According to Aquiles Pérez (1960, 129), the lake was christened Chicapán when the Páeces people attempted to put a stop to the destruction of their corn (*pan* or *pang*) harvests caused by the chica insect by placating the lake with human sacrifices. It is from this event that the lake took the name Chica-pán.

The lake's Kichwa name, Imbacocha, on the other hand, according to Haro, originated in a period when the area teemed with the *imba* or *preñadilla* fish. According to lake lore, the Caras, one of several native peoples who thrived in the lake basin prior to Inka expansion, would spend dark nights along the banks of the *Río Desaguadero*, Lake San Pablo's overflow stream, attempting to catch the small fish with traps and lures prior to their escape over the Peguche waterfall (Jijón y Caamaño 1945, 391). Naturally this *cocha* (Kichwa for lake) with all of its *imbas* came to be known as Imbacocha.

## *Totora*

As noted in the introduction, Friedrich Hassaurek (1967, 147), while traveling through the Ecuadorian northern sierra in 1863, was unimpressed when he came across Lake San Pablo. Initial observations of the lake's serenity and the presence of lakeside haciendas and *huasipungos* gave way to contempt for the native scenery.

Further comments about the size, temperature and depth of the lake[4] and the pervasiveness in the lake's shallow waters of the *preñadilla* were counterbalanced by his criticism of the technology employed by Lake San Pablo's Indigenous residents in traversing the lake.

> The Indians, when they want to cross from one side to the other, construct of reeds, which grow along the shore, a kind of balsa, on which they ride

---

[4] "The lake is about a league and a half in circumference; its waters are exceedingly cold; its depth is very great" (Hassaurek 1967, 147).

astraddle up to their hips in water, and paddle themselves across. But even this primitive system of navigation is but little in use. It is perhaps less troublesome to walk around the lake than to construct a balsa of reeds (Hassaurek 1967, 149).

Haussarek's derision for the material culture of the Indigenous communities around Lake San Pablo reflected a widely held ethno-centric perspective that white Ecuadorian society also held. For native Andeans of this region, however, the totora reed (*Scirpus californicus*) had for centuries represented their most important resource other than water.

In the early twentieth century this native plant was ubiquitous along the shoreline of Lake San Pablo. Those who had access to the banks where this plant grew were considered fortunate. In fact, many forward looking *huasipungueros* of the local haciendas created their *chozas* (huts) along the shores of the lake San Pablo in order to have access to this versatile reed. Totora was used to manufacture many domestic items. Bedding (*petate*), *estera* (large totora mats), table mats, floor mats, burial wraps, thatch, fans, baskets, canoes (*caballitos de totora*), and even paper have all been created with this multifunctional native plant. Lake San Pablo's totora artisans have traditionally been considered specialists on par with the region's textile producers. Indeed, highland Andean society's culture of totora draws from a long history of cultivation, utilization and appreciation dating back at least to when items made of totora were used as tribute for the Inka and had distributive value for market exchange (Mardorf Rosas 1985, 17).

Totora-derived goods were ever present in Indigenous households upon the arrival of the Spanish in the early sixteenth century. In fact, throughout the colonial period Spanish chroniclers made observations regarding the use of this reed throughout the Andes. In the 1570s, for example, the Canon of the Cathedral of Quito, Lope de Atienza noted that totora mats were used by native Andeans as beds and sitting pads and also floor mats on which to place food (cited by Mardorf Rosas 1985, 15-16).[5] In that same period Polo de Ondegardo marveled at the floating house rafts that the Urus made from totora on Lake Titicaca. The chronicler Antonio Vásquez de Espinoza recorded that the Indigenous peoples of Arica (in northern Chile) utilized totora to assist them in their *mita* labor responsibilities on the haciendas and in the mines. Totora carriers were created to transport wine, and totora baskets were made to carry mercury.

---

[5] The Spanish referred to this reed by several names, including "espadaña," "enea," "junco," or "junquillo."

References to totora use in the late eighteenth century indicate that the plant was also used to make bridges, in the construction of rafts, and in the manufacture of *estera* floor covers. In the markets of Quito, it was bought and sold, and at Lake San Pablo, the reed was valued for its presence in all of the said applications and also as food (the root is edible) and as a nesting ground for the water fowl, such as ducks and *garzas* (herons), that supplied the local inhabitants with eggs, one of their main sources of protein (Mardorf Rosas 1985, 17).

Totora as a commodity did not command the attention of elites whose household tastes rarely included the *esterilla vieja*.[6] Nor did it appeal to the sociologists sent to Ecuador's northern Andes in the early twentieth century to investigate Otavalo households. Nevertheless, totora has been ever present in Indigenous markets throughout the twentieth century, and the latter half of the century has seen the demand for totora grow, with Lake San Pablo artisans supplying Ecuador's national markets in the sierra, the Oriente, the coast, and the Galapagos, and international markets in Colombia and Venezuela.

To the Indigenous communities of the early twentieth century who relied on Lake San Pablo for their livelihoods, the benefits of cultivating totora transcended its economic value. Totora grew naturally along the lakeshore and served as a natural filter, absorbing toxins in the water. Periodic harvesting, thus, removed this contamination from the lake. Often growing alongside totora were *nenúfares del agua* (water lilies). The combination of both plants created an ideal habitat for numerous creatures including *preñadillas* (*imbas*), frogs, *garzas* (herons), and insects.

Totora at San Pablo Lake grows most abundantly on the east, south, and northwest sides of the lake for the communities of San Rafael, Villagrán Pugro, Cachibiro, Pucará Bajo, and La Compañía. However, on the north side, totora does not grow at all. This is primarily due to the fact that whites have displaced Indigenous peoples along this segment of the lake's shoreline and have neither the desire nor the wherewithal to cultivate this reed.

The growing, processing, and marketing of totora are activities that cement important family and communal bonds. Totora is grown either on private or communal lands. When it is time to harvest, families sometimes call on *mingas* to help with the work. Men, women, and children all participate in the cutting of totora. After it is cut, it is allowed to dry for two weeks until it is yellow. Then it is wrapped into fifty-pound bundles. Finally, it is sold to artisans who sort it and use it in their craft.

---

[6] A pejorative reference often made by elites to totora.

## San Pablo's Ecological Zones and Sacred Space

Lake San Pablo sits at the western base of Volcano or Taita Imbabura. In general, lakeshore communities have conceptualized the relationship of Lake San Pablo to the Volcano Imbabura in terms of ecological zones. At the base level where Lake San Pablo adjoins the land is Huambo allpa. This zone teems with life as aquatic plants such as totora reeds,[7] watercress, alder trees are found in the lake's shallow waters and are part of an ecosystem that also includes *garzas* (herons), ducks, lizards, frogs, baby clams, *preñadillas*, and other fish. In addition, domesticated animals, such as cattle, sheep, and llamas also pasture along the shoreline. The Indigenous communities regarded this area as an ideal place to hunt and fish, as well as a place that bears sustenance both for households and livestock (CEPCU 1998, 5-6). It is also at this first ecological level where communal lands were tended, where Indigenous peoples had access to pasture lands and well waters, and where communities grew corn and beans. The second level from 2700-2800 meters above sea level is Ura allpa; it is here that settlements were established and seasonal farming was conducted. The third level from 2800 to 3200 meters above the sea is Jahua allpa. Forests and occasional agricultural fields characterized this zone. The fourth zone from 3200 to 3400 meters above sea level is Sacha allpa. This region is semi-arid and was conducive only to the growth of thickets and scrubland. The Ucsha allpa is the fifth zone, reaching from 3400 to 3700 meters above sea level. These páramo lands were suitable only for the pasturing of animals. The final zone, the Rumi allpa, from 3700 meters on up, provides no resources for human occupation and is above the timberline (Vicuña C. and de la Torre 2002, 78).[8] These zones were viewed as essential, constituent parts of the sacred space that manifested itself on the mountain Taita Imbabura.

The Indigenous communities that called the environs of San Pablo home perceive the value of the lake in more than utilitarian terms. Certainly harvesting the totora reeds to create *caballitos*, *estera*, and other items was important to the subsistence economies of these communities, as was retrieving water for domestic use, herding community livestock to the adjacent pasturelands, and growing corn along the banks of the lake. However, the waters of the lake and the surrounding mountains also were

---

[7] The residents of the lakeshore communities use the lake to cultivate and harvest totora, which they then dry and weave into mats, hats, and other products (CEPCU 1998, 20).

[8] Note that the altitudes are approximations and may vary with the community and/or institution conducting the study.

imbued with a cosmological significance that was central to Otavalos' identity.

Legends demonstrated the high regard that the Indigenous peoples of Imbabura had for their waterways. This is particularly true of creation stories that conceptualized the origins of humans and their natural surroundings. For Otavalos, Imbacocha or Lake San Pablo was the cradle of civilization for ancient Andeans of the region.[9] It was also a place favored by the Andean gods. In one account, the Creator, depicted as larger than the mountains, was found meandering through the most scenic valleys and waters, appreciating his handiwork. Upon getting to Lake San Pablo, however, he lost his balance (due to the lake's depth) and was forced to grab the neighboring volcano, Imbabura, to break his fall. The impact of the stumble dislodged rocks at the top of the volcano creating the geological formation that appears to be a window to those who view it from the level of the lake.

Another important native species that defines ethnic relations in the Lake San Pablo basin is the lechero tree. Its importance stems from its unique appearance and its medicinal properties, which include its ability to alleviate liver pain, headaches, and earaches, as well as eliminating warts. As for its appearance, the tree typically has a straight, thick trunk and then its branches spread out laterally, giving it a cross-like appearance. Indigenous communities frequent the trees as part of a ritual, or to ask for help in dealing with health issues. Typically a visit includes leaving an offering at the base of the trunk. There are few trees in the region, and it is not clear whether selective planting has been intentional as it is considered a sacred tree, or whether it has been subject to deforestation. Those that do exist occupy an important place in the northern Andean pantheon of sacred spaces. A 2002 publication on Lake San Pablo, *Imbakucha: Estudios para la sustentabilidad*, citing area yachaks or healers, identified thirteen lechero trees in communities around the lake basin and pointed out that they correspond to the thirteen months of the lunar calendar (Vicuña C. and de la Torre 2002, 59).

In addition, according to Aníbal Buitrón and John Collier in *El valle del amanecer* (*The Awakening Valley*), the lechero tree that sits atop the Rey Loma hill is not only considered sacred for the Indigenous peoples of the communities Desagüadero, Pucará, and La Compañía, but it also helps delineate the white-mestizo world from the Indigenous one. Everything to the north of Rey Loma is part of the white-mestizo world and to the south

---

[9] Jeanette Sherbundy (1982, 1992) identifies the same phenomenon among Indigenous peoples around Lake Titicaca who also saw this body of water as the source of their origins.

the Indigenous one, which also includes Lake San Pablo and Volcano Imbabura.

## Andean Dualism at Lake San Pablo

Andean dualism and reciprocity also relate to the sacred aspects of San Pablo geography. The notion of dualism or parallelism is an essential component to Andean cosmology. It is based on the premise that all entities have a complement (sun/moon, earth/sky, land/water, volcano/lake, man/woman) and that the actions of one stimulate reciprocal actions in the other. As Irene Silverblatt (1987, 20) explains, "[c]hains of women paralleled by chains of men formed the kinship channels along which flowed rights to the use of community resources." These concepts had religious expression as gods, spirits, and *huacas* since "Andean peoples paired gender symbols with cosmological forces" (Silverblatt 1987, 29). Harmony was maintained as long as the duality or "mutuality" existed and the reciprocal obligations were met.

Chantal Caillavet found the gendered Lake San Pablo landscape the ideal setting for observing notions of Andean duality. For Caillavet (2000, 397), "[h]uman settlements do not just transform their surroundings through their economic and material relationship to it, rather they also inscribe on their territory their conception of the cosmos, giving it both a political and spiritual dimension." As such, Lake San Pablo's native communities ascribed gender and sacred meanings to the region's physical geography, including mountains, valleys, hills, and streams.

Having already established the original location of the powerful Otavalo *ayllu* along the shoreline of Lake San Pablo in a 1981 article, Caillavet (2000, 402) makes the case that Otavalo's cosmological harmony was generated by *huaca* gender duality perceived within the Otavalo ayllu's line of vision. For the ancient Otavalos, the sexual duality manifested by the presence of the masculine Volcano Imbabura and the feminine Lake San Pablo at essentially the same point (as viewed from ancient Otavalo) would have been a powerful sacred image and would have legitimized the rule of the Otavalo ayllu in the region. This same sexual duality is evident in other visual lines radiating from the ancient settlement of Otavalo.

Pucará Bajo, for example, is a small Indigenous town that sits to the east of Eugenio Espejo and on the northwest banks of Lake San Pablo. It is part of the visual alignment that connects the site identified as Rey Loma, where the native lechero tree lives, with the feminine Na Sa de Agua Santa and with the feminine lake and masculine mountain Cusin. Moreover, the reverse direction of the alignment connects the masculine Rey Loma with another feminine site San Juan. These networks of masculine and feminine sacred spaces around Lake San Pablo problematize the views of Haussarek and others regarding what they viewed as a drab, unproductive lakeshore environment.

## State-Sponsored Development Projects

Throughout the early twentieth century, Otavalo's municipal government, Ecuador's Ministry of Public Works, and local and regional economic elites had their sights set on lands and waters that native communities controlled. Waters and adjacent lands were coveted by those who wanted to increase water accessibility for purposes of irrigation, use these waterways to create energy for hydraulic textile factories and hydroelectric plants, and use bodies of water as recreational and tourist attractions.

San Pablo Lake in the early twentieth century was the site of frequent contestation over control of the lake, its tributaries, and its downstream rivers. These conflicts stemmed from a variety of sources, including efforts by industrialists to control lands and waters of the River Jatunyacu, attempts by the Hacienda Cusin to keep lakeshore communities off of communal grazing lands and waters, plans developed by Otavalo's municipal government to create a road that would circumnavigate the lake, proposals by Ecuador's Air Force to utilize the surface of the lake as a landing strip for its hydroplanes, and designs by local and national authorities to utilize Lake San Pablo and its basin as an experimental laboratory where exotic flora and fauna would be introduced to the region in order to promote tourism and "beautify" the lake. However, these designs by Ecuador's highland elites to control Lake San Pablo and its surrounding lands and waters were invariably met with resistance. Physical confrontation, sabotage, land occupations, petitions, and litigation represent a mere sampling of the strategies adopted by natives and local communities to challenge elite measures to control lands and waters (Kincaid 2005).

## Modernizing the Lakeshore and Resistance

In the early 1920s, Otavalo's municipal government began promoting tourism in the region. The timing for this decision had much to do with the completion of the transprovincial railroad that would link the highland capital, Quito, to the coastal cities of the province of Esmeraldas. The obvious site for this endeavor was the scenic lake, San Pablo, as it was also near the railroad line. However, before tourism would take root as a viable economic enterprise, certain municipal projects would have to be developed and completed. For one, city leaders viewed a lakeside road as essential. They also planned to build new docks and a hotel along the shore. They aimed to beautify the lake by planting eucalyptus trees along the banks of the lake. Finally, they wanted to conserve fish and fowl for the tourist industry, and thus prohibited hunting and fishing on the lake. Cloaked in terms of progress, these projects were designed to bring Otavalo into the twentieth century. Municipal leaders did not anticipate the reaction of Indigenous peoples along the lake to these notions of progress.

In May of 1924, the *Junta de Fomento Agrícola e Industria de Otavalo* began construction on the road with the goal of "improving" and "beautifying" Lake San Pablo.[10] In addition, it was considered essential for the promulgation of tourism in the canton.[11] The road was to measure fifteen kilometers in length and six meters in width and would cost over 40,000 sucres. The project would also destroy the lands and streams belonging to several Indigenous communities.[12]

Conflict with Indigenous communities over the alteration of Lake San Pablo's natural environs was nothing new. In August 1919, Indigenous peoples of Eugenio Espejo challenged the construction of a road leading to the lake's only dock.[13] Projects that altered the physical landscape of the lake invariably met with organized resistance by the area's native communities.[14] Whereas the members of the Junta viewed the road as a symbol of "progress" and a means to make the region more attractive and accessible, Indigenous peoples rejected that vision of the lake. Offers to pay for lands lost and harvests destroyed were countered with complaints about the destruction that the road would bring to their lands, the danger of having traffic so close to areas that they often frequented, the reduction of access to the water of the lake, and the effect that this construction and the traffic would have on the *totora* grown along the lake's shores.[15]

In 1925, political power was restored to Conservative hands in the name of the Julian revolution. The transfer of power, however, did not

---

[10] Archivo de la Jefatura Política del Cantón de Otavalo (AJPCO)/Libro Copiador de los Oficios (LCO), May 17, 1924, no. 115, p. 340.
[11] AJPCO/LCO, November 29, 1925, no. 3, p. 66.
[12] AJPCO/LCO, November 29, 1925, no. 3, p. 66.
[13] AJPCO/Libro de Correspondencia de la Junta de Fomento Agrícola (LCJFA), August 15, 1919, p. 23.
[14] AJPCO/Libro de Correspondencia de la Junta de Fomento Agrícola (LCJFA), November 26, 1925, p.225.
[15] AJPCO/LCO, November 29, 1925, no.3, p. 66.

alleviate the tensions at Lake San Pablo between lakeside communities and Otavalo's municipal government over the public works projects being initiated at the lake. More than ever before, Indigenous dissidents attempted to persuade national leaders to side with them in this conflict. In addition to this pacific form of protest, Indigenous peoples employed more confrontational strategies, including physically blocking roads and paths that led to project sites, the destruction of completed segments of public works, and threats to sabotage, if not destroy, the municipality's machinery. In response to the violence, the Jefatura Política, in agreement with Otavalo's *Junta de Fomento Agrícola e Industria*, "resolved to suspend temporarily the project," until the Governor could station an armed company permanently in Otavalo.[16]

Another letter to the Governor, also dated November 29, 1925, reveals another problem that the municipal government was having with San Pablo's lakeside communities. Municipal lands on Lago San Pablo's south side had been the target of an invasion by members of a local village. The *jefe político* responded to this situation by requesting that the Governor send someone to patrol these fields, until they could be sold.[17]

In December of 1925 and January of 1926, complaints from several different lakeshore communities opposed to the road construction project were filed with the Ministry of the Interior and with the Ministry of Social Welfare charging local police authorities with unlawful arrests, police misconduct, and arbitrary fines.[18] Otavalo's *jefe político* denied the charges. He did, however, make a countercharge, stating that the Indigenous peoples of these communities were unruly because of their propensity for drink and because of meddling outsiders who made trouble by stirring the passions of naïve Indigenous peoples.[19]

As the city continued its work on the road and initiated other projects in the vicinity of San Pablo, lake residents' threats became more severe. In April of 1926, following several heated exchanges between workers and foremen that led to threats of physical violence, Otavalo's *jefe político* once again asked military commanders, stationed near Otavalo, to send troops in order to assist the police in defending engineers and laborers working on the project.[20]

---

[16] AJPCO/LCO, November 29, 1925, no. 417, p. 5.

[17] AJPCO/LCO, November 29, 1925, no. 418, p. 5.

[18] AJPCO/LCO, December 2, 1925, no. 428, p. 10; AJPCO/LCO, January 8, 1926, no. 13, p. 44.

[19] AJPCO/LCO, January 8, 1926, no. 13, p. 44.

[20] AJPCO/LCO, April 21, 1926, no. 206, p. 115.

Attacks on state properties at Lake San Pablo were not confined to the road construction project. In November 1928, Indigenous peoples from the parroquias of San Rafael and Eugenio Espejo gathered along the shores of Lake San Pablo at a point called "Araque" to harvest totora. While there, according to the *teniente político* of San Pablo, they also absconded with the covering to the Ministry of Government's boat.[21] The lakeshore road envisioned by local leaders would eventually be built. Other projects designed to "improve" the lake also met with such resistance, however, and many of the plans were dropped or changed dramatically.

## Uprooting the Future?

In 1926, Juan E. Valencia, representing several Indigenous peoples from the community of Eugenio Espejo, forwarded a complaint to the office of the governor of Imbabura regarding the city's attempts to plant eucalyptus trees in fields adjacent to the road that led up to the pier on San Pablo Lake. Indigenous members of Eugenio Espejo responded to the encroachment onto their lands by uprooting the trees and carrying them away. Responding to the governor's inquiry regarding the events of those days, Otavalo's *jefe político* stated that the eucalyptus project was designed to "beautify" the lake's environs and was being carefully elaborated to avoid any unnecessary damage to peasants' lands. The *jefe político* added that the *teniente político* of Espejo was justified in his reprisals against those whom he deemed accountable for the vandalism and theft. Perhaps the most significant part of this *oficio*, from the perspective of attempting to understand how Indigenous peoples responded to the municipality's public works projects, was the *jefe político*'s disclosure that "all Indigenous [were] in opposition to [these] projects."[22]

Two years later a similar incident occurred on municipal lands at the *fundo* (estate) called Pusaco. According to the *teniente político* of San Pablo, local Indigenous communities were responsible for the felling of several eucalyptus trees at the estate.[23]

Otavalo's municipal and Ecuador's national governments claimed that the eucalyptus projects were essential for development in that they would beautify the region; provide lumber for construction purposes; serve as windbreaks; fight soil erosion; and provide a fuel source. The fact that the trees grew to such impressive heights of between 30 to 60 meters in a

---

[21] AJPCO/LCO, November 28, 1928, no. 442, p. 624.

[22] AJPCO/LCO, November 12, 1924, no. 220, p. 369.

[23] AHIOA/LCAMO, August 22, 1928, p. 106.

relatively short period of time made it the tree of choice for local and state planners (Cooper 1876, 32).

## Impact of Eucalyptus Trees

The response of some Indigenous communities to the introduction of eucalyptus trees to the San Pablo basin should not be evaluated solely on the redistributive act of uprooting them and taking them away. The presence of these trees had significant ecological and cosmological consequences for the inhabitants of this area. The proliferation of eucalyptus trees profoundly affected the relationship of Indigenous communities to their natural world. The tree's physical properties above and below the soil altered the ability of Indigenous communities to maintain their material culture and posed a challenge to their cosmology.

Whereas ecologists as well as rural and urban planners heralded the eucalyptus tree in the early twentieth century, today that praise is considerably more restrained. From the most superficial level to the most utilitarian, the imported tree was celebrated for making the valleys, mountains, and hilltops more aesthetically pleasing. They were also praised for their ability to grow rapidly, thus providing significant stores of firewood, construction material, shade, and natural fencing. The medicinal properties of the leaf and its fragrance were also lauded. What was not considered, perhaps, or not known, when deciding to make eucalyptus plantations the cornerstone of conservation efforts in the Ecuadorian highlands, were their potential social and ecological consequences. First and foremost, the imported tree exacts an extraordinary toll on aquifers and all local vegetation. Studies of highland ecologies, such as those in the Ecuadorian Andes, show that eucalyptus trees are responsible for the lowering of water tables, depriving soils of moisture, and limiting the types and amounts of adjacent or under-story vegetation, including farms crops (Doughty 2000, 154; also see Poore and Fries 1985). Second, the eucalyptus leaves are quite acidic and their decomposition in soils has the effect of sterilizing them (Chacón-Vintimilla, Gagno, Paré, and Proulx 2003). To be sure, the planting of eucalyptus trees along the banks of Lake San Pablo reduced the amount of water available to totora plants and other native flora that drew from the same aquifer. It also reduced the ability of basin soils to support crops and other vegetation.

The presence of eucalyptus trees at Lake San Pablo would have affected the spiritual relationship of Indigenous communities with the lake and the nearby volcano Taita Imbabura. Rows of trees standing 30 to 60 meters tall in front of Lake San Pablo or around local *tolas* or other *huacas* would upset the visual spatial alignment so important to Otavalo's native cosmology. In addition, deep eucalyptus roots would have also invaded the sacred spaces of Otavalo's ancient ancestors.

In reflecting on the actions Indigenous communities took to the introduction of eucalyptus trees in 1926, it is important to recognize that a series of previous confrontations with local authorities and elites over water and lands in the basin have conditioned their responses. Moreover, throughout the first quarter of the twentieth century, Indigenous peoples had witnessed the growth of these trees as well as the impact that these trees had on water supplies and native vegetation. It is likely that in the course of these observations, many native peoples in the San Pablo basin came to the conclusion that eucalypts challenged their ability to subsist and became the basis for resistance to "progress."

## Reexamining a Classic

The 1949 ethnographic classic *El Valle del Amanecer* by Aníbal Buitrón and John Collier provides a sympathetic depiction of the lives of Indigenous peoples in Otavalo and around San Pablo. In addition to discussing the repression that native peoples have traditionally encountered and the ways that Otavalo's Indigenous peoples have been able to overcome these challenges, Buitrón and Collier also provide a fascinating account of the relationship of Otavalo's Indigenous peoples to their natural world and to the sacred spaces that surround them.

A re-reading of this work through the lens of sacred space reveals an Indigenous world that was still holding onto its cosmology in the early twentieth century despite the efforts by local and state officials to transform it. For example, Buitrón and Collier point out that members from Lake San Pablo's Indigenous communities who must travel to Otavalo invariably take the path that goes by the lechero tree, avoiding the roads created by municipal authorities, which were much too windy. Upon the return trip from Otavalo to Lake San Pablo, Indigenous peoples typically stop at the lechero and pay their respects to the tree, then put down whatever they are carrying and cast their gaze on Lake San Pablo and Volcano Imbabura. Whereas Buitrón and Collier suggest that this custom is primarily done so that the individual might catch his or her breath after the climb up the hill and that the exclamations in Kichwa reflect merely their happiness at seeing their homes and fields, a reading of this ritual through the lens of sacred space suggests that those Indigenous peoples would also have been venerating Lake San Pablo and the Imbabura Volcano.

The photographs in the *Awakening Valley* (Buitrón and Collier 1971, 109) also make clear that the sacred spatial alignments so important to native Otavalos that linked settlements and roads with revered mountains, hills and lakes were becoming more and more obstructed by eucalyptus trees and their foliage. Buitrón and Collier go on to reflect on the psychology of the Otavalos especially as it relates to how native peoples respond to the humiliations to which they are frequently subjected. They write that the Otavalos' silence is often wrapped in a cloak of thoughts relating to the mountains, the rains, the sun, and the winds. They point out that "if [he] were to find his mountains profaned, his sacred lake destroyed, his ancestral lands, stolen from him, he would perish immediately."

Other images taken from Buitrón and Collier's camera, however, show an Indigenous people who had come to accept, at least in part, eucalyptus trees in their sacred basin. The photographs depict Indigenous peoples gathering in the shadows of eucalyptus trees. They also show native peoples constructing edifices with the hardwood. The decision by Indigenous peoples and communities to exploit eucalypts seems to be one based primarily on practicality as the foreign species quickly outgrew and outnumbered native trees, though native peoples soon found that the use of eucalypts for lumber and/or fuel had consequences. On one hand, it pulled them into the market economy (more so than totora did). On the other, buildings that were made with eucalypts tended to be taller than the *chozas* in which they had previously lived, and were draftier, making them unsuitable for the in-house raising of guinea pigs.

In the 1950s the federal government addressed conservation issues with the creation of the Forestry Service. With a goal of planting 6,500 hectares of trees per year, the Forestry Service hoped to reverse the rate of forest loss that had been plaguing Ecuador throughout the early twentieth century. Though tree species was not indicated, the unstated standard practice was to plant eucalyptus or pines. Drawing upon the free labor of high school students and army conscripts, the federal government planted trees on both public and private estates. The net result of a half of a century of reforestation of plantation trees was 120,000 hectares of eucalypts and pines and the virtual annihilation of native forests.

# Politicizing the Eucalypt

For Ecuador's large landowners the 1964 Ley de Reforma Agraria y Colonización (Agrarian Reform and Colonization Law) posed a threat to their holdings, their labor base, and the social hierarchy. Not only did the law abolish all forms of coerced labor, such as the *huasipungo*, requiring that all workers receive payment for services rendered, it also capped the amount of land that a person could own at one thousand hectares. The reform law did little to alleviate rural suffering, though, as it was inconsistently enforced. Moreover, there were loopholes in the law that could be easily exploited that could thwart Indigenous peasant land claims.

One way to sidestep agrarian reform was to demonstrate that lands were being used productively. This was a problem for many latifundistas, however, since it was often the case that a sizeable portion of their estates was completely unused and eligible for expropriation. In need of some type of flora to indicate land use, landowners turned to the eucalyptus. By planting rows of this fast-growing tree, landholders could demonstrate use and avoid having their lands appropriated. The hacienda El Topo, for example, by October 1972 had over seventy-five hectares of eucalyptus tree and the Hacienda Angla registered over ninety hectares of the same. According to landowner and former president of the republic, Galo Plaza, the reason that he planted such large quantities of eucalyptus trees was to "avoid turning the land over to the *naturales*" (the Indigenous peoples) (Rosero Garcés 1982, 87).

Eucalyptus trees thus served hacienda owners who sought to evade land reform stipulations by demonstrating land use, thereby nullifying native claims to said lands. For native peoples it represented another instance where eucalypts were used to undermine claims to land and traditional uses of the lakeshore basin.

# Conclusion

Today, in highland Ecuador Indigenous communities, NGOs, and international aid agencies are working together to re-Andeanize native landscapes. They are doing this through massive reforestation campaigns designed to stop soil erosion and to reduce the ratio of non-native to native trees. These alliances have netted positive results as soil erosion has diminished, stream, lake, and subsoil pollution have lessened, and native leaders have imbued their communities with a pride in native species and landscapes.

In Otavalo, the Centro de Estudios Pluriculturales (CEPCU), an Ecuadorian NGO made up primarily of Indigenous professionals and technicians, the Federación Indígena y Campesina del Imbabura (FICI), and Oxfam America have worked together since 2000 in order to address environmental and social issues surrounding Lake San Pablo. Problems that Lake San Pablo and the Indigenous communities of the basin face have been developing over the course of a century. Soil erosion, lake and stream contamination, and a declining water level threaten subsistence as well as production for local economies. Central to the plan is a reforestation campaign that in the course of six years planted over one hundred thousand trees in and around the basin, eighty percent of which are native species.

In Muisne, peasants have taken a page out of the book of peasant resistance Indigenous peoples previously authored at Lake San Pablo. In addition to contacting local organizations to seek redress for their loss of resources, the Muisne peasants have also engaged in direct action campaigns invading eucalyptus plantations and cutting down trees. Moreover, echoing the laments of local authorities at San Pablo and in Otavalo in the 1920s, EUCAPACIFIC officials have criticized peasant protestors as being opposed to progress.

# References

Acosta Solís, Misael. 1949. *El eucalipto en el Ecuador*. Guayaquil: Editorial "Ecuador."
—. 1960. *Maderas económicas del Ecuador y sus usos*. Quito: Editorial Casa de la Cultura Ecuatoriana.
Buitrón, Aníbal and John Collier. 1971. *El valle del amanecer*. Otavalo: Instituto Otavaleño de Antropología.
Chacón-Vintimilla, Gustavo and Daniel Gagno, David Paré, and Dominique Proulx. 2003. "Impacto de la deforestación, pastizales, plantaciones de eucalipto y pino en suelos de bosque montano alto, en la sierra sur del Ecuador." *Revista de Investigaciones de la Universidad del Azuay* 11 (February):19-34.
Caillavet, Chantal. 2000. *Etnias del norte: Etnohistoria e historia de Ecuador*. Quito: Ediciones Abya-Yala/Lima: Instituto Francés de Estudios Andinos (IFEA).
Centro de Estudios Pluriculturales (CEPCU). 1998. *Cachiburo: Autodiagnóstico comunitario*. Otavalo: CEPCU.
Cooper, Elwood. 1876. *Forest Culture and Eucalyptus Trees*. San Francisco: Cubery & Company.

Cuvi, Nicolás. 2005. "Dos cajones con semillas de Eucalipto." *Ecuador: Terra Incognita* 37 (Sept.-Oct.).

Doughty, Robin W. 2000. *The Eucalyptus: A Natural and Commercial History of the Gum Tree*. Baltimore: Johns Hopkins University Press.

Guha, Ramachandra. 1989. *The Unquiet Woods: Ecological Changes and Peasant Resistance in the Himalaya*. Berkeley, CA: University of California Press.

Gerber Julien-François and Sandra Veuthey. 2010. "Plantations, Resistance and the Greening of the Agrarian Question in Coastal Ecuador." *Journal of Agrarian Change* 10(4) (October).

Hassaurek, Friedrich. 1967. *Four Years among the Ecuadorians*. Edited and with an introduction by C. Harvey Gardiner. Latin American Travel Carbondale: Southern Illinois University Press.

Herrera, Amable Agustín. 2002. *Monografía del Cantón de Otavalo*. Quito, Ecuador: Instituto Otavaleño de Antropología. Universidad de Otavalo.

Jaramillo Alvarado, Pio. 1997. *El indio ecuatoriano*. 2 vol. 7th ed. Quito: Corporación Editora Nacional.

Jijón y Caamaño, Jacinto. 1945. *Antropología prehispánica del Ecuador*. Quito: La Prensa Católica.

Kincaid, Kenneth. 2005. "Currents of Dissent: Water, Identity, and the State in North Ecuador, 1924-45." Ph.D. dissertation, University of Kansas.

Mardorf Rosas, María Cristina. 1985. "Artesanía y ecología de la totora de la provincia de Imbabura, Ecuador." *Sarance* 10 (July).

Peluso, NancyLee. 1992. *Rich Forests, Poor People: Resource Control and Resistance in Java*. Berkeley, CA. University of California Press.

Poore, M.E.D. and C. Fries. 1985. *The Ecological Effects of Eucalyptus*. FAO Forestry Paper, no. 59. Rome: FAO.

Rosero Garcés, Fernando. 1982. "El proceso de transformación-conservación de la comunidad andina: el caso de las comunas de San Pablo del Lago." In *Estructuras agrarias y reproducción campesina: lecturas sobre transformaciones capitalistas en el agro ecuatoriano*, ed. Cristian Sepúlveda. Quito: Pontificia Universidad Católica del Ecuador, Instituto de Investigaciones Económicas.

Sherbundy, Jeanette. 1982. "El regadío, los lagos y los mitos de origen." *Allpanchis* 17(20):3-32.

—. 1992. "Water Ideology in Inca Ethnogenesis." In *Andean Cosmologies through Time*, ed. Robert Dover, Katharine Seibold, and John McDowell, 46-66. Bloomington: Indiana University Press.

Pérez T., Alquiles R. 1960. *Quitus y Caras*. Quito: Instituto Ecuatoriano de Antropología y Geografía.

Silverblatt, Irene. 1987. *Moon, Sun, and Witches: Gender Ideologies and Class in Inca and Colonial Peru*. Princeton: Princeton University Press.

Vicuña C., C. Azucena and Segundo de la Torre. 2002. *Imbakucha: Estudios para la sustentabilidad*. Quito: Indugraf del Ecuador.

# CHAPTER NINE

# STRUGGLES FOR THE MEANING
## OF "INDIGENOUS" WITHIN INCULTURATION
## THEOLOGY IN ECUADOR

# CARMEN MARTÍNEZ NOVO[1]

Andrew Orta (2004, 105) has defined the theology of "Inculturation" as a trend within the Catholic Church to "codify and reinforce Indigenous religiosity as part of the Church's broader effort to embrace "local theologies" and "inculturate" itself within specific cultural contexts." After centuries of preaching that Indigenous peoples turn away from their traditional cultural practices to embrace Christianity, many Catholic missionaries now insist that Indigenous ways were Christian all along: Indigenous peoples must become more "Indian" and return to the ways of their ancestors that missionaries see as local cultural expressions of Christian values (Orta 2004, vii). Orta argues that "Inculturation" Theology follows on the heels of Liberation Theology, which proposed that Christians were called upon to correct the sinful social injustices of poverty and oppression, and that tended to downplay ethnic distinctions and emphasized instead the homogenizing identity of "the poor." He suggests that the Theology of Inculturation is a response to the relative failure of Liberation Theology to take hold in rural and Indigenous contexts where the rationalizing and homogenizing discourses of the liberationists did not resonate strongly. For instance, Liberation Theology rejected popular religiosity based on the sacraments and syncretic Catholic rituals and emphasized instead evangelization based on reasoning and the written word. The move from Liberation to Inculturation also signals, according to this author, the Catholic Church's accommodation to the shift in global politics from class-based movements to identity politics.

---

[1] Some of the data for this article was previously used in Carmen Martínez Novo (2009).

In this paper, I explore the indigenist project of Inculturation Theology in Ecuador based on field and archival research that I have been doing since 2002 in the highland and Amazonian missions of the Salesian Order. Is Inculturation in this case an altogether different project from Liberation Theology? Is the turn towards multiculturalism in the Catholic Church comparable to the turn from class politics and an emphasis on redistribution, to the politics of recognition (Fraser 1997)? What is the relationship between the indigenist project of Inculturation Theology and so called "neo-liberal multiculturalism" (Hale 2005)? Is Inculturation like "neoliberal multiculturalism" a form of symbolic recognition that distracts Indigenous peoples from more substantial struggles, and co-opts them for the Church and/or the state? And, last but not least, what critiques are coming from Indigenous quarters to the indigenist project of Inculturation?

The Salesian order has been a very influential agent of different kinds of indigenismo in Ecuador since the late nineteenth century. In 1893, president Luis Cordero, a fervent Catholic and an indigenista who wrote a Kichwa-Spanish dictionary (Cordero Crespo 2010 [1892]) and Kichwa and Spanish poems, granted the Salesians the authority to "civilize and Christianize" the Shuar in the Southeastern lowlands of Ecuador. Originally, the Salesians sought to transform Shuar ways and teach the Shuar the Spanish language to make them Christian and subjects, if not citizens, of the state. The "Jívaros," as the Shuar were called at the time, were perceived according to Ann Christine Taylor (1994) as an anarchic group that rejected authority and social hierarchy, inhabited a dispersed habitat, and were in a permanent state of internal war. Neither the Inkas, nor the Spaniards, or earlier missionaries, had been able to subdue this group, a task in which only the Salesians succeeded. The Shuar were also known for their custom of shrinking the heads of dead enemies to make "tsantsas," and for the practice of polygyny. At the end of the nineteenth century, the rationalism, materialism, and perceived lack of spirituality and rituals of this group irritated missionaries. Missionaries called the Shuar "a barbarous and atheist race...resulting from all the savage forces combined like cascades, ravines, the claws of beasts, and the venom of snakes" (Taylor 1994, quoting Pierre and Alvarez, 84). Because of their alleged cynicism, the missionaries argued that Shuar culture was of satanic inspiration. For the missionaries in this period, cultural change was a way to eradicate the work of Satan. The Salesians were also preoccupied by the lack of sexual morals of the Shuar, which they associated with the custom of polygyny.

However, by the 1960s, the Salesians began to reflect on the importance of preserving an Indigenous culture that was increasingly threatened by their own work as well as by the colonization of Amazonian regions by peasants from the highlands, particularly after the 1964 Agrarian Reform and Colonization Law. According to the missionaries' own accounts, their experiences with the Shuar made them aware of the importance of cultural preservation and, consequently, they became pioneers in promoting the awareness of the Catholic Church for cultural and ethnic diversity in the Barbados conferences (1971, 1977) (J. Botasso, FLACSO Conference 2005; J. Manangón, personal communication 2002). Because of this history, in the work of the Salesians with the Shuar I perceive two tensions. The first is the difficulty of shifting from an effort towards acculturation to an emphasis on cultural preservation. The change puzzles the Shuar who wonder about this change. A second tension in the case of the Shuar is how to preserve a cultural tradition that was in many ways marked by the practice of violence.

The second example that I am using is the mission of Zumbahua, located in the central highlands of Ecuador at approximately 4000 meters of altitude and where Kichwa speaking peasants live. Different from the *Oriente* Missions, this one, which started in 1971, was informed from its start by the Theology of "Inculturation." From the sixteenth until the beginning of the twentieth century, Zumbahua was a large hacienda property of the Agustinians, a Catholic order (Weismantel 1988). Due to the high altitude of most of its lands, the hacienda consisted largely of pastures used for sheep-raising, an activity that provided wool for a textile factory that the order owned close to the provincial capital of Latacunga. In 1908, with a law that nationalized Church assets, Zumbahua became property of the Social Assistance, a public institution that rented lands to finance hospitals, orphanages, and other charities for the urban poor. Paradoxically, labor conditions were often harsher on public haciendas. The Zumbahua hacienda subjected its workers to the systems of *concertaje* and later *huasipungo*, contracts based on custom through which the worker exchanged his and his family's labor for the usufruct of a small plot of land (*huasipungo*), a nominal salary that most of the time was not paid, and some other benefits. In 1964, with the first agrarian reform law, Zumbahua, like other public haciendas, was distributed among Kichwa peasants. Social differences that originated in the hacienda period were reproduced in the land distribution process, causing inequalities and tensions. The challenges that the Salesians confronted in Zumbahua were very different from those they earlier faced in the "Oriente." They did not confront the contradictions of their own earlier assimilation work, or of how to preserve a culture in which violence was an important part. On the contrary, the traits of solidarity and reciprocity of Andean peasants were

easier to claim as Christian values. The question here was how to construct
a self-sufficient agrarian community on high-altitude pastoral lands that by
the 1960s were divided in increasingly smaller and badly eroded plots.
Another challenge for the Salesians was how to create a new man, highly
spiritual and altruistic, among people who experienced poverty,
malnutrition, and discrimination on a daily basis.

In order to discuss the indigenista work of the Salesians as inculturation
theologists and the interaction of their indigenista theology with
Indigenous goals and wishes, I am going to focus on two examples: their
attempt to create a rural peasant utopia, and their struggle for cultural
preservation and for the purification of Indigenous culture.

## The Making of a Rural Peasant Utopia

In the mission of Zumbahua, opened in 1971, the Salesians, inspired by
a Liberation Theology that they already complemented with cultural
overtones, sought to combine peasant evangelization with what they called
"human development." They understood human development as helping
and advising peasants in their struggle for access to the land and for a
better exploitation of this resource. In order to make the agrarian reform
law effective, or to get government credit, or to have access to development
funds and technical advice, peasants needed to organize. Therefore, the
Salesians promoted social and political organization through consciousness
raising in intercultural bilingual education classrooms, or by directly
creating and strengthening peasant organizations at the community, second-
tier, and provincial levels.

From the point of view of rural development, the Salesians had goals
that may seem contradictory to us: They sought both to promote a self-
sufficient peasant community based on the Kichwa tradition *and* to
modernize agriculture in the style of the green revolution. They wanted
peasants to appropriate the rural modernity that Ecuadorian landowners
were already enjoying in the 1970s. Among the first goals of the mission
were the improvement of roads, the introduction of enhanced seeds and
new agrarian techniques, the selection of animal species, and so on. These
noble goals and intentions, however, confronted important limitations due
to the low quality of eroded land, the difficulty of cultivating steep slopes,
the small size of land plots, and the lack of water.

Given these limitations, peasants in the Cotopaxi highlands have not
been able to live solely on agriculture. They typically combine several
economic activities that include trade, smuggling, temporary or permanent
migration to Ecuadorian cities, and more recently internationally, crafts in

the case of Tigua, and incipient tourism (Colloredo-Mansfeld 2009). Despite this reality, the Salesian priests still perceived the inhabitants of this area as peasants and criticized migration as a source of social disorganization, violence, and destruction of traditional culture.

This "campesinista" focus is reflected in the kind of education the mission promoted, which focused on rural needs. The Salesians educated rural teachers and experts in agrarian and animal husbandry techniques. The Salesians also adapted the school calendar to rural needs, teaching the whole elementary curriculum in four years instead of six to allow impoverished rural children to finish their elementary education, and implementing weekend and distance education for high school and college age highlanders. They also adapted the school calendar to agricultural seasons.

Young highlanders, aware of the limitations of agriculture in Zumbahua, have questioned this rural-oriented curriculum and prefer a professional urban-like education based on the use of computers and knowledge of English and other modern languages. In their own words, highlanders want to be ready for what they perceive as the "modern" world. However, they seek this kind of education without detriment to the study of the Kichwa language and culture, as well as Indigenous politics that have been useful for young peoples' insertion into the Indigenous movement, an important source of social mobility in the last decades. It is important to note, to the Salesians' credit, that mission education has adapted to the desires of the youth, offering classes in computers and modern languages. Again, the Salesians have not perceived a contradiction between the reinforcement of ethnic traditions and the education of youth in those aspects related to modernity. The point of contention is whether this modernity should be rural, urban, or cosmopolitan.

Nevertheless, the Salesians still think in terms of a peasant-oriented project. To confront the agrarian crisis of the Zumbahua area they proposed reforestation and the migration of highland peasants organized in cooperatives to sub-tropical lands. The Salesians do not perceive craft making, tourism, or migration as solid alternatives. Commerce and smuggling, a long tradition in highland communities since pre-conquest times, are not even present in Salesian discourse. This enduring representation of Indigenous peoples as localized subsistence peasants is also reproduced by scholars and by Indigenous organizations themselves, and has important political consequences as more complex economic realities and identities are often not taken into account in political strategies.

In the missions of the Oriente, in the Morona-Santiago region, the Salesians also tried to transform the Shuar, a semi-nomadic group, into settled peasants in the 1960s. This strategy was a response to the Agrarian Reform and Colonization Laws of 1964 and 1973. Whereas the agrarian reform benefited Zumbahua's peasants with the distribution of public hacienda land among its workers or granting huasipungos to those who lived in nearby private haciendas, the Shuar perceive this law as harmful. These agrarian reform laws established that those lands that were not in cultivation or used for cattle raising activities could be distributed to other peasants in need. This meant that the Shuar who used to move periodically when their plots were exhausted and their hunting prey dwindled, had to become sedentary in order to keep their land. The Salesians encouraged the Shuar to do so, promoting agriculture and particularly cattle raising to lay claim to the territory. Instead of living in disperse habitats, the Salesians encouraged the creation of Shuar centers, or groups of houses around a main square. In order to defend Shuar territory, these centers joined a federation organized by the Salesians in 1964, the FICSH (Interprovincial Federation of Shuar Centers). This was one of the first modern Indigenous organizations in Latin America. In later years, FICSH became part of the Indigenous movement and CONAIE, whose first president was Miguel Tankamash, a Shuar. FICSH's leaders, however, did not seek a return to an Indigenous tradition. According to Steve Rubenstein (2005) the hierarchical character of FISCH, its well-defined territorial limits that mimicked the Ecuadorian state, and the concentration of the population in towns or centers that evoked colonial *reducciones*, contrasted with traditional Shuar understandings of diffuse authority and vague territoriality.

In ways similar to the Zumbahua area, Amazonian lands are not the best for intensive cultivation. Due to abundant rainfall, Amazonian soils are superficial, and the traditional strategy of slash and burn agriculture seems to make sense in this environment when using rudimentary techniques. Salesian education in Shuar territory also promoted the formation of rural teachers and agrarian technicians. Nevertheless, like the peasants of Zumbahua, the Shuar also combine several strategies to make a living, including urban and international migration, incipient tourism, and collaboration with NGOs. For the leaders, building a political career provides another option. The Salesians have also adapted their strategies to this cosmopolitanism. For example, Salesians help the Shuar and the Achuar produce or gather forest goods for export abroad through the Chankuap Foundation.

The Salesians seem to strongly identify Indigenous with subsistence peasant. However, this is not a strategy to keep Indigenous peoples in the past as part of the "culture" emphasis of Inculturation Theology. For the Shuar, to become settled peasants and cattle raisers was something new. Zumbahua highlanders had just changed from being landless peons to owning small plots of poor land in the early 1970s. In both cases, the Salesians promoted the modernization of agriculture to raise the living standards of these peoples. When the Salesians perceived that Indigenous peoples wanted a more professional and urban education, they struggled to provide them with this.

## The Purification of Indigenous Culture

Although Andrew Orta (2004) situates the origins of Inculturation Theology in the mid-1980s and claims that this current was introduced in Bolivia in the early 1990s, it seems to have started much earlier in Ecuador. In the project that the Salesians wrote to start the Zumbahua mission in 1971, there was already a very clear concern for the preservation and reinforcement of Indigenous culture as part of their human development and evangelization goals. The formation of the Federation of Shuar Centers in 1964 was also a sign of an early concern with reinforcing an Indigenous identity to protect the Shuar from the external world. In fact, missionaries in Ecuador locate the starting point of Inculturation directly in the Second Vatican Council, and the discontinuity or shift from Liberation to Inculturation is not all that clear to me from the archival documents. They give importance in order to understand the multicultural turn of the Catholic Church to the Decree Ad Gentes on the Missionary Activity of the Church written by Pope Paul VI in 1965. The main idea behind "Inculturation," according to missionaries, is that the Church after Vatican II no longer considers non-western cultures profane. These cultures are believed to contain the "seeds of the word of god," an idea that was already present in colonial times (Orta 2004) but that was revitalized after the Second Vatican Council. Pastoral agents should identify these seeds, those elements within a culture which are positive from the point of view of Catholic ethics or that can be used for evangelization purposes such as solidarity, love for the earth, spirituality, and so on. Pastoral agents should learn the language and other cultural elements of the people among whom they work, and should use them for evangelization and Catholic rituals. Although this theology focuses on respect for diversity and cultural preservation, the Decree Ad Gentes argues that cultures should be purified from those elements that are negative from the point of view of Christian ethics. It reads:

> [Mission activity] liberates from evil traits all the truth and grace that existed among the peoples as the veiled presence of God and restitutes it to its author, Christ, that subdues the presence of the Devil and separates wickedness from sinners. Thus, all that is good in the heart and mind of men, in the rites and cultures of the peoples, does not perish, but is purified, elevated and perfected for the glory of God (Ad Gentes, 1965, 7).

Despite the interest of the Salesians in the recovery of Shuar culture starting in the 1960s, the profound transformations effected in Shuar ways and language during the first half of the twentieth century could hardly be reversed. Let us take a look at the same process from the point of view of some Shuar individuals.

José Vicente Jintiach, a historic leader of the Shuar Federation and one of the first to access higher education at the Catholic University, published his reflections on the difficult adjustments facing the Shuar youth who entered Salesian boarding schools (Jintiach 1976). Jintiach's book portrays the Shuar as a people fully integrated into, and fond of, modernity, who enjoyed the music of The Beatles and the few movies to which they had access in the town of Sucúa. Evoking the egalitarian traditions of Shuar culture, Jintiach is highly critical of Salesian authority. Acording to Jintiach, Shuar adolescents find the lack of personal liberty and the sexual repression they encounter in the Salesian boarding schools particularly painful. However, Jintiach unambiguously recognizes the importance of the opportunity that the Salesian schools provided to educate themselves in the dominant culture. This book portrays both a process of cultural change and also some cultural continuity because the Shuar had been traditionally fond of those things coming from outside their own culture (Descola 2005).

A Shuar woman and her elderly father from the Salesian Mission of Sevilla Don Bosco in Morona Santiago, explain the transformations of Shuar culture and the role played by the Salesians in them in the following way. The woman notes,

> When we went to school they did not want us to speak the Shuar language. We spoke Shuar with our classmates because we did not speak correct Castilian, but the nuns thought that we were insulting them. Today, they do not want us to speak Spanish. "Speak Shuar," they say. They used to call the parents and tell them that they [the Salesian nuns] commanded us to speak Castilian. And because we were little, we gradually lost our language. Today, our kids at the Shuar centers speak only Spanish. We still

know a little, but our children don't. And now they [the Salesians] want us to return to our past. Of course, I identify as Shuar. Wherever I go I say: "I am Shuar, I am from the Amazon, I am Ecuadorian." And people look at me with surprise. However, it is also unfair that today's schools teach only Shuar. How can children learn if they don't teach them good Spanish? When we went to school we had well prepared teachers from Quito and Guayaquil. At least thanks to those teachers we learned to speak good Spanish. We want to get education for our children. Because we do not have good education, we get delinquency. They [the Salesians] taught us well. They taught us how to do things, how to cook, how to greet people, how to eat properly, how to use the broom.... But, today schools don't teach children good manners... (Interview, February 19, 2006).

This quote illustrates some of the complexities of the process of cultural transformation endured by the Shuar. The Shuar are first forbidden to use their language and customs, and when the process of cultural change is almost complete, they are asked to retrieve them. As seen in the quote, both processes are perceived as an imposition from outside. Like Jintiach (1976), this Shuar woman argues that the process of cultural transformation has been both painful but ultimately useful for the Shuar, because it helped them integrate into, or at least to survive within, the dominant culture.

Her father also makes reference to the misunderstandings enmeshed in the process of cultural recovery undertaken by the missionaries. He complains of the new Catholic mass implemented by the Salesians that makes use of Shuar language and music in the liturgy. This elderly Shuar notes,

Here, they celebrate the mass in Shuar. If God had been here and had made a miracle, if God-Arutam [a Shuar deity] had said, "come with me," I would believe. But I don't. That Father said that Arutam is God. He is writing a Bible [in Shuar]. I don't want the Shuar mass. My father and my grandfather used to sing that music [that they use in mass] when they killed. They are singing a song from the times of the hard *chonta* [kind of palm of the Ecuadorian Amazon]. My father would drink *chicha* and sing that song with our own rhythm. The priests should not use that [in mass]. That song is what they sang when they killed a person. I told the Father that the Bible that God wrote couldn't be amended. We cannot change what Christ has written. What Christ said we must follow. But now they are writing another book, a book with Arutam, Iwia, and what else. My father and grandfather used to say that Iwia [a mythological Shuar giant] ate people.... And, there he was, Father José, I came in and he was there, standing and singing "Ahhhhh." Then, he raises the holy host and he invokes Arutam and Christ. If Christ were that powerful, why would he need Arutam to help him? Then, I said "that's enough," I won't come back to mass. If they would sing in Shuar, speaking about God that would be

nice. But they mix everything. The song that they sang when they killed
humans and made *tsantsas* [shrunken heads], the song that they sang to
attract women, songs for demons and snakes... [they use in mass]. I say
no. I told them to be careful with Arutam. Arutam is a powerful Demon.
They [the Salesians] taught us that. They told us that Arutam was a Demon
almost equal to God. Arutam knows how to deceive. We did not know well
before. All the Salesian priests and nuns who have sung to Arutam have
died or become ill. That Arutam gave strength to commit crimes. That is
why I say that this is not a mass. They already fed us that there is only one
God. Why do they have to bring in Arutam now? (Interview, February 19,
2006).

The interviewee highlights again the contradictions of the colonization
process. First their culture is stigmatized and changed. Later, the Salesians
want to retrieve it. However, they do so as if one culture was translatable
into another, as if one God was equal to another God. Probably the priest
is using the Shuar word Arutam to say God in the native language. This
elder's sharp exercise in cultural analysis tells us, however, that cultures
are not equivalent. Furthermore, the missionaries have convinced the
Shuar that there were negative elements in their own culture, particularly
those related to violence. And it is problematic to return to these elements
both for the Church and for the organizations. Thus, the interviewee
refuses to accept the new stereotyped and stylized version of his own
culture that the Salesians seem to be attempting to promote in their search
for "cultural preservation." He says, "I know everything, nobody can lie to
me because my grandfather told me: "This is like this, and that is like
that...." And, now they are creating a new law. That is why I don't like
when they do Shuar things." He rejects the "purification" of culture that
the theology of inculturation proposes as unauthentic. Consequently, this
Shuar elder perceives the process of "preservation and recovering" as yet
another colonial imposition, or, in his own words, as a new "law."

In the case of Zumbahua, the retrieval of Indigenous culture is also
perceived as a process originating from above and has been somewhat
resisted by Indigenous peasants. The missionaries taught the Kichwa
language and philosophy, but they did not extract this knowledge from the
Indigenous peasants. On the contrary, they believed that the peasants'
Kichwa was corrupted with profuse influences from Spanish and sought to
teach a purified, more classic version of the language, one used by
university-based linguists and priests.

Kichwa culture should also be preserved while purifying it from those
aspects considered by the Salesians contrary to ethics such as the
oppression of women. Father Javier Herrán, a Salesian who organized the
Zumbahua mission, tells the following anecdote. When intercultural

bilingual education promoted by the Salesians started in Zumbahua many families did not want to send their daughters to school. Seeing that there were few girls in school, Herrán asked the peasants to send them to school. They answered that women did not need to study to take care of the home, children, and domestic animals. Father Herrán asked: Then, do you think that women are not human beings equal to men? If that is what you think, then from now on I would not baptize women. According to Herrán, the peasants were scared by this threat and decided to send the girls to school.

Another Salesian priest, Father Luigi Ricchiardi, added that the well-known trait of Andean reciprocity should be transformed into the Christian value of gratuity. He argued:

> From the point of view of the Church, or those of us who want to help Indigenous peoples, this moment of change is a good moment to help introduce within their own culture new elements that help the culture to develop in a certain way. The element that we want to emphasize is the element of solidarity. But from solidarity, they should evolve into gratuity. Indigenous culture is a solidarity culture. But their form of solidarity is randi-randi, meaning you give something to me, and I give something to you. This is what we call Andean reciprocity. But Andean reciprocity mixed with the capitalist perspective becomes selfish. Then, we have to inject the value of gratuity that immunizes Andean reciprocity against the neo-liberal mentality of exploitation of others. I use the other for what he can give me, and I help him expecting something in return.

Father Luigi does not see Indigenous culture as something that must change to adapt to modernity, but as a mixture of Indigenous and capitalist modern values that must be purified from the point of view of ethics to make up a more altruistic and utopian pattern. This new Indigenous utopia should be an example against the neo-liberal logic.

As in the Shuar case, this particular way to reinforce Indigenous culture, which the Salesians connected with improving self-esteem, confronted resistance by Indigenous peasants. Communities did not always trust Indigenous teachers and many peasants thought that teaching in Kichwa was a waste of time. Wasn't the whole point of going to school to learn Spanish in order to become stronger, less vulnerable, in relation to the dominant culture? For instance, Rodrigo Martínez, a white-mestizo teacher who collaborated for decades with the Salesian project states:

> Why did we emphasize the philosophy of bilingual education? Because Indigenous peoples themselves were not convinced of the value of Indigenous education. They always thought that it was a second-class situation. They were not convinced that an education that is relevant to the cultural reality could also be an education with possibilities to achieve

quality. Then, we spent our time convincing them that the Indian is a person with value, that Indigenous peoples are valuable as a people, that their culture includes valuable things. And so we spent our time, until they were able to consolidate their collective identity (Interview, July 2002).

The intercultural bilingual education program implemented by the Salesians in Zumbahua created a political consciousness based on ethnic pride and formed a new generation of leaders. The Salesians also promoted political organization in direct ways. The Zumbahua Project (1971, 20) gave priority to this aspect:

> In order to solve the Indigenous problem, Indigenous peoples themselves have to become agents in liberating actions...through a consciousness raising process that leads them to transform every unfair socio-economic structure. Therefore, the main goal of all our action should be to conduce the Indigenous community to a true self-management. Our work as agents of change is just temporary, transient, and subsidiary.

Again, the Salesians did not aim to preserve Indigenous social and political organization, but to transform it in ways that made it more just and efficient. For instance, the Salesians had to struggle against forms of exploitation and inequality among peasants that came from hacienda times. Because of their fight against local *caciques*, the Salesians were close to being lynched and expelled from the Zumbahua area.

Both in the Oriente and Zumbahua, cultural "recovery" really meant cultural change. Some elements of the culture were kept and purified, new elements were introduced, and others were transformed. In both cases, Indigenous peoples were suspicious of the strategy of cultural recovery because they perceived the cultural change that they had already achieved as a more effective way to integrate to and survive within a global world to which they were already connected. On the other hand, they hardly recognized the purified version of their own culture that the missionaries were offering back to them, and saw the "recovery" more as an outside imposition.

Indigenous peoples who have become priests within the Catholic Church and who have been forced to leave this institution, have even more poignant critiques of Inculturation Theology. Some of these priests have left Catholicism and joined Protestantism because they perceive the Church, even in its Inculturation stream, as a discriminatory institution. They complain that white-mestizo inculturation theologists still want to hold power over Indigenous peoples, and that they do not want Indigenous peoples to become independent from their white mestizo "ventriloquists." They also accuse inculturationists, whom they label "Pachamamas," of stereotyping Indigenous culture. Another common accusation is that the Church has used Indigenous peoples to get development funds that are then invested more in the white-mestizo hierarchies than in the Indigenous communities.

## Conclusion

How should we characterize the indigenist project of Inculturation Theology looking at it from the specific case of the work of the Salesian order in Ecuador? I would argue that it is a utopian project that goes beyond a superficial or symbolic reclaiming of identity. The Salesians did try to put together recognition with redistribution. The recovery of culture and self-esteem went together with structural transformations such as the struggle for agrarian reform, land, and territory. Furthermore, the separation between Liberation and Inculturation Theologies, particularly in the case of Zumbahua, does not emerge that clearly in the documents. Both currents seem to be entangled in a single project of liberation and in the construction of a new, more ethical Indigenous person that also enjoys a better, more modern standard of living.

However, Indigenous peoples who seem to have had a different understanding of themselves challenged the focus of the Salesians on a purified version of local culture, subsistence agriculture, and a new more ethical Indigenous person. They thought of themselves as already culturally transformed, more cosmopolitan, and more practical than what the Salesians would have wanted.

The relationship of the multicultural church with neoliberal multiculturalism is paradoxical. As I pointed out above, in the work of the Salesians, the emphasis on identity does not seem to be accompanied by distancing oneself from struggles for structural change. Furthermore, they are reinforcing identity and political organization specifically to fight capitalism and more recently neo-liberalism. In the case of Ecuador, the Indigenous movement, strongly supported by the Salesian order from its inception, was able to bring the neo-liberal project of privatization to a halt (Zamosc 2007). Moreover, I would argue that the Salesians have been central to the shift from neo-liberalism to a "post-neoliberal" state in Ecuador. First, I would argue that with their work with the social movements they created the kind of anti-neoliberal environment in which the shift away from neo-liberalism was made possible. Second, President Correa himself was a lay Salesian missionary who lived and learned in the Zumbahua Mission. However, as the post-neoliberal state becomes stronger and more authoritarian, and as the new government collides with social movements because of its lack of tolerance for dissent and over the issue of the extraction of natural resources, the Salesians find themselves in a difficult position. On the one hand, the Order wishes to support the anti-neoliberal turn. On the other, they perceive that alignment with the government could have the effect of separating them from the social movements that are fighting increasing authoritarianism and extractivism, the very social movements that for so many years the Salesians have nurtured.

# References

Colloredo-Mansfeld, Rudi. 2009. *Fighting Like a Community: Andean Civil Society in an Era of Indian Uprisings*. Chicago: The University of Chicago Press.

Cordero Crespo, Luis. 2010 [1892]. *Diccionario Quichua-Castellano, Castellano-Quichua*. Quito: Corporación Editora Nacional.

Descola, Philippe. 1998. *The Spears of Twilight. Life and Death in the Amazon Jungle*. New Press.

Hale, Charles R. 2005. "Neoliberal Multiculturalism: The Remaking of Cultural Rights and Racial Dominance in Central America." *Political and Legal Anthropology Review* 28(1):10-28.

Jintiach, J.V. 1976. *La integración del estudiante shuar en su grupo social*. Sucúa: Mundo Shuar.

Martínez Novo, Carmen. 2009. "The Salesian Missions of Ecuador: Building an Anti-Neoliberal Nation with the Indigenous Movement." In *Bridging the Gaps: Faith Based Organizations, Neoliberalism, and Development in Latin America and the Caribbean*, ed. Tara Hefferan, Julie Adkins, and Laurie Occhipinti. Lanham, MD: Lexington Books.

Orta, Andrew. 2004. *Catechizing Culture. Missionaries, Aymara, and the New Evangelization*. New York: Columbia University Press.

Rubenstein, Steven. 2005. "La conversion de los Shuar." *Iconos* 22:27-48.

Taylor, Ann Christine. 1994. "Una categoria irreductible en el conjunto de las naciones indígenas: Los jíbaro en las representaciones occidentales." In *Imágenes e imagineros*, ed. Blanca Muratorio, 75-108. Quito: FLACSO.

Weismantel, Mary. 1998. *Food, Gender, and Poverty in the Ecuadorian Andes*. Prospect Heights, IL: Waveland Press.

Zamosc, León. 2007. "The Indian Movement and Political Democracy in Ecuador." *Latin American Politics and Society* 49(3):1-34.

# CHAPTER TEN

## POWER RELATIONS AND STRUGGLES WITHIN INDIGENOUS CHURCHES AND ORGANIZATIONS

## JUAN ILLICACHI GUZÑAY[1]

> "Good Christian, good citizen;
> good Christian, good Indian;
> good Christian, good wife."
> —Pastor Simón Gualán

### Background

Ecuador is an Andean country with a population of 14,306,876 inhabitants, according to the recent 2010 census. Population data compiled during this census indicates that Indigenous and Afro-Ecuadorian populations have grown. There are 1,018,176 Indigenous people, an increase from 2001. Afro-Ecuadorians, in turn, make up 1,041,559 people, which amounts to 437,550 more than in the population count of 2001.

Chimborazo, one of Ecuador's twenty-four provinces, is situated in the central part of the country's inter-Andean valley. Tall and gorgeous mountain ranges make up the natural scenery, giving way to an infinite array of beautiful landscapes enjoyed by those who have lived there since

---

[1] This article forms part of my doctoral thesis research in Social Anthropology at the Center for Advanced Research and Study in Social Anthropology (Centro de Investigaciones y Estudios Superiores en Antropología Social, CIESAS) in Mexico City; for that reason, some parts of the text may seem disconnected. My analysis is based on fieldwork conducted in two Indigenous communities between May 2010 and September 2011. I studied Protestantism in Majipamba and Catholicism in Licto. Translated from Spanish to English by Kathleen C. O'Brien, Ph.D. Candidate in Sociocultural and Linguistic Anthropology at the University of Illinois, Urbana-Champaign.

antiquity. The province was made a political entity on June 25, 1826 under the presidency of the liberator Simón Bolívar, president of Gran Colombia. Currently, the province is divided along political and administrative lines into ten cantons, seven urban parishes, and forty-four rural parishes. It covers 6,000 square kilometers, representing 2.34 percent of the nation's territory. It is bordered by the province of Tungurahua to the north, the province of Cañar and part of Guayas to the south, the province of Morona Santiago to the east, and the provinces of Bolivar and Guayas to the west.

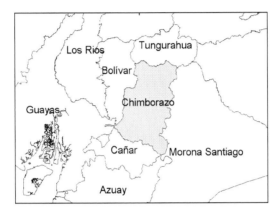

Source: Ramón Valarezo, 2007

Chimborazo comprises 3.1 percent of the national population. An estimated 236,124 inhabitants, or 58 percent of the provincial population, are Indigenous, making Chimborazo one of the provinces with the greatest numbers of Indigenous peoples in the country.[2] Almost 40 percent of Chimborazo's population can be found in urban areas, while 60.91 percent reside in rural areas.

According to the recent population and housing census, the illiteracy rate within the economically-active population of Chimborazo province for the year 2010 was 17.6 percent; the rate of illiteracy among women at 23.4 percent was higher than the rate among men at 13.7 percent. Of those living in urban areas, 3.5 percent were illiterate, with the percentage being higher among women at 4.9 percent than among men at 2.5 percent. Illiterates made up 26 percent of the rural population. Following the

---

[2] According to census data INEC compiled in 2001, the province has 403,632 inhabitants, 190,667 of who are men and 212,965 of who are women. In addition, 157,780 of the inhabitants live in urban areas while 245,852 reside in rural areas.

general trends outlined above, women showed a higher rate of illiteracy at 34.7 percent, compared to men at 20 percent.

## In The Field

I have enjoyed the privilege of doing research in the culture where I was born and currently live, as well as listening to testimonies, sermons, conversations, and interviews in my native tongue, Kichwa. At times I think that I am studying myself and indeed I am in a way. I speak from my subjectivity as an Indigenous person more so than in my affiliation with one church or another.[3] When I donned my poncho in the field, nobody realized that I was acting as an investigator; only my camera marked the difference between my *hermanos* (brothers and sisters of faith) and myself, not as a researcher but rather as a photographer. For that reason, people would say: "Hermano, take this picture of us. We'll pay you later. Give us your business card." In addition, my digital recorder marked the difference between us, not as a researcher but as a good Christian. For that reason, they would say to me: "You are a good hermano. I congratulate you on making a recording and listening to it again later." My notebook did not create a barrier between the researcher and the researched, either; rather, it positioned me as the secretary of the event.[4] These conversations and messages confirmed my subjectivity as an Indigenous person, colleague, and hermano. While these experiences may not interest others, they do carry tremendous methodological implications, though I hesitate to call my research collaborative (Mora 2008; Rappaport 2008).[5] While recognizing some limitations, I have had the methodological "privilege" of carrying out ethnographic fieldwork from within and not from outside of the culture. I have considered the suggestions of some anthropologists (Hernandez, Mattiace and Rus 2002) to break with traditional anthropological research that conceives of Indigenous peoples as mere "objects of study" to be theorized from the vantage point of a distant and

---

[3] I should mention my previous position as a catechist at my local church in Flores Parish and my longstanding connection to, and solidarity with, those involved with the progressive Catholic Church. During my fieldwork, however, my Indigenous identity carried more weight than my religious identity.

[4] I refer to my evangelical hermanos as well as my Catholic ones. I entered their churches with permission, having explained my motives for being there. I was never questioned or restricted from conducting my fieldwork, but rather was invited to convert. Some pastors considered me "Tayta Illicachi" or "Tayta Little Priest," but not their spiritual brother.

[5] I explore this issue in greater depth in one of the chapters of my thesis.

apolitical academy. Therefore, it has become essential to position my work within a collaborative research framework that considers those studied to be intellectuals in their own right and active subjects of their own history.[6]

## Power Relations and Struggles within Catholic and Evangelical Churches

In this chapter I raise the following questions: Have Protestant and Catholic churches reproduced power relations? When do power struggles emerge? During evangelical conferences, especially during special performances called "especiales," individual and collective power struggles among evangelical women occasionally emerge underneath the conference tent. Resolution occurs only once members of the judging panel declare their final decision, placing the women on different levels according to their scores. This religious field of contention underneath the tent or inside the church does not take place against the opposite gender but rather among evangelical women themselves of different ages and places of origin. The women exhibit their ability to sing, pantomime, and dance in front of the men, showing an incredible outpouring of love for and faith in an omnipotent and omnipresent Being.

"Santiago de Quito" Choir

---

[6] According to Gramsci, modern intellectuals are not simply writers but also directors and organizers involved in the practical tasks of constructing a society.

"El Corderito" (The Little Lamb) Choir

Pastors: Members of the Judging Panel

Liturgical dance, which is performed exclusively by young women and girls, also plays a role in this dynamic of struggle over power and prizes despite the fact that the participants say they perform in order to praise God and pray, not to win a prize. It is worth noting that prizes are not always given out nor are they always sought after in these large encounters; praising God is the primary motivation. In other words, saving souls takes precedence; social transformation will come later, as a result of saving souls (García 2008). In Catholic life, women also compete with each other but not with the same fervor and intensity nor with the same level of organization as the evangelical women. Their performances sometimes seem to take on an improvisational quality, but this is not to negate their contributions and agency in spiritual, social, and political settings. Within these contests, rules of the game established by the same Kichwanized or "Indianized" (Santana 1995) churches come into play. Performers are judged on the following criteria: presentation, rhythm, harmony, vocalization, and doctrine. This new religious experience, especially within Indigenous Protestantism of Chimborazo, makes possible the rise of what Berger calls "communities of life" with their own mechanisms for the shared experience of cohesion, struggle, alliance, reciprocity, organization, and affect in daily life (García 2008).

According to my research findings, Indigenous evangelical churches propose, advocate, and exercise discipline. The pastor or the deacon exercises "disciplinary power" (Foucault). The deacon in his administrative capacity is not meant to take the place of the church pastor, or at least not with the same kind of legitimacy or influence as the pastor. In terms of hierarchical relationships, the Protestant church holds the pastor in highest esteem after God. On earth, the pastor governs and presides exclusively over all baptisms, weddings, and restitutions, and leads the evangelists, deacons, and members of the congregation. One testimony from a representative of the Council of Pastors (COPAEQUE) demonstrates this hierarchy and sphere of influence: "As president of the Council, I minister to all of the pastors, evangelists, teachers, workers, deacons, and also to the missionaries by offering ideas, managing, motivating" (Simón Gualán). The converted sense the pastor's exercise of power and feel the weight of the organization. They know how and by whom they are being controlled and led, and give their consent ("ideological consensus") to being regulated and controlled by evangelical church authorities (Roseberry 2007). To get beyond reducing power relations to a simple opposition between the controlled and the controllers (Gledhill 2000; Restrepo 2005), one has to consider the multiplicity of encounters between individuals or groups, and the pastors and deacons, taking into account various processes and different levels of complexity. Certainly, within these millions of encounters (Trouillot 2001), the Indigenous evangelical church authorities are present in a variety of scenarios, starting with the daily life of individuals and families:

> In spite of the pastors' moralistic messages favoring women (respect, good treatment), physical and psychological aggression persists. No matter how long it takes, spiritual leaders and deacons gather late at night to deal with and negotiate *machista* practices taking place within churches or homes. They offer advice and intervene by employing Biblical passages such as 'man cannot separate what God has united,' using the technique of prayer, transmitting messages of gender equality before God, laying the Bible on the violator, and eliciting repentance and tears. The resolution is made in secret under the pastor's guidance (Interview: Teresa Pagalo).

The pastor's direct relationship with members of his congregation and his unfaltering vigilance are evident. Sanctions are applied according to the level of the infraction and are based on Biblical text. "The pastor and the deacons are authorized to discipline and restore the disciplined" based on the following texts: Philippians 1:18; 2 Corinthians 2: 5-10; 2 Corinthians 10:8, 13-10; 1 Timothy 3:8; Titus 1:7-5 (COPAEQUE Regulations). In other words, the Word of God (the Bible) has to be carried out verbatim, just like the rules established by the pastor and deacons of the church, although the forms of discipline and sanctions are not the same across all evangelical churches. Not complying with the norms of the church involves being subjected to a series of sanctions. For example, those who do not actively participate in church or who have sexual relations prior to marriage marry without honor and cannot wear a veil or have music played during their wedding.

Catholic Church of Licto

At the same time, Licto Convent continues to be the central meeting ground for affiliated Indigenous Catholic communities. I suggest that the center of power is located here, at the Licto Temple. One might say the "panopticon"[7] can be found here, not because it is a prison but because it is set up as God's "inspection house," an architectural construction from which small churches located in Indigenous communities across Licto are directed and surveyed. This is done in a productive, rather than prohibiting, way. Baptisms, weddings, workshops, meetings, planning sessions, etc. are conducted here. In other words, this is the center of decision making, among other activities.

---

[7] A panopticon can also be called an "inspection house." It is not limited to the organizational model of the prison. As a new principle of architectural construction, it is applicable to any kind of establishment. It consists of a building whose periphery takes the form of a ring and whose center features a tower with large windows that look towards the interior of the ring, which also have windows. One guard in the central tower can see all of the prisoners (Lechuga; 2007: 204).

I observed the reproduction of surveillance and discipline in Indigenous Catholic churches and gatherings; on occasion, disciplinary practices were re-enacted on stage. The dramatization involves a "major of the Armed Forces" who introduces two police officers.[8] In reality, one is dressed as a military officer and the other a police officer, as you can see in the following photographs:

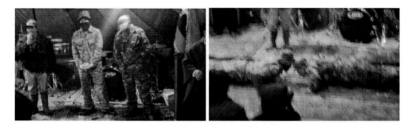

This kind of half-formal, half-joking surveillance takes place at evangelical conferences as well. Security and surveillance forces (the "sergeant" and the "lieutenant") can be found "everywhere," both inside and outside of the tent, watching the behavior of the Catholics gathered and the evangelical conference-goers. The phrase one could hear over and over again was: "Those who fall asleep lose their hat, *bayeta*, poncho." Some people at the event had garments taken away from them; the garments were returned afterwards without a fee. The watchmen were in charge of looking after and controlling "everything," as well as imposing disciplinary action on a variety of subjects. The ongoing surveillance mechanism over bodies and minds was achieved through the designation of specific "uniformed" officers for that specific event. The uniformed

---

[8] In nearly all of the evangelical conferences and Catholic gatherings, members of the disciplinary unit ("Armed Forces" and "National Police") were presented in a pretend fashion. However, on March 4, 2011, the official bodyguard of the president of Licto's Parish Board (Junta Parroquial) was present.

people exercised power over the watched, who demonstrated consent and obedience in both Catholic and evangelical Indigenous churches. For that reason, those being watched would give over articles of their clothing without any resistance. Church authorities and members in attendance support watchmen in their endeavors. In other words, authorities such as catechists and pastors, through "the forces of order," look to assert hegemony, in the Gramscian sense of the term. They attempt to convince their subordinates in ideological fashion that they are being controlled of their own accord and for their own wellbeing (Scott 2007).

## Relationship between Indigenous Organizations in Chimborazo

Through my conversations with members of Kichwa Indigenous organizations in Chimborazo affiliated with the Gospel Missionary Union (GMU) denomination, I have "discovered" that they are directed by the Council of Quichua Evangelical Pastors (Concilio de Pastores Evangélicos Quichuas del Ecuador, COPAEQUE) and their organizational arm the Confederation of Evangelical Indigenous Peoples, Organizations, Communities and Churches (Confederación de Pueblos, Organizaciones, Comunidades e Iglesias Indígenas Evangélicas de Chimborazo, CONPOCIIECH), whose headquarters are located in the community of Majipamba-Colta. They do not identify themselves as Protestant, but rather as evangelical or Christian. Those who share this identification consider themselves to be hermanos (brothers) and hermanas (sisters) and grant the pastors the right to be spiritual fathers. In addition, the Council of Pastors declared Majipamba-Colta the "center and capital of the gospel."

The popular base of the Confederation of the Indigenous Movement of Chimborazo (Confederación del Movimiento Indígena de Chimborazo, COMICH) is made up of thirty-two parish and cantonal organizations, according to the movement's archives. In contrast, evangelical congregations from Indigenous communities constitute the organizational backbone of the Confederation of Evangelical Indigenous Peoples, Organizations, Communities and Churches. COMICH belongs to the Confederation of Indigenous Nationalities of Ecuador (CONAIE), and CONPOCIIECH is an affiliate of the Ecuadorian Federation of Indigenous Evangelicals (FEINE).

Together, these two organizations (COMICH and CONPOCIIECH) have constructed their own local "micropower" and their own histories. Both organizations are affiliated with or form part of a religion, whether Catholic or evangelical. Ever since the beginning, these organizations have come into contradiction and have different objectives. To give an example, COMICH emerged in alliance with the Dioceses of Riobamba and had three main objectives: "to maintain our own culture, politics, and economics." By contrast, CONPOCIIECH was formed under the direction and the auspices of North American missionaries with the objective of converting more people and defending the converted from "attacks" on the part of Indigenous Catholics. In some cases these attacks were instigated by members of the Indigenous Catholic hierarchy who sought to "defend their historical positions, whereas Protestantism is about conquering new members of the faith" (Santana 1995). Added to this thorny project was the fight to make the dominant or "hegemonic" church, as Gramsci would say, recognize and accept them at the very least as "separate hermanos," not because they really needed acknowledgement to continue their operations, but rather to avoid conflict, violence, and tension in spaces that the Catholic Church dominated.

COMICH was not expressly created or defined as a confessional organization or a practicing and/or militant Catholic organization. However, one cannot deny its relationship with and close tie to the reformed Catholic church. Without denying the organizational capacity of the Indigenous movement of Ecuador and of Chimborazo, it certainly would have been difficult to burst onto the international stage, at least during the 1990 Indigenous uprising, without the help of the progressive Catholic Church.[9] To lend substance to the idea that COMICH is not exclusively Catholic, one need only search the Government Council archives and note the testimonies of its leaders, at least one of whom is evangelical and belongs to one of the Christian churches:

> Our organization and its popular base do not care if its members are Catholic or evangelical…. When I was president of COMICH (2002-2005), Pascual Cuzco, an evangelical hermano from Alausí, assumed the position of vice-president. During that same time, the president of COCIF, a local organization in Flores affiliated with COMICH, was pastor Angel Chacha. His contribution was important and we never encountered problems belonging to different religions (Interview: Pedro Janeta).

With the support of Monsignor Leonidas Proaño, one of the biggest proponents of the Theology of Liberation in Latin America, the Catholics have promoted an organization that is both of Indigenous peoples and for

---

[9] "Without the support of the Church, the actions of the Indigenous movement of Ecuador would not have been successful. Indigenous peoples almost always used to have a localist perspective, one that was very insular. Their local protests prevailed on a local level but not on a national one" (Anonymous).

Indigenous peoples. It is an organization with an ethnic philosophy, not a Catholic one. COMICH has never officially declared itself a Catholic organization, nor said that it belonged only to Catholics in Chimborazo. However, its close-knit connection to the Church of Riobamba, at least during the first decade of its existence, is undeniable. Likewise, one cannot hide the fact that some of its leaders have at one point or another been part of the formation of the Catholic Church. Such is the case of Delfín Tenesaca, the current president of Ecuador Kichwa Llaktakunapak Hatun Tantanakuy (ECUARUNARI).[10] Evidently, those involved in the Catholic hierarchy, including Indigenous and non-Indigenous priests, do not make decisions within the organization. At least today, a quasi-separation exists, unless Indigenous peoples seek input on a specific point.

On the other hand, since the beginning CONPOCIIECH has declared itself a confessional evangelical organization. In other words, evangelicals have chosen to organize themselves around their faith, as one can see in the way they categorize themselves as "evangelical Indigenous churches." The organization's structure brings evangelical hermanos together. Those who aspire to become leaders of the organization find support in the form of letters of recommendation from their spiritual fathers (pastors) and the deacons of their churches. Moreover, evangelical churches advance demands, discourses, and practices in favor of themselves. Pastors always participate actively in the decision-making processes of evangelical churches as well as the provincial organization. This reflection demonstrates one of the points of contention between the two provincial organizations (COMICH and CONPOCIIECH).

Another source of tension is the political participation of both Indigenous evangelicals and Catholics through their respective political parties Amauta Yuyay and Pachakutik. Amauta Yuyay adopts conciliatory discourses and warm actions towards the national government. Pachakutik espouses aggressive discourses (without ruling out reconciliation). The two approaches involve different degrees of dialogue and conflict between local or national governments on the one hand and Indigenous organizations on the other (León 2010). The political fighting and tensions between the two organizations (COMICH and CONPOCIIECH) are generated by their respective political movements, Pachakutik

---

[10] A few priests met with Indigenous leaders from various provinces of the Andes. This led to the First Constitutive Congress of Ecuador Runacunapac Riccharimuy (ECUARUNARI) in 1972. More than two hundred Indigenous people from Tepeyac Community in Chimborazo participated (Bretón 2001; León 1993). ECUARUNARI is a regional Indigenous organization with an ethnic agenda tied to the progressive Church, particularly to that of the Diocese of Riobamba.

Plurinational Political Movement (*Movimiento Político Plurinacional Pachakutik*) and Amauta Yuyay, which become more visible during election time. The search for bureaucratic spaces and political alliances has generated tension and divisiveness between the two provincial organizations. In this way COMICH, together with Pachakutik on a more national scale, and CONPOCIIECH, together with Amauta Yuyay on a more local scale, appear to be in competition during elections. The struggle over voters and leaders or key political issues involves competition as well as mutual distrust and contempt. However, the construction of these political movements has undoubtedly played a part in instigating an Indigenous political awakening that challenges and upsets (post) colonialist politics. This means that "they are not just fighting for access, incorporation, participation, or inclusion in the 'nation' or the 'political system' under the terms set by the dominant political culture." Rather, as Dagnino underscores, what is at stake these days for social movements (including Indigenous ones) is the right to participate in the very definition of the political system, the right to define that of which they seek to be a part (Escobar 2001, 44).

The issues described above illustrate some of the fissures and communication breakdowns that divide the two organizations. However, this is not to deny completely the existence of goodwill, contributing to at least some cohesiveness between the two provincial organizations. For this reason, an intermediary body or agency at the provincial level that binds the two is needed: "We need to create a provincial coordinating entity, an organization that coordinates both organizations (COMICH y CONPICIIECH)" (Pedro Janeta: COMICH) "that coordinates authorities, that represents both Indigenous organizations" (Víctor Malán: CONPOCIIECH).

An "intermediary space" exists between COMICH and CONPOCIIECH (Bhabha 2002). The proposition of creating an organization that mediates the two, with the potential to open up dialogue between COMICH and CONPOCIIECH, means working together according to an agenda that addresses topics of mutual interest. This "interstitial" organism would be active rather than passive. It would serve as a dialogic and impartial organizational space of mediation between COMICH and CONPOCIIECH. This interstitial proposal thus "becomes a necessity." Working for and within an intermediary space is a project that both organizations need to pursue in order to avoid confrontation. This organizational initiative of creating a point of intersection—"Puruwa Nation" or "Provincial Coordinator"—between COMICH and CONPOCIIECH under common goals would serve as a space of dialogue between the two Indigenous organizations.

# References

Bhabha, Homi. 2002. *El lugar de la cultura*. Buenos Aires-Argentina: Manantial.

Breton, Víctor. 2001. *Cooperación al desarrollo y demandas étnicas en los andes ecuatorianos*. Quito-Ecuador: Universitat de Lleida (UdL).

Escobar, Arturo and Sonia Alvarez. 2001. "Introducción. Lo cultural y lo político, en los movimientos sociales latinoamericanos." In *Política Cultural y Cultura política*. Bogotá-Colombia: Instituto Colombiano de Antropología e Historia (ICANH).

Foucault, Michel. 2007. *Sexualidad y poder*. Barcelona-España: Folio, S.A.

García, Andrés. 2008. *Chiapas para Cristo. Diversidad doctrinal y cambio político en el campo religioso chiapaneco*. Ciudad de México: Miguel Carranza.

Gledhill, John. 2000. *El poder y sus disfraces. Perspectivas antropológicas de la política*. Barcelona-España: Ballatella.

Hernandez, Aída and Mattiace Shannan. 2002. *Tierra, Libertad y autonomía: impactos regionales del zapatismo*. México, D.F.: CIESAS e IWGIA.

Hernandez, Aída. 2008. "Diálogos e Identidades Políticas: Génesis de los procesos organizativos de mujeres Indígenas en México, Guatemala y Colombia." In *Etnografías e Historias de Resistencias. Mujeres Indígenas. Procesos organizativos y Nuevas Identidades Políticas*, 45-127. México D.F.: CIESAS-PUEG-UNAM.

Lechuga, Graciela. 2007. *Breve introducción al pensamiento de Michel Foucault*. Ciudad de México: Universidad Autónoma Metropolitana.

Leon, Jorge. 2010. "Las organizaciones indígenas y el gobierno de Rafael Correa." *Revista Iconos* 37.

Ramón Valarezo, Galo. 2007. *El presupuesto participativo del gobierno provincial de Chimborazo*. Quito-Ecuador: COMUNIDEC.

Restrepo, Eduardo. 2005. *Política de la teoría y dilemas en los estudios de las colombias negras*. Bogotá-Colombia: Editorial Universidad de Cauca.

Roseberry, William. 2007. "Hegemonía y el lenguaje de la controversia." In *Antropología del Estado: Dominación y prácticas contestarías en América Latina*, ed. María Lagos and Pamela Calla, 40-117. Cuaderno de Futuro No. 23. Bolivia: PNUD.

Santana, Roberto. 1995. *¿Ciudadanos en la etnicidad? Los indios en la política o la política en los indios*. Quito-Ecuador: Abya-Yala.

Scott, James. 2007. *Los dominados y el arte de resistencia*. México, D.F.: ERA.

Trouillot, Michel-Rolph. 2001. "The Anthropology of the State in the Age of Globalization: Close Encounters of the Deceptive Kind." *Current Anthropology* 42(1) (February): 125-138.

# CHAPTER ELEVEN

## ÁNGEL GUARACA:
## '*EL INDIO CANTOR DE AMÉRICA*'
## CONTESTING THE IDEOLOGY
## OF THE ECUADORIAN MESTIZO NATION

## KETTY WONG

Indigenous music in Ecuador is often associated with Otavalan folkloric ensembles and the traditional music of Indigenous festivities such as Inti Raymi and Corpus Christi. However, Indigenous peoples in Ecuador are not only involved in folkloric and traditional music. In fact, a large part of their musical life falls under the popular music realm. I am referring here to a commercial and mass-produced type of Indigenous popular music that the elites pejoratively call *chichera* music. This paper explores the ethnic, racial, and class tensions associated with the musical production of Ángel Guaraca (b. 1975), a charismatic Indigenous singer and songwriter from the province of Chimborazo who has a large following among Indigenous peoples and lower-class *mestizos*. His work has been innovative in his rendition of Indigenous song-dance genres, particularly the *sanjuanito* and the *yumbo*, whose lyrics address sentiments of Indigenous pride and the experiences of Ecuadorian migrants in the diaspora.

Unlike previous *chichera* singers who were largely ignored by the mainstream media, Guaraca is often invited onto television programs and introduced as the new *música nacional* phenomenon. *Música nacional*, literally "national music," is a term that elite Ecuadorians have appropriated to designate a specific body of music they regard as most representative and encompassing of Ecuador's nationhood. *Música nacional* comprises a selected repertoire of *pasillos*, *pasacalles*, *albazos,* and *fox incaicos*, whose refined lyrics and musical arrangements for guitar and *requinto* (small guitar) represent the musical aesthetics of the elite. Because of the particular connotations this term has in Ecuador, the labeling of Guaraca as a "*música nacional* phenomenon" by TV show hosts signals a subtle change in Ecuadorians' view of *música nacional* and the position of Indigenous peoples within the Ecuadorian nation.

Guaraca's music is challenging elite notions of *música nacional* with its commercial visibility, the widespread popularity of his songs among Ecuador's working classes, and the attention it attracts from the mainstream media, even if this is done with the sole purpose of catering to their lower-class viewership. I argue that Guaraca's musical production and performances have become sites where Indigenous peoples contest the elite ideology of *mestizaje* (racial and cultural mixture) and propose their view of an Ecuadorian "Indigenous" nation through music.[1] As a nation-building discourse, the ideology of *mestizaje* seeks to unify the heterogeneous Ecuadorian population, but marginalizes the non-*mestizo* population for its non-mixed character (Whitten 1981). Just as the ideology of *mestizaje* excludes Indigenous and Afro-Ecuadorian populations from the imagined nation, the elite notion of *música nacional* excludes Indigenous and Afro-Ecuadorian popular music from the Ecuadorian musical canon.

## Chichera Music

As with *chicha* music in Peru, *chichera*[2] in Ecuador is a style of music that emerged in the early 1970s in the aftermath of massive rural migrations to the cities and intensive processes of modernization and urban growth. Its lyrics usually express double entendres or deal with topics about everyday life or, since the early 2000s, international migration experiences. Upbeat danceability, the use of electronic and percussion instruments, and the blending of Ecuadorian folk music with Caribbean rhythms, particularly the *cumbia* from Colombia, characterize its music. That being said, *chichera* is not so much defined by its musical traits as by its extra-musical features, such as the social contexts where it is performed and the ethnicity and low social status of both the singers and the audiences. The term *chichera* is wielded by the elites and has negative connotations implying bad taste, cheapness, and kitsch culture, expressions that reflect how the elites view Indigenous peoples.[3]

---

[1] The 1998 Constitution declared Ecuador as a pluriethnic and multicultural nation, thus abolishing "mestizaje" as the nation's goal.

[2] Ecuadorians use the term "chichera" to refer to this type of music.

[3] It is worth noting that *chichera* music is rarely used as an Indigenous cultural symbol by either Indigenous social movements or intellectual elites; instead, traditional music and rituals tend to be held up as emblematic expressions of Indigenous culture.

It must be noted that Indigenous peoples and lower-class mestizos do not normally call their popular music "*chichera*" but "*música nacional bailable*" (danceable national music). The adjective "*bailable*" distinguishes this type of music from "*música nacional antigua*" (old national music), a term they often use to refer to a repertoire of Ecuadorian *pasillos* generally perceived as having a sad character and a slow tempo, which makes them not suitable for dancing. The appropriation of the label *música nacional* for a style of music scorned by the elites is symptomatic of changes in the popular classes' ethnic and racial perception of the Ecuadorian nation. Although this appropriation does not imply an actual change in Ecuador's racial and social power structures, it is a way for lower-class people to define nationhood for themselves using a term already acknowledged to designate "the nation."

While urban versions of the *sanjuanito* and the *yumbo* certainly fall into the category of *mestizo* music,[4] not all are deemed *chichera* music. The *yumbo* has remained a traditional form of Indigenous music and, to my knowledge, no *mestizo yumbo* has entered the *música nacional* repertoire. *Sanjuanitos mestizos* recorded in Quito and Guayaquil in the mid-twentieth century by Discos Granja and IFESA were considered *música nacional* and were performed by renowned singers, such as Dúo Benítez-Valencia, Hermanas Mendoza-Suasti, and Carlos Rubira Infante. One example is "Pobre corazón" (Poor Saddened Heart) by Guillermo Garzón (1902-1975), one of the most popular urban *sanjuanitos* in the *música nacional* anthology. Neither are *chichera* music the *sanjuanitos* played by pan-Andean folkloric ensembles with guitar, panpipes, *quena*, and *bombo*.[5] This type of *sanjuanito* is considered to be "folkloric" and signals a cosmopolitan Indigenous aesthetics associated with Otavalo Indians. It does not conform to *chichera* aesthetics, though its basic rhythm features prominently in *chichera* music. Finally, stylized renditions of *sanjuanitos* and *yumbos* for symphony orchestra, written by academic composers such as Segundo Luis Moreno (1882-1972) and Luis Humberto Salgado (1903-1977), are considered nationalist art music. It is important to note that, unlike *chichera* music, none of these types of

---

[4] The *sanjuanito* and the *yumbo* are performed in the ritual context of the *Inti Raymi* and the *Corpus Christi* festivities, respectively. Both types of music are typically played with flutes and drums.

[5] Lynn Meisch (2002) provides a detailed history of the formation of Otavalan folkloric ensembles, which have adopted the pan-Andean ensemble instrumentation of panpipes, *quena*, *charango*, and *bomba*, with the addition of the violin and the *rondador*, idiosyncratic instruments of Indigenous music in the Otavalo area.

*sanjuanitos* and *yumbos* has incorporated electronic instruments or has been broadly disseminated on the radio or on records.

*Chichera* is an urban popular music associated with Indigenous peoples and lower-class mestizos who have migrated to the cities, the people the elites identify as *cholos* and *longos*. The term "*chichera*" was relatively unknown in Ecuador prior to the 1970s (Naldo Campos, 1997). It appears concurrently with the recording and dissemination of Indigenous commercial music in the cities and the emergence of *chicha* music in Peru. For Ricardo Realpe, the quintessential *chichera* composer, this term indicates modern performances of *sanjuanitos* by ensembles consisting of synthesizers, electric bass, and drum kit. Rock Star, a group founded in the early 1970s by Jaime Toaza, pioneered this trend in Quito. According to Realpe, Toaza arranged *sanjuanitos* using a particular high-pitched timbre on the Yamaha 270 electric keyboard, which is "loud (*chillón*), screaming, but at the same time, sweet and bitter" (personal interview, 2004).[6]

Most *chichera* groups in the 1990s recycled decades-old songs with new arrangements and lyrics. Rock Star, for example, adapted Segundo Bautista's *fox incaico* "Collar de lágrimas" to the *cumbia* rhythm. Bautista composed this song out of nostalgia for Ecuador in the early 1950s during a tour of Peru. Considered a classic within the *música nacional* repertoire, "Collar de lágrimas" has become the popular anthem of Ecuadorian migrants because its lyrics make reference to the yearning that people experience when they are far away from their homeland, mother, and loved ones. These lyrics speak to the sentiments that many Ecuadorian migrants share when they leave their country seeking better opportunities. Rock Star altered the slow tempo and sorrowful character of the song, changing it into an energetic and fast-tempo dance that the popular classes regard as "*música nacional bailable.*"

Bautista was upset with these changes because he felt that the sentiment he had intended to convey with this song had been distorted and he did not appreciate that it had moved into the realm of *chichera* aesthetics (personal interview, 2004).

---

[6] The typical instrumentation of *chichera* music in Ecuador and *chicha* music in Peru are different. In the latter, the melodies are played by the electric guitars and based on the *huayno*. Also different are the type of performance style. Besides a few music bands like Rock Star, most *chichera* singers are soloists and sing to the accompaniment of recorded tracks, while *chicha* music in Peru always includes the accompaniment of a live band.

*Así será mi destino, partir lleno de dolor*
*Llorando lejos de mi patria,*
*Lejos de mi madre y de mi amor.*

*Collar de lágrimas dejo en tus manos*
*Y en el pañuelito consérvalo mi bien.*

*En las lejanías será mi patria,*
*Que con mis canciones recordaré.*

*A mi madre santa le pido al cielo*
*Me conceda siempre la bendición.*

[This will be my destiny, to leave full of pain
Weeping far from my homeland,
Far from my mother, and from my sweetheart.

A necklace of tears I leave in your hands
And in the little handkerchief keep it safe, my love.

In the distance will be my homeland,
that I will remember with my songs.

I ask the holy mother in heaven
She always blesses me.]

Los Conquistadores, a group from Ambato made up of singer Francisco Manobandas and three dancers performing set choreographies, recycled "El conejito" (Little Rabbit), an old *sanjuanito* from the 1950s. This song embodies what most Ecuadorians believe *chichera* music is all about. "El conejito" employs a rabbit figure to tell the story of a man who visits a woman at midnight and jumps into her bed without underwear. When Los Conquistadores perform this song, they wear rabbits' ears and tails and dance at a fast tempo. This song was very popular in the early 2000s among the working classes and was performed by various *chichera* singers and female *tecnocumbia* groups with great success.

*Ay mi conejito era tan vanidón, ay caramba*
*Subiendo a la cama no quiso bajar, ay caramba*
*A la media noche llegó sin calzón, ay caramba.*

[Ay, my little rabbit was so vain, ay caramba
Jumping into bed, he did not want to get out, ay caramba
At midnight he came in without underwear, ay caramba.]

Needless to say, upper-middle-class Ecuadorians stigmatize and ridicule this song, accusing it of lacking in artistic qualities and dismissing the lyrics as crude. Many young people of this social sector I spoke to acknowledged occasionally watching the video on the television program *Diez sobre Diez*, which airs on a UHF television channel in Quito. The lyrics, the body gestures, and the singers' outfits were the subject of mockery because they were considered coarse and tasteless. However, *chichera* fans reacted enthusiastically to this and other happy *chichera* songs.

## *Chichera* Trends at the Turn of the Twenty-First Century

Ricardo Realpe once pointed out in a personal interview that the figure of a charismatic solo singer was the only thing that *chichera* music lacked to reach national prominence. Until the mid 1990s, music bands appealing to the lower classes and little-known *mestizo* singers had recorded *sanjuanitos* with moderate success in the highlands.[7] However, it was only in the late 1990s that *chichera* reached higher levels of popularity, with the appearance of two charismatic singers, Ángel Guaraca and Bayronn Caicedo, a mestizo singer from the eastern province of Pastaza. Unlike Rock Star and Los Conquistadores, Guaraca and Caicedo do not recycle or modernize old songs; rather, they write new ones in *sanjuanito, yumbo,* and other hybrid musical genres.

Guaraca often performs in the United States and Europe for Ecuadorian migrant communities, which see him as a messenger bringing news from the homeland. He is unreserved on stage and immodestly refers to himself as "the musical revelation of the millennium." Before his success as a singer, Guaraca was a peasant who worked the land. Later he earned a living as a plumber and a taxi driver in his home province. He began singing in the rural areas and recorded his first songs as a cassette that he sold on the streets. A short visit to Mexico in 1997 allowed him to explore *música norteña* and exchange musical ideas with local musicians. Upon his return to Ecuador, he recorded his first CD for Producciones Zapata Internacional, a well-known *chichera* music label. As of now he

---

[7] In the 2000s, *mestizo* singers, such as Azucena Aymara and María de los Ángeles, boosted their artistic careers when they switched their *chichera* repertoire to *tecnocumbia*, a Peruvian type of popular music very popular in Ecuador in the early 2000s.

has released a total of six CDs; Producciones Guaraca Internacional, his own record label, produced the last two.

Figure 1: Ángel Cuaraca on stage with his typical stage outfit (2003). Photograph by the author.

Guaraca projects an image of modernity with his carefully selected outfits featuring a cowboy hat, leather pants with fringes, leather gloves with metal studs, leather boots, and a vest woven with Indigenous designs or the Ecuadorian coat of arms.[8] He wears his long hair loose rather than in a braid, thus maintaining an Indigenous cultural trait (long hair), but displayed in a modern way.

---

[8] Guaraca may have gotten some of these ideas from the flashy *norteña* outfits he saw in Mexico.

Unlike *tecnocumbia* singers, Guaraca performs without the accompaniment of dance choreographies on stage. In addition, he changed the typical lyrics of *yumbos* and *sanjuanitos*, which usually deal with aspects of everyday life, to highlight sentiments of Indigenous pride for being Ecuadorian. He has also innovated the traditional *yumbo* with lyrics that point to the Indigenous and diasporic component of the Ecuadorian nation. Finally, he incorporated electronic instrumentation and pop music elements into the arrangements, thus making *yumbo* a commercial music.

In the *yumbo* "Campesino de mi tierra" (Peasant of My Land), Guaraca promotes the unity of Ecuadorians living in and outside the country and employs the poncho as a symbol of national Ecuadorian culture. With statements such as, "Para todos mis compatriotas que están fuera de nuestra patria" (For all my compatriots who are away from our homeland), Guaraca acknowledges the idea of a de-territorialized Ecuadorian nation with a diasporic population united by emotional bonds and recognition of a common origin.

The traditional *yumbo* is easily recognized for its rhythmic pattern of short-long notes in a fast-tempo duple-meter.

*Soy campesino de mi tierra, sí señor*
*Con mucho orgullo cantaré para Ecuador.*

*Miles descubren la vencida sí señor*
*Pobres hijos y humildes somos Ecuador.*

*Este es mi poncho, es la cultura nacional*
*Ángel Guaraca es el vocero del pueblo indio de mi patria.*

[I am a peasant of my land, yes sir
With great pride I will sing for Ecuador.

Thousands of people discover our land, yes my Lord
Poor and humble sons we are Ecuador.

This is my poncho, it's the national culture
Ángel Guaraca is the spokesman of the Indian people of my homeland.]

In this *yumbo*, Guaraca regards himself as a "speaker" for the Ecuadorian Indigenous peoples and underscores the idea of an Ecuadorian nation made up of poor and humble peasants like himself.

His song "El migrante" (The Migrant) features an upbeat tempo in a *sanjuanito* rhythm.[9] It tells a well-known story for thousands of Ecuadorian migrants who have left their children at home under the care of their grandmothers. The song starts with a phone conversation between a migrant father and his little son, who tells his father that he wants to see him instead of receiving beautiful toys and clothes by mail. The father explains to him that he is working to improve the family's economic situation and cannot return to Ecuador. The song narrates the experiences of undocumented migrants who risk their lives to cross the border and suffer for not being close to their children. In the lyrics, the migrant asks God to bless his children and the grandmothers, who have become substitute parents. This song has had a great impact on Indigenous and lower-class *mestizos* because it addresses the common Ecuadorian migrants' experience of not being able to see their children grow.

While Guaraca has many followers in both rural and urban areas, he is criticized and mocked by upper- and middle-class *mestizos*, who view his songs as the music of *indios*, *cholos*, and *longos*. In Ecuador, *cholo* and *longo* are pejorative ethnic labels often used as insults. They point to Indigenous peoples and lower-class mestizos who strive to climb the social ladder in order to become *whites*. "Whiteness," in this case, has less to do with race than with social distinction and socioeconomic status among different-social-class *mestizos*. These are features used as a means to build social boundaries between upper-middle-class *mestizos* and lower-class *mestizos*.

Karem Roitman (2009, 2) rightly points out that upper-middle-class *mestizos* (white *mestizos*) tend to deny their Indigenous heritage and see little or no connection to an Indigenous past, while lower-class *mestizos* (simply called "*mestizos*") are associated with people who have been acculturated and are "no longer Indians." By denying their Indigenous heritage, upper-middle-class *mestizos* disregard the long history of racial and cultural miscegenation resulting from the encounter between Europeans, Amerindians, and Africans during the colonial period. This process of *mestizaje*, highlighted in the well-known saying "*El que no tiene de Inga tiene de Mandinga*" (That person who does not have Indigenous blood [*inga*] has African blood [*mandinga*]), is ignored by white *mestizos*.

This denial of Indigenous heritage can be observed in the opinions of both fans and detractors left as comments on Ángel Guaraca videos on YouTube. Some of the comments reveal very clear racist attitudes towards

---

[9] This song is available in various YouTube videos.

Indigenous peoples. These may be obscene, employ vulgar language, or come across as more literate, but all point to the existing social tensions between Indigenous peoples and upper-middle and lower-class mestizos. The comments appear here as they appear on YouTube.

> "Angel Guaraca hace música chichera y les gusta solo a los longos e indios."

> [Angel Guaraca makes *chichera* music and only the *longos* and Indians like it.]

> "La cara de ese puto indio se parece al culo de una gallina jajaj fuk up!"

> [The face of that fucking Indian looks like a chicken's asshole, ha hah what a fuck up!]

> "jajajajaja muy chistoso el cara de la verga. Prefiero ser descendiente de los marcianos en vez de Los Puruhaes, [y] Atahualpa que son unos indios de mierda igual que tu chichero de porqueria."

> [ha-ha-ha, very funny that asshole. I would rather be descended from Martians than from Puruhaes, (and) Atahualpa who are shitty Indians like you, crappy chichero.]

In contrast, Guaraca's fans point to their pride of being Indigenous and criticize *mestizos* who do not acknowledge their ethnic roots.

> "Bravo guaraca haces bailar hasta los criticones aunque los que te critican sean tus coterráneos."

> [Bravo, Guaraca. You make even your picky critics dance, even though the guys who criticize you are your countrymen.]

> "Mi humilde opinión, en Ecuador la mayoría somos decendientes de indígenas y el que es blanco ojos azules ese no es un auténtico ecuatoriano yo orgulloso de ser 100% indígena carajo."

> [In my humble opinion most people in Ecuador are descendants of Indigenous peoples and someone who is white and has blue eyes is not an authentic Ecuadorian. I am proud of being 100% Indigenous.]

> "Hola no entiendo xq se averguenzan de su musica si es tan linda y muy alegre para bailar... ayq sntirseorgullosos [sic] de lo que es nuestro [z] yo soy peruana pero me gusta mucho la musica ecuatoriana... gracias a que tengo muchas amistades ecuatorianas y si he visto personas en mi instituto que son de Ecuador y se averguenzan de su musica o prefieren no oirlas."

[Hi, I don't understand why [Ecuadorians] are ashamed of their music. It is so beautiful and lively to dance to. One should feel proud of one's own culture. I'm a Peruvian but I really like Ecuadorian music . . . because I have a lot of Ecuadorian friends. And I've seen people in my institute who are from Ecuador and are ashamed of their music or prefer not to listen to it.]

un agradecimiento a todos y saludos ala ves a quienes les agrada(.) y a aquellos hp que no les agrada simplemente no los vea (...) Y ACUERDENSEN QUIEN NIEGA A SU TIERRA TAMBIEN NIEGA ALA MADRE QUE LOS TRAJO A ESTE MUNDO(,) NO HACE DIFERENCIA EN DONDE SE ENCUENTRE UNO.

[Many thanks to all and greetings to those people who like it (the song) and to those jerks who do not like it, don't watch it (the video). AND REMEMBER THAT WHO DENIES HIS HOMELAND ALSO DENIES THE MOTHER WHOEVER BROUGHT THEM TO THIS WORLD(,) THERE IS NO DIFFERENCE IN WHERE YOU LIVE.]

These comments reveal the complex dynamics of ethnic relations in Ecuador and the reluctance of certain social groups to acknowledge the Indigenous component in both their individual and collective *mestizo* social identities.[10]

## Conclusion

Ángel Guaraca proudly self-identifies as "Indio cantor de América" (the Indian singer of America) and promotes images of an Ecuadorian "Indigenous" nation with his song lyrics and by singing in Quichua and Spanish to his audiences in Ecuador and abroad. Guaraca is symbolically articulating a popular nationalism that projects a more realistic view of the true ethnic and racial configuration of the Ecuadorian nation than the elite nationalism projected by elite *música nacional*. He does so by sending messages about pride in Ecuador's Indigenous culture, by making his music visible at national and international levels, and by envisioning an Ecuadorian nation beyond its national borders, which encompasses all compatriots who share emotional bonds with the homeland regardless of their socio-economic and ethnic backgrounds.

---

[10] See Wong 2012 (Chapter 1) for more information on *mestizaje* and the ideology of the *mestizo* nation.

It is safe to say that the label "*música nacional bailable*" used by the popular classes is more inclusive of the heterogeneous Ecuadorian population than the elite *música nacional*, which disparages Indigenous popular music. The prominence in the twenty-first century of *chichera* music, or *música nacional bailable*, as Indigenous and working-class Ecuadorians call it, reflects how the popular classes are destabilizing the paradigm of the ideology of *mestizaje* and how Ecuadorians in general are changing commonly held notions of elite *música nacional*, Indigenous peoples, and the Ecuadorian *mestizo* nation.[11]

# References

Ángel Guaraca's website. http://www.angelguaraca.com.ec
Meisch, Lynn. 2002. *Andean Entrepreneurs. Otavalo Merchants and Musicians in the Global Arena*. Austin: University of Texas Press.
Roitman, Karem. 2009. *Race, Ethnicity, and Power in Ecuador: The Manipulation of Mestizaje*. London: First Forum Press.
Whitten, Norman Jr. 1981. *Cultural Transformations and Ethnicity in Modern Ecuador*. Urbana: University of Illinois Press.
Wong, Ketty. 2012. *Whose National Music? Identity, Mestizaje, and Migration in Ecuador*. Philadelphia: Temple University Press.
YouTube Videos Comments.

**Personal Interviews**

Segundo Bautista, August 2004.
Naldo Campos, June 1997.
Ricardo Realpe, September 2004.

---

[11] It bears mentioning that the popular classes' appropriation of this label for *chichera* music parallels changes in the official vision of the Ecuadorian nation as a pluriethnic and multicultural nation according to the Constitution of 1998.

# CONTRIBUTORS

**Marc Becker** is Professor of Latin American history at Truman State University. His research focuses on constructions of race, class, and gender within popular movements in the South American Andes. He is the author of *Pachakutik: Indigenous movements and electoral politics in Ecuador* (Rowman & Littlefield Publishers, 2011) and *Indians and Leftists in the Making of Ecuador's Modern Indigenous Movements* (Duke, 2008); co-editor (with Kim Clark) of *Highland Indians and the State in Modern Ecuador* (University of Pittsburgh Press, 2007); and editor and translator (with Harry Vanden) of *José Carlos Mariátegui: An Anthology* (New York: Monthly Review Press, 2011).

**Cristina Echeverri Pineda** is a historian and is in her third year of PhD studies in political science at the Universidad de los Andes in Colombia. She has a scholarship for doctoral studies from the Departamento Administrativo de Ciencia, Tecnología e Innovación de Colombia (Colciencias). Her current research interests are the recent constitutional processes in the Andean region and their relationship with Afro-Latin American social and political movements, in particular the cases of Colombia (1991), Ecuador (2008), and Bolivia (2009).

**Kathleen S. Fine-Dare** (PhD Anthropology, University of Illinois at Urbana-Champaign) is Professor of Anthropology and Affiliated Professor of Gender and Women's Studies and Native American and Indigenous Studies at Fort Lewis College in Durango, Colorado. In 2005 she taught as a Fulbright Lecturer at the Salesian Polytechnic University in Quito, Ecuador. In 2006 she was selected as Fort Lewis College's Featured Scholar, and in 2009 she received the college's first Distinguished Professor award for excellence in teaching, scholarship, and service. Fine-Dare has published articles in journals such as *Dialectical Anthropology*, *Radical History Review*, and *Journal of Social Archaeology* and is the author of *Cotocollao: Ideología, Historia, y Acción en un Barrio de Quito* (Quito: Abya-Yala Press, 1991), and of *Grave Injustice: The American Indian Repatriation Movement and NAGPRA* (Lincoln: University of Nebraska Press, 2002). She co-edited (with the late Steven L. Rubenstein) *Border Crossings: Transnational Americanist Anthropology* (University of Nebraska Press, 2009) in which she has two-articles co-written with Rubenstein and one chapter of her own entitled "Bodies Unburied, Mummies Displayed: Mourning, Museums, and Identity Politics in the Americas." She is currently writing a book based on more than 20 years of research on performance, identity, and indigeneity in northwestern Quito.

**Linda Jean Hall** earned a Master's in Latin American and Iberian Studies and is currently completing a second year of study towards a doctorate in Anthropology. Linda's research extends over a five-year period and the ethnographic data consisting of extensive interviews examines the social ramifications of migration, assimilation, and constitutional change to Afro-Ecuadorians in metropolitan Quito.

**Juan Illicachi Guzñay** has a Master's in Higher Education from the University of Cuenca, a Master's in Ethnic Studies at FLACSO-Ecuador, and is a doctoral student in Social Anthropology at CIESAS in Mexico City (class of 2009-2013). He is a former leader of the Confederation of the Indigenous Movement of Chimborazo-CONAIE, and is currently teaching at the Colegio Intercultural Bilingüe Santiago de Quito.

**Víctor Hugo Jijón** is a petroleum engineer and geologist/geophysicist who has studied at the Central University of Ecuador, the French Petroleum Institute in Paris, and the American Institute of Human Rights in Costa Rica. He has taught at the Escuela de Gobierno y Políticas Públicas in Ecuador, and has been an adviser to the Confederación de Nacionalidades Indígenas del Ecuador (CONAIE) and the Pachakutik Movement. He is also the National Coordinator of the Comisión por la Defensa de los Derechos Humanos (CDDH).

**Kenneth Kincaid** is Assistant Professor of history at Purdue University North Central. He has a PhD in Latin American History from the University of Kansas.

**Carmen Martínez Novo** is Associate Professor of Anthropology and Director of the Latin American Studies Program at the University of Kentucky. She is the author of *Who Defines Indigenous? Identities, Development, Intellectuals and the State in Northern Mexico* (Rutgers University Press, 2006) and the editor of *Repensando los movimientos indigenas* (FLACSO, 2009). She has written numerous articles and book chapters on *indigenismo* and Indigenous identities in Mexico and Ecuador.

**Manuela Lavinas Picq** is Professor of International Relations at the Universidad San Francisco de Quito, Ecuador. Her research bridges international relations and comparative politics to tackle issues of gender, ethnicity, and the state in Latin America. She has been a Junior Scholar for the Study of Democracy at the Woodrow Wilson Center and a Loewenstein Fellow at Amherst College. In 2013-2014, she is based at the Institute of Advanced Studies developing a history of international relations in the Amazon. She has published in venues such as the *Journal of Latin American Politics and Society* and *Cahiers du Genre*, and is a regular opinion contributor to Al Jazeera English.

**Rachel Soper** is a PhD candidate in Sociology at the University of California, San Diego. Her research centers on the relationship between agro-export commodity chains, Indigenous communities, and Indigenous movement organizing. She is currently carrying out dissertation research in the highlands of Ecuador, comparing food sovereignty activism in three agro-export production areas.

**Ketty Wong** is Associate Professor of Ethnomusicology at The University of Kansas. She is the author of *Luis Humberto Salgado: Un Quijote de la Música* (2004) and *Whose National Music? Identity, Mestizaje, and Migration in Ecuador* (2012). A Spanish version of the latter book received the Casa de las Americas Musicology Award in 2010. Her research interests focus on Latin American art and popular music, Chinese ballroom dancing, migration, nationalism, and identity.